GUIDE TO
montréal

GUIDE TO
montréal

CHRIS and DIANE KEATING

McGRAW-HILL

New York, Toronto, London, Sydney, Mexico City

GUIDE TO MONTREAL

94777

Library of Congress Catalog Card No. 67-18805

1 2 3 4 5 6 7 8 9 0 PL67

0 9 8 7

Printed and bound in Canada

To Muriel and Ernest Heys

CONTENTS

AUTHORS' NOTE

No financial contributions have been made by any establishments listed in this guidebook.

Prices mentioned in the book are subject to change.

We wish to thank Paul Leduc and the Montréal Municipal Tourist Bureau for their help in furnishing information.

All colour separations are a courtesy of the monthly magazine published by the City of Montréal.

1.

MONTREAL AT A GLANCE . . . A FASCINATING HYBRID OF OLD AND NEW WORLD

People arriving for the first time in Montréal usually anticipate a large, raw-boned city, populated by a volatile French-speaking people whose primary passions are hockey, separatism, and pea soup. If this is what you expect, *mes amis,* slip this book in your pocket. You are in for a delightful surprise.

A short stroll down central Mountain Street will take you past stately 19th-century mansions, once owned by aristocratic Victorians, but now elegantly housing some of the city's most distinguished French restaurants . . . past a noisy bistro with gay awnings, from which wafts the agreeable odour of Camembert cheese and roast chestnuts . . . past a bizarre, spiralling chain-mail facade of a licensed pharmacy and a post office where, in addition to filling prescriptions and mailing letters, you can buy *avant-garde* clothes, eat *gourmethèque* meals, and browse through a pop art gallery.

After dark the bright lights of St. Catherine Street reflect the pulsating life of a Montréal evening. Whatever your taste it will be satisfied here, from the bump and grind of burlesque, to the classical concerts at the magnificent Place des Arts, to the evocative intense singing of a French *chanteuse*.

A short distance from the bustling crowds of the business district and you are in a haven of wooded slopes and rolling parks called Mount Royal. Its natural beauty and panoramic view of the city can be enjoyed leisurely by foot, comfortably by car, or romantically by horse-drawn *calèche*. There is something for everyone on this people's mountain. Snack at the modern pavilion, watch the children sailing boats on Beaver Lake, or on a warm summer's night, listen to a symphony concert under the stars at the Chalet.

Don't miss the opportunity of an afternoon stroll through the narrow streets of 18th century *le Vieux Montréal*. Then at dusk conclude your tour by relaxing with a cocktail and watching the sunset from the 45th floor of a nearby skyscraper, or if you prefer, watching the girls from a sidewalk *café* on *chic* Sherbrooke Street.

Not only can you spend an afternoon wandering through the large, century-old Montréal Museum of Fine Arts, but also in surrounding streets you will find tiny galleries and boutiques tucked away in the most unusual places . . . above grocery stores, beside laundromats, and even inside restaurants.

Outside the whirling doors of an immense, ultra-modern department store, a one-armed hurdy-gurdy musician grinds out squeaky tunes while pathetically eyeing the bustling crowds in hope of nickels and dimes for his tin cup.

This is Montréal, an unusual place with seemingly incompatible characteristics.

She's awesome New York, skyscrapers sprouting from narrow Dublin lanes.

She's London Conservatism tipping his bowler to Parisian *joie de vivre*.

She's San Francisco's miles of harbours; she's Rome's churches on every corner.

She's a delightfully schizophrenic city, bubbling with sights, sounds, and flavours . . . often perplexing, always exciting.

Simply stated, she's a unique city that seems to have everything.

A QUICK ORIENTATION . . . "THROUGH A BIRD'S EYE"

To the stranger, Montréal has an endless variety of sights and activities. To enjoy your stay and gain the most from our city, here is how we would begin a visit.

Upon arriving in Montréal the first consideration is finding accommodation (details appear in our section on hotels.) Then, after depositing your bags and perhaps changing your shoes, follow the natural impulse to head for the centre of town and the cruciform Place Ville Marie complex on Dorchester Blvd. In the lobby look for an elevator marked "Observation" which rises to the lofty top of the skyscraper, from which unfolds a magnificent panorama of city, sky, and distant Vermont mountains. Admission to the Observation tower at this writing is 75¢, and we hear it's elevating even higher.

HINT: For the price of a drink and with the same spectacular view you can relax in plush comfort and sip a cool drink. Simply take the elevator one floor higher to the glass encased Altitude 737. Up to 9 p.m. the cocktail lounge has no minimum charge.

South Side—St. Lawrence River

The most noticeable geographical feature from the south side of the observation platform is the wide, swift-flowing St. Lawrence River which, with its tributaries, girdles the city, forming a thirty-mile long, ten-mile wide island . . . a thousand miles from the sea! Stretching along the waterfront are the concrete piers and tall grain elevators of the world's largest inland seaport. During the trading season the moaning horns of the seafaring ships penetrate the air as they line up to enter the billion-dollar St. Lawrence Seaway.

From the southeast corner of the lookout, you can see the various transit systems of bridges and boats converging at an oblong island, partly manmade, partly natural, in mid-St. Lawrence. There are really two islands, a network of canals, islands, and tiny lakes which gives a gay Venetian atmosphere to the area. What could be a better site for the Universal and International Exhibition of 1967 than this impressive synthesis of land and water, which exemplifies Expo's theme of "Man and His World"?

Oldest Montréal runs along the waterfront from the western end of the Exposition site. It is bound on the west by a building with green, six-foot-high letters reading, "Bank of Montreal". This is also where our foot tour of *le Vieux Montréal* begins (see chapter 2). To the east Old Montréal is bound by the round, grey dome of the reconstructed Bonsecours Market Building. Between, the narrow, irregular streets with their centuries-old, storeyed buildings provide hours of happy strolling. You can browse through antique shops, art galleries, and fashion boutiques, or dine in quaint restaurants on authentic French-Canadian food. Whatever your interests, don't miss this sector of town!

Head now for the southwest corner of the Place Ville Marie platform. Scanning the industrial districts below you, with their tall, smoking chimneys, your attention will be caught by a towering building clothed in bright white concrete with tiers of half-moon-shaped windows. This is the new Canadian Pacific Hotel, Le Château Champlain, which stands on Place du Canada. The green patch with cement paths that lies directly north of the hotel is Dominion Square, the focal point of activity for tourists because of its many hotels, large travel agencies, and regularly departing tour buses. It is hard to believe that this was once the official cemetery of the city.

Easily visible between where you are now standing and Dominion Square is the silver, circular dome and golden cross of Mary Queen of the World, Montréal's Roman Catholic cathedral. This church (definitely worth a visit) is a faithful replica of St. Peter's of Rome, but slightly less than half as large. If you lean over the railing and look down, you can see the thirteen statues on the top of the facade which were gifts from the city's most important parishes.

North Side—The Mountain

From any point on the north side of the Observation Tower, the most conspicuous and characteristic physical feature is the mountain, sprawled like a sleeping green giant in the centre of a metropolis of two and a half million people. The first white man to climb this 764-foot hill was Jacques Cartier. Some say he was so impressed with the view that he called it Royal Mountain, or Mont Réal in French. Previously it was thought that this was how Montréal derived its name, but historians now claim "no", giving two different versions of the origin. Some claim Cartier was told by the king to name "a high place he discovers" Montréal, to flatter Cardinal de' Medici, Archbishop of Montreale, Sicily. Others claim that the name came from a Breton nobleman, who was aboard Cartier's ship. He was a godson of the queen and lord of the family estate known as "Montréal" in France.

From a northeast position on the platform, you have the best view of the world's largest illuminated cross, which commemorates Sieur de Maisonneuve's first crude symbol of Christianity. He erected it in 1643 after his prayers to stop the flood waters from wiping out Ville Marie were answered. It towers 103 feet from the top of Mount Royal, and its arms have a 36-foot span. The city's most

Central Montréal.

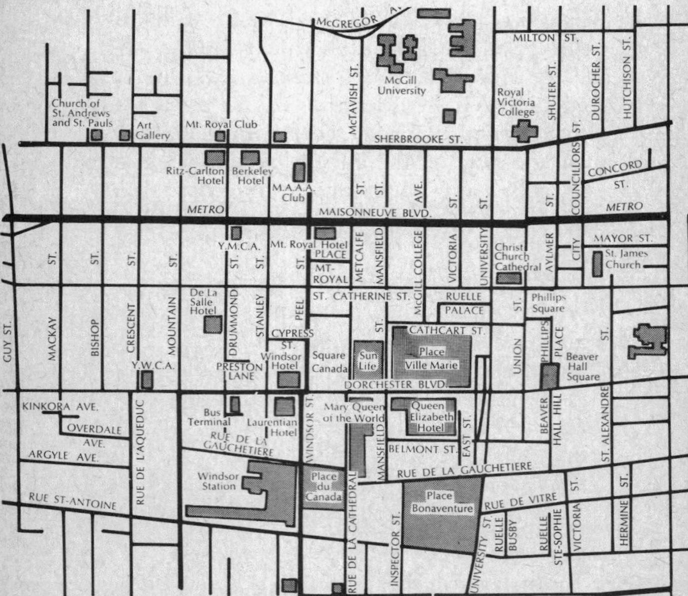

familiar landmark, it can be seen thirty miles downstream on the St. Lawrence River.

Montréal's oldest university is located directly below the cross where the mountain meets the city, or more explicitly, in the only grass and tree patch visible from this side of the tower. McGill University combines neo-Gothic and contemporary buildings around lawns which once formed part of the country estate of its founder, James McGill.

Looking over your right shoulder, you will see the big "Q" of the Hydro Québec Building. The street at its feet, which runs straight north and south, is St. Lawrence Boulevard, one of the most colourful and interesting thoroughfares in Canada. Every nationality is represented in its string of grocery shops, restaurants, second-hand stores, and markets. Be sure to stop at one of the stalls for freshly boiled corn-on-the-cob, or a steamed hot dog. And feel free to munch as you saunter—we Montrealers do! "The Main", as St. Lawrence Blvd. has been affectionately termed, is the east-west dividing line of the city's street-numbering system. It was once considered the demarcation line between the French- and English-speaking populations. However, this is no longer true as bilingualism and biculturalism have spread through the city.

By walking to the northwest corner, you will have the best view of Westmount Mountain with the huge copper dome of St. Joseph's Oratory silhouetted against the sky. This great modern shrine has become one of the famous sights in Montréal, with over a million visitors a year.

Below, on the slopes of the mountain, the beautiful homes and gardens of one of the best residential districts in the country enhance the quiet charm of the area. This is the City of Westmount, an independent municipality which, along with 84 other cities, towns, and parishes on the Island, makes up Greater Montréal.

Looking east along the top of the mountain, you can see the tower of the University of Montréal. This is the second largest French-speaking university in the world, but then Montréal is the second-largest French-speaking city in the world. Continuing east, you cannot miss seeing the immense T.V. transmission tower which stands in a natural mountain park. The chalet below the tower serves as a lookout for a magnificent view of the city. Inside is displayed the coat-of-arms of Montréal and scenes from the early history of Canada.

Between the foot of the mountain and your own feet is the shopping district of Montréal, where even department stores have their own personalities, setting one apart from the other. The tall concrete structures that dot the area are modern, prestige apartment towers that boast swimming pools, health clubs, filtered humidified air, and even heated sidewalks to clear unwanted snow. Understandably, the tickets to enter through the gates of these earthly paradises are very high in price!

You have had a look at Montréal from every corner of the P.V.M. Observation Tower. We began this quick orientation from a bird's point of view for two reasons: First, to give you a sense of position in relation to the surrounding environment so you will feel more at home; and second, to show you Montréal in all her glory so you will want to stay awhile and get to know her.

Now that you have had a sampling taste of Montréal's attractions, it is time to descend to ground level and take a closer look at its distinctive character.

THE FRENCH FACT

What draws millions of visitors a year to Montréal? Usually it's the promise of something different—a foreign country without crossing the ocean. To quote facts and figures, Montréal is the second largest French-speaking city in the world. Paris, of course, is the largest. Roughly two-thirds of the two million citizens of Greater Montréal have French as their mother tongue. However, since almost everyone in the central district speaks English, the visitor arriving for the first time may feel this is just another city.

But it isn't long before he realizes the "French fact". It's revealed subtly in the *chic* of the women, in the numerous French restaurants, in the great number of churches, in the young, handsome policemen. On a drive through the rest of the province, it becomes more obvious. French words on billboards; monasteries and shrines that dot the countryside; and huge churches that loom above every village are a few of the signs.

The French were the first white men to arrive in Canada 300 years ago. Although they succumbed to British rule in 1760, they never lost their national identity, and it's this nationalism that gives Canada her dual personality and prevents her from being culturally swallowed by her more powerful American neighbour.

Québec is "the ancient" of Canadian culture. For centuries strong tradition, religion, family life, and classical knowledge were the essence of everyday living. *L'avocat, le curé,* and *le docteur* were at the top of the deeply entrenched social hierarchy—especially the priest, who was more concerned with tradition and heritage than commercial progress. For this reason very few French-speaking Canadians entered commerce or industry. If they did, it was at the risk of losing their French-Canadian identity.

In the meantime the commercially minded English in Québec gained control of the economy. They, too, isolated themselves, forming a tightly knit community in Montréal. Up until the last decade it was not unusual for an English-speaking Montrealer to grow up without learning French.

In recent years there's been a change of direction and a metropolitan rebirth. The French-speaking Canadian has leaped from the 18th century to the 20th, enthusiastically entering the fields of commerce and science. This renaissance has been termed the Quiet Revolution—a bloodless attempt by the French Canadian to acquire economic control of his province's destiny. Although this transition has erupted in angry words, and even a few bombs, generally speaking there's been little violence and a great deal of progress. Today there is a refreshing atmosphere of co-operation between the French and English businessmen. Large companies are giving preference to bilingual employees, and English-speaking executives are taking crash courses in French.

How far Québec has come in this Quiet Revolution was driven home to us by a conversation overheard at a cocktail party. A sweet young English Montrealer was introduced to a distinguished diplomat, and in the course of the conversation she mentioned that, although born and brought up in Montréal, she spoke no French. “Good God,” exclaimed the diplomat, his voice rising in shock, “a monolinguist! I didn’t realize there were any left in Montréal!”

The next morning she registered at the Berlitz School of Languages.

2.

A FOOT TOUR OF OLD MONTREAL . . . LE VIEUX MONTREAL

HOW TO GET THERE: The Métro is the easiest and quickest way. Take the Métro east to De Montigny Blvd. and transfer to the No. 2 line south to Place d'Armes. If you have your own car, locate the intersection of Dorchester Blvd. and Beaver Hall Hill on our map of the city. Turn south down Beaver Hall Hill onto McGill Street and then left at Notre Dame Street. Take Notre Dame to the first square, which is Place d'Armes, the starting point of our tour.

GATEWAY TO THE WEST

The far-flung results of Montréal's unique birth make a walk through the oldest quarter a must for every visitor. The founding of Montréal was based upon the almost simultaneous religious vision of two zealous French-Catholic men. Compelled by their dreams, they formed a society in Paris and in 1642 sent twenty-four French settlers to establish a settlement, to serve God, and to save the souls of the Indians.

For over 150 years this struggling community on the banks of the St. Lawrence River was the gateway to the interior for thousands of canoe-bearing explorers, missionaries, fur traders, and *voyageurs*. These pioneers, caught up by the adventure of the unknown, paddled, laughed, sang, and drank their way to the discovery and development of the northeastern United States, the Mississippi Valley, and western Canada.

In recent years, an interest has been generated in the restoration of this historical section of the city. On warm Sunday afternoons, groups of Montrealers stroll through the narrow streets, discussing the renovation of the 18th- and 19th-century buildings and examining the numerous historic tablets. In four years the city of Montréal has poured over five million dollars into the restoration of the old quarter. This has stimulated individual citizens to buy rat-infested warehouses and old fruit-storage plants and to convert them into fashionable homes and shops of the Victorian era.

Because of the maze of narrow streets and the one-way traffic, the best method of visiting Old Montréal is by foot. To aid you in your wandering, we suggest the following foot tour. It should not take more than two hours and can be done in considerably less. In describing it we shall attempt to bring history out of the textbook into the present by discussing the buildings, the streets, and the monuments that represent three centuries of architecture and history. Unfortunately, we cannot say much about the 17th century, because little of the architecture has survived. However, because of the unique concentration of 18th- and 19th-century buildings, it is possible to envisage the character of the town and the lives of its inhabitants.

PLACE D'ARMES

To begin the tour, we have chosen a square in the heart of oldest Montréal that has been the setting of many dramatic scenes in the city's history. Let's take a few minutes to look at some of the surrounding buildings. Dominating the square in its Gothic grandeur is the twin-towered Notre Dame Church. The fieldstone Seminary of St. Sulpice that adjoins it is the oldest building in Montréal, dating back to 1683.

Turning clockwise we see the tall building which is the new head office of La Banque Canadienne Nationale. Its brash, clean lines add a modern dash to the Old World square. We like to think that the proud figure on top of the centre monument has unfurled his flag to shield his eyes from its glistening newness, so out of place with the grey of the surrounding antiquity.

On the north side of the square, the Bank of Montreal building with its stately columns and domed roof resembles the Pantheon in Rome. It once contained a trunk full of documents smuggled here by Jefferson Davis's sister-in-law. He was the American Confederate President who lived in Montréal for a short time after the Civil War. If you are interested in old coins and bills, the Bank of Montreal has a museum open weekdays from 10 a.m. to 4 p.m. Admission is free.

Above you on the east side is the large, round face of an old, broken clock, ignored alike by repairmen and historians. To the right of it is the former Aldred Building, now La Prévoyance, which was the tallest building in Montréal when it was built in 1929, the same year that the Empire State Building was erected.

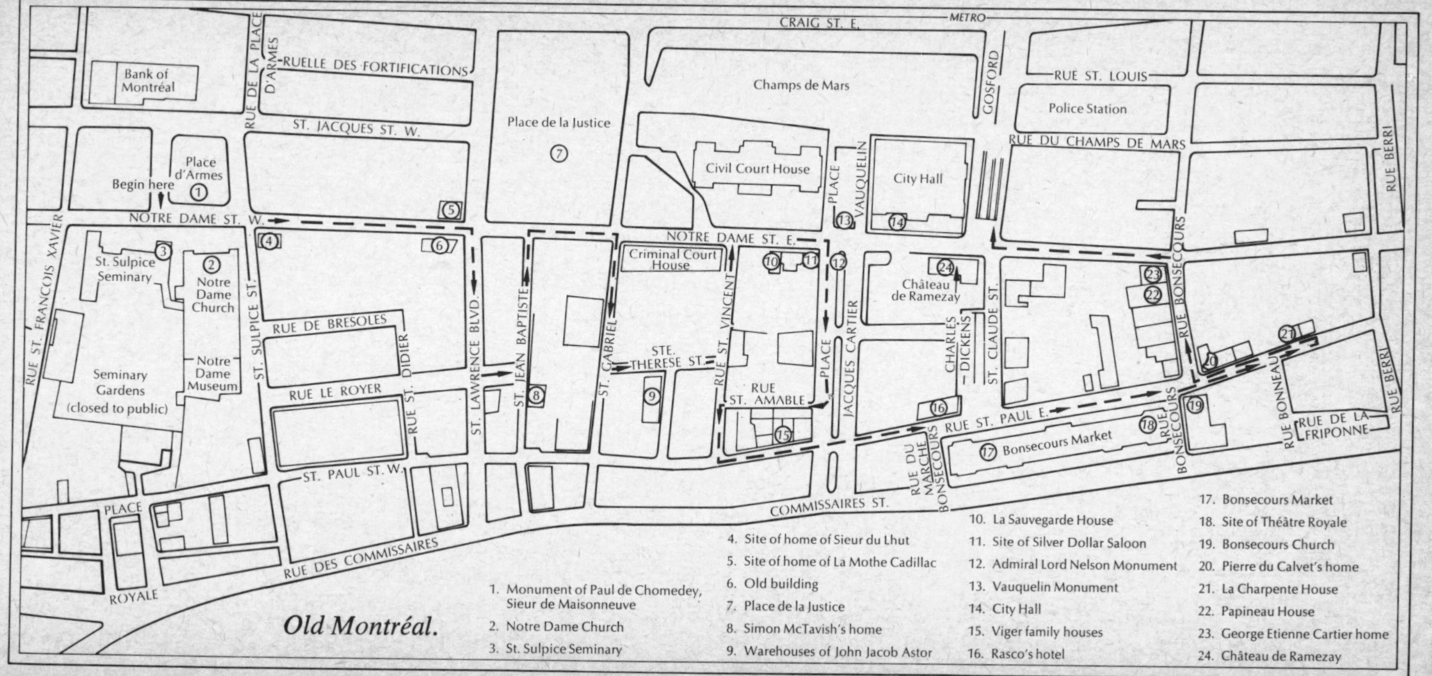

Old Montréal.

1. Monument of Paul de Chomedey, Sieur de Maisonneuve
2. Notre Dame Church
3. St. Sulpice Seminary
4. Site of home of Sieur du Lhut
5. Site of home of La Mothe Cadillac
6. Old building
7. Place de la Justice
8. Simon McTavish's home
9. Warehouses of John Jacob Astor
10. La Sauvegarde House
11. Site of Silver Dollar Saloon
12. Admiral Lord Nelson Monument
13. Vauquelin Monument
14. City Hall
15. Viger family houses
16. Rasco's hotel
17. Bonsecours Market
18. Site of Théâtre Royale
19. Bonsecours Church
20. Pierre du Calvet's home
21. La Charpente House
22. Papineau House
23. George Etienne Cartier home
24. Château de Ramezay

The Monument—Paul de Chomedey, Sieur de Maisonneuve

In the centre of Place d'Armes, you will see a large granite and bronze monument, which is the work of the well-known Québec sculptor, Philippe Hébert. Since this monument vividly depicts the story of Montréal's founding, a close inspection will give an insight into the hardships of the first settlers and will provide the necessary background for continuing the tour.

The ten-foot bronze figure on top is Maisonneuve in the attire of a well-dressed count, proudly gripping the Bourbon flag of France. The founding father of Montréal, his courage and determination matched his words, "I would go there (Montréal) . . . if every tree were an Iroquois." At the corners are four figures who played important roles in the early history of the colony.

When you are facing Maisonneuve, with your back to Notre Dame Church, the figure by your left-hand is Jeanne Mance tenderly dressing the wound of a small child. She founded the first hospital in the settlement, only a short distance from this square. Her bravery and humanity earned her the title, "Mother of Montréal".

To your right, the crouched figure of Major Lambert Closse and his dog Pilotte adorn the southeast corner. Many tales tell of the Major's bravery during the Indian attacks. Pilotte, his dog, had an extraordinary ability to sense approaching Iroquois and earned the name, "The Watchdog of Ville Marie". Ville Marie de Montréal was the name of early Montréal from 1642 to 1706.

On the northwest corner stands Charles le Moyne, soldier and entrepreneur. His legacy of eleven sons was a great boon to the population-starved early settlement. Seven of them were awarded seigneuries for their work as explorers and navigators.

Last of all, on the northwest corner crouches the figure of a warlike Iroquois. It was tastefully placed by the sculptor Hébert at the furthest point from the watch-dog, Pilotte.

The bas-reliefs between the four figures depict scenes from the treasured memories of French-Canada. Again take a position face to face with Maisonneuve and turn counter-clockwise. In front of you is a scene depicting the signing of the charter for the founding of Montréal. The east scene describes the first Mass celebrated in the new colony on the arrival of the pioneers. Father Vimont in addressing the settlers says, "What you see is only a mustard seed . . . but it is so animated by faith and religion it must be that God has great design for it." The bas-relief on the north is the death of Dollard, hero of Long Sault. He and sixteen companions volunteered to try and stop an attack of eight hundred Iroquois. The battle lasted nine days, but ended with the massacre of Dollard and his men. The east side shows Maisonneuve killing an Indian chief. About to be taken captive by the chief, he raised his gun only to have it misfire. Luckily, the gun in his other hand did work and killed the Indian. In the ensuing confusion Maisonneuve escaped.

From this brief description of the figures and scenes around Maisonneuve's monument you can appreciate some of the dangers and hardships that marked the life of Montréal for its first three years.

Notre Dame Church

Before leaving Place d'Armes Square, you will want to examine the impressive Notre Dame Church. From where you are now standing, you can gaze undisturbed at its austere facade and high towers. However, do not let its simple grandeur prevent you from looking both ways in crossing the street, for the traffic moves quickly, with little heed to slow-moving pedestrians.

Before we discuss the architecture of the church, here is a quick historical sketch. The history of Notre Dame is intertwined with the history of Montréal. They began at the same time and at the same place. As soon as the settlers landed in 1642 at Pointe-à-Callière (a ten-minute walk from here), they hastily erected a log chapel, which carried the name of Notre Dame. Over the years the first chapel was moved and enlarged as the size and religious needs of the population increased. Finally, in 1672 a substantial edifice was built in the middle of Notre Dame Square, dividing it into two parts. Again the church became too small for the number of parishioners, and in 1824 the present church was begun. It opened for worship in 1828.

EXTERIOR: The Notre Dame of today is an enormous chunk of Montréal limestone, measuring 260 feet in length and 132 feet in width. It is a chaste example of the severe architectural style known as perpendicular Gothic, and in this class it has no superior in North America. Unfortunately the Irish-American architect, James O'Donnell, died before it was completed, but his work was continued by John Ostell. It is interesting to note that both men were Protestants whose studies in ecclesiastical architecture led them to become Roman Catholics.

You will note that the portal is formed by three identical arches repeated above as niches for Québec's three patron saints, the Virgin Mary, St. Joseph, and St. John the Baptist. Framing it are two square bell towers, which are only 2½ feet shorter than the famous ones of Notre Dame Church in Paris. The parapet between the towers has battlements like a fortress and is topped by a small iron cross.

THE BELLS: The tower on the left, called Temperance, contains ten bells, ranging in weight from 897 to 6,011 pounds. Each bell has been christened with the name of its godfather or benefactor. The custom of the Catholic Church symbolizes the large part bells play in the spiritual life of the faithful. The carillon was cast by Charles and George Mears in the Whitechapel Bell Foundry in London. Their pleasant harmony induced the churchwardens to ask the Whitechapel Foundry for the biggest bell that they had ever produced to hang in the "tower of perseverance" on the left of the church. Unfortunately, a few months after its inauguration it cracked. Since it was found lighter in weight and poorer in material than agreed upon, it was returned. The Whitechapel Foundry then produced a greater new bell (Gros Bourdon) weighing 24,780 pounds. It took an entire day and many horses and men to raise it to the top of the tower, and at the last minute, a window had to be enlarged to allow it through. For 120 years Montrealers have stopped and listened to its full, majestic voice proclaiming great church festivals. Le Gros Bourdon, baptised St. Jean Baptiste, bears in Latin this legend relating its history:

> I was cast in the year 1847 of the Christian era, the 202nd since the founding in Montreal, the 1st of the Pontificate of Pius IX, the 10th of Victoria, Queen of England; I am the gift of the merchants, farmers and artisans of Ville Marie.

INTERIOR: It is for its interior that Notre Dame has gained the reputation of being one of the most impressive churches of the Roman Catholic faith on this continent. As you walk through the arches into the vast nave, your attention will immediately rest on the magnificent high altar, which like a jewel seems to be cut with facets so as to have special brilliance. Gradually you will become aware of the flickering candlelight, the rich colour, and the profuse detail that is so characteristic of the interior. It could be said that here is represented the double heart of Montréal – the conservative, somewhat austere exterior exemplifying the English character, the colourful, ornamental interior responding more to the French-Canadian temperament.

Let us continue with a closer inspection of the interior upon which so much wealth of the Sulpicians has been spent. First, a few statistics to appreciate its huge dimensions: The nave measures 220 feet long with the chancel and is 69 feet wide, not including the side aisles. There are fourteen side windows, each 40 feet high, and three stained-glass rose windows in the ceiling. There are nine chapels in Notre Dame, including Our Lady of the Sacred Heart, which is the size of an average church. The church has a double row of galleries which can accommodate 5,000 seated and 2,000 standing. The parishioners of 1824 had either considerable optimism or great religious zeal, as

Montréal's population was only a little over 22,000 at the time.

As you walk up one of the centre aisles to the main altar, you will note the clusters of colourful slender columns. They gracefully support the vault, which is suspended above like a star-filled sky. While you are gazing upwards, do look at the centre rose window. It shows Mary bearing Jesus in her arms surrounded by twelve angels singing her praises. We hope that by the time this book is published the large spotlight has been removed from the middle so that the beauty of the window is not hidden.

A noteworthy feature of the church is the carved pulpit and canopy on the left-hand side of the nave. It was designed by Victor Bourgeau, creator of the main altar, and features sculptures by Philippe Hébert. At the base of the pulpit are two prophets, Ezekiel and Jeremiah. The figures on the canopy above the pulpit represent four teachers of the church. Finally, crowning the intricate structure is the symbol of religion – a young man resting on a cross and holding a chalice to his heart.

The aisle ends at five steps which lead to the sanctuary above the nave. The sanctuary can be viewed from every part of the church, for the floor of the nave is sloped like an amphitheatre (a first in religious architecture). If you turn your back for a moment on the main altar, you will see the organ in the upper gallery over the front entrance. You cannot help but be impressed by the huge proportions of its 5,772 pipes which range from 32-foot giants that you can readily see, down to ½-inch midgets in its interior. One of the largest in America, it was made in shops of the Casavants at St. Hyacinthe, 40 miles east of Montreal. When the four keyboards and thirty pedals are played by a skilled organist, the church seems alive with the powerful sound of music.

Turn again to the main altar and take a few minutes to gaze at this remarkable masterpiece. Once the general effect of its beauty has been felt, it is time to concentrate on the detail to gain an understanding of the architect's theme, which is the Sacrifice of Jesus Christ as foretold in the Old Testament and related in the New.

To the right of the central Crucifixion are two Old Testament pre-figures of the Bloody Sacrifice. You will see the Sacrifice of Isaac, and in the niche directly above, a priest of Aaron offering the sacrifice of a spotless lamb. To the left of the Crucifixion are the two Old Testament prototypes of the Eucharistic Sacrifice — Melchisedech, Archpriest and King of Salem, and above, Moses before the Ark.

Both sacrifices are then depicted as they are related in the New Testament. Above the Tabernacle is Christ on the Cross (Bloody Sacrifice), and beneath the Tabernacle is the Last Supper (Eucharistic Sacrifice). Now raise your eyes to the top of the altar, and there is Mary being crowned by her son. Notre Dame, which is French for "Our Lady", is dedicated, "To the Queen of Heaven, to the Queen of Angels." In the niches on both sides of the main altar are six statues representing the evangelists who spread the gospel throughout the world.

It remains only to say that the men responsible for this striking monument were Victor Bourgeau, a Canadian architect, and a French sculptor, Bouriché. We hope that through this rather detailed discussion the main altar has been vividly painted in your memory, for it contributes largely to the unique character of the church.

If you wish to have a closer inspection of the chapels, the stained glass windows, and the Stations of the Cross, walk down the aisles under the galleries. The ground-floor windows illustrate the chief events in the early history of Montréal. Although all the chapels and windows deserve to be mentioned, we shall pick out the ones we feel to be of special interest. Moving in a counterclockwise direction around the church, we see first, directly behind the pulpit, the chapel which is dedicated to St. Ann, the patron saint of French Canadians. The painting is by a Roman artist, Carnavali. The window to your right depicts Jeanne Mance, whom we saw sculptured on the Maisonneuve monument in Place d'Armes. Continuing toward the rear of the church, we come to the large wooden crucifix which is worth noting because of the lifelike expression on the rough-hewn face of Christ. The last window on this side pictures Notre Dame partly constructed. One tower is finished and the big bell waits on Place d'Armes to be hauled into place. Crossing to the other side of the church, we approach the second chapel after the Baptistery which is dedicated to St. Amable. This 17th-century altar is of special interest because it served as the main altar in the old church. Its graceful lines were designed by Louis Quévillon. The paintings above the tabernacle came from Rome. The Chapel of the Holy Rosary is the last chapel on the aisle, next to the main altar. Note the exquisite Florentine Madonna on the door of the tabernacle and the finely carved bas-relief. The painting is a copy of one of Andrea del Sarto's masterpieces representing Mary giving the rosary to St. Dominic while Jesus lays a crown of thorns on the head of St. Catherine of Sienna.

CHAPEL OF OUR LADY OF THE SACRED HEART: Don't miss seeing it! Located in the apse of the church, you reach it by going through the door at the end of either side aisle. Our Lady of the Sacred Heart Chapel was built as an afterthought to accommodate private ceremonies and is of no recognizable style. Although it has been criticized for its profusion of detail and lack of focusing theme, the broad effect suggests a warm and luminous intimacy — a striking contrast to the panoramic grandeur of the big church. It is entirely finished in Canadian white wood without the use of a single nail. At least so it is said! It is lit from above, showing to advantage the paintings done by Canadian artists in their youth. Above the main altar the *Descent of the Holy Ghost* is a copy from Lebrun. At the back of the chapel, above the entrance door, is a large replica of Raphael's *Disputation of the Holy Sacrament*. The symmetrical twisting staircases lead to balconies supported by Roman columns. We were particularly fascinated by the Stations of the Cross, which are skillfully carved so as to produce a three-dimensional effect. Note, too, the intricate detail of the figures, such as the muscles on the arms and the ties of the sandals.

When you have finished looking at the Chapel of Our Lady of the Sacred Heart, turn right at the exit and, if you wish, visit the small church museum. It contains a variety of historical objects including furniture, cutlery, paintings, and personal effects. At the back of the museum is the Chapel of the Catacombs, holding the relics of numerous saints. The admission price is 25¢ for adults. Before leaving Notre Dame Church, you may want to stop at the booth near the museum entrance, where a wide variety of mementos are sold.

St. Sulpice Seminary

When you are once again facing Place d'Armes, take a few minutes to look at the old seminary adjoining Notre Dame Church. Erected in 1683, it is the best preserved and the oldest 17-century building in Old Montréal. A few steps to your left, and you are beside the high, rough-stoned fence dating back to 1712. The gate opens into a quiet, rather unkept courtyard. Its serenity contrasts greatly with the confusion of traffic and people in the square. Walk into the courtyard or, if it is muddy, continue on the sidewalk and look through the iron bars of the wood-roofed main gate. The most noteworthy feature is the clock ornamenting the four-foot-thick walls of the Seminary. Dating back to 1701, the clock is not only the oldest in Montréal, but also the oldest in North America. Its inner workings are made of wood. Even as this book is written it records the correct time, although the chimes are no longer operating. The commodious but stern-looking Seminary has been the administration quarters of the Society of St. Sulpice since the end of the 17th century. The Sulpicians had a profound influence on the history of Montréal and, in part, are responsible for its unique character. The following paragraphs will explain why this is so.

LANDLORDS OF MONTREAL: Although the Society was founded mainly for spiritual reasons, the Sulpicians eventually became the owners of the Island of Montréal. This occurred for two reasons. First, the founders, Maisonneuve and the Company of One Hundred, were either dead or crippled by debts. Secondly, the Gentlemen of St. Sulpice were recruited from men of good family and education, who brought professional experience and private capital to the order. In 1963, in return for paying the colony's debts, they received the title deeds of the island. For two hündred years they held temporal and spiritual power, but always in the best interest of Montréal. Under François Dollier de Casson, the third Sulpician *seigneur,* streets were laid out, the Lachine Canal started, and the Fort de la Montagne built. The latter was erected in 1676 as a fortified Indian mission. The original fort was destroyed, but two of the watchtowers still stand on the north side of Sherbrooke Street, just a few minutes west of Guy Street. They share the distinction with the Seminary of being the oldest structures in Montréal.

When Montréal became a city in 1832, the huge seigneury of the Sulpicians was divided into parishes, but "The Gentlemen" did not stop extending aid. As an example, during the period from 1873 to 1930 they gave five million dollars to worthy projects. Unfortunately, most of their wealth was lost during the Depression years. Nevertheless, there remains lasting evidence of their work in the churches (especially Notre Dame), hospitals, schools, and universities throughout Montréal.

Continuing your *promenade dans le Vieux Montréal,* turn now to our map of Old Montréal and look for Notre Dame Street, which runs east from Place d'Armes. Note as you are leaving the seminary the two grilles on either side of the roofed gate. It was from here that the guards used to watch for hostile Iroquois Indians.

NOTRE DAME STREET

Notre Dame was the first street actually laid out. The commercial activity was located closer to the river on St. Paul Street. We will head now for this area, picking out points of interest along the way. As you cross St. Sulpice Street, the corner building on your right houses the General Trust of Canada. However, as the plaque indicates, it was once the home of Sieur du Lhut who founded Duluth, Minnesota. As you continue east along Notre Dame, you will pass seemingly uninteresting retail stores. But look above the ground-floor level to the ornamental facade on the upper floors. These buildings were erected during the mid-19th century, a period of prosperity in Montréal when the fur trade was producing America's first millionaires. On fashionable Notre Dame Street, old stone houses were replaced by dressed limestone, mud paths became wooden sidewalks, and the first whale-oil street lights were installed. In those days a bottle of beer cost five cents and a house could be rented for $3.50 a month.

The last house before St. Lawrence Boulevard, (No. 1 on the left hand side of Notre Dame Street), is the site of the home of La Mothe Cadillac, the famous *voyageur*. Cadillac came to Montréal to engage in the fur trade, but unable to resist the call of the wandering life of the *voyageur,* he set out to discover new lands. History books inform us he founded the city of Detroit in 1701 and also was the Governor of Louisiana for a few years.

After crossing St. Lawrence Boulevard, you are in the eastern section of the city. In 1700, St. Lawrence was the main highway in Montréal, extending right across the island. Today, it is the demarcation line between west Montréal and east Montréal. Glance back at the old house across Notre Dame Street from the Cadillac building.

Built in the late 1700's, it was part of Notre Dame Convent and is one of the oldest houses on this street.

On the left is the site of the fifty-million-dollar Place de la Justice, to be completed by 1968. The construction has been deliberately delayed so as to avoid building and spending clashes with Expo '67. The finished complex, spreading over two city blocks, will include a main thirty-storey courthouse, a smaller building, and a mall with works of art, fountains, and other decorative features.

Simon McTavish's Home

The next street to the right is St. Jean Baptiste, one of the earliest streets of Montréal and one of the few that has retained its original narrowness. This is a good time to mention that Montréal was originally a fortified town. Although the 18-foot-high walls have gone, their influence is still felt in the irregular pattern and narrow dimensions of the streets. It is also felt in the position and design of the houses. They were built on the front edge of the property, with any unused land serving as a walled garden at the back. Usually it was planned so that the ground floor was used for commercial enterprise and the upper floors for living quarters. A look at the city from the river revealed a long, narrow, walled town with compact rows of solid stone houses capped by tin roofs. A citadel, which was demolished in 1821, could be seen on a hill at the end of Notre Dame Street, where a gun was fired at sunrise and sunset.

During the week St. Jean Baptiste is crowded with trucks unloading produce. If this is so, then go down St. Lawrence, turning left at Le Royer. The building we are interested in stands on St. Jean Baptiste Street at the corner of Le Royer. This rundown warehouse was built in 1765 as the show home of Simon McTavish, Canada's first millionaire and founder of the North West Fur Company. He was nicknamed "the Marquis" because of the many parties he held while courting his beautiful, young French fiancée, Marie Marguerite Chaboillez. After marrying her, McTavish spent a fortune refurnishing their home. Over the years the house has been greatly altered, and the original pitched roof has been replaced by a brick storey. You can still see the arched *porte cochère* or carriageway that used to lead to the stables at the rear. Today it leads to a modern stable — a parking lot!

McTavish planned to erect a *château* on the side of the mountain for his bride, but she died before it could be completed. Its ruins overlooked the city for fifty years, gaining the reputation of being a haunted house.

Fifty feet in front of McTavish's house, on the corner of Le Royer and St. Lawrence, a plaque denotes the site of the first permanent school of Ville Marie. It was built one block west in 1657 by Marguerite Bourgeoys, an important figure in the early history of this city. We shall discuss her contribution to the colony when we reach Notre Dame de Bonsecours Church, a few blocks from here. The attractive but roughly hewn figures in the plaque represent this zealous woman with two pupils, an Indian girl and a little French-Canadian boy.

Return to Notre Dame Street and continue east to St. Gabriel. Before turning right, notice the row of stately columns on the facade of the Criminal Court House. Originally this land was the estate of Lambert Closse, the intrepid Indian fighter whose figure stands on the Maisonneuve monument in Place d'Armes. It was Maisonneuve, a close friend, who gave him this land as payment for his bravery. It was indeed a small token when we think of Closse's courage in fighting off the attack of two hundred Iroquois with only a dozen men.

As you walk down St. Gabriel Street, watch for a small sign reading "Auberge le Vieux St. Gabriel". This ordinary-looking building now houses the oldest continuously operating restaurant in America. It dates back to 1754, when Auberge le Vieux St. Gabriel was a hotel as well as a restaurant. Although the present building is not that old, some of the original furnishings have been preserved, including the dark-stained wooden bar and the stone fireplace in the first dining room. Now is the time to mention their delicious *tarte au sucre Québec* or sugar pie — a French-Canadian dessert that should be tried. Pie and coffee will cost you fifty cents.

BEAVER HATS GAVE CANADA HER START

Continue down St. Gabriel until you come to Ste. Thérèse, the street behind the court house. The area of the parking lot on the corner is the site of the home of Simon Fraser, fur trader and explorer who discovered the Fraser River in British Columbia. Turning down Ste. Thérèse you will notice a building between the parking lot and rue de Vaudreuil which was erected in 1759 as a warehouse for John Jacob Astor, the American fur baron. Like the home of Simon McTavish, the original roof has been removed and a brick storey added. The interesting features of this rather nondescript building are the pieces of original eaves which still jut out at the point where brick meets cement. The owner must certainly have been in a hurry to increase his storage space! Whoever is to restore this rejected warehouse will have to tear down the brick addition, scrape off the cement hiding the original stone, and put on a pitched roof. Then *voilà!* – an authentic 18th-century construction.

Since John Jacob Astor is so intimately connected with the fur trade, let us disgress briefly to the time when fur was king.

It all began in the 16th century when a craze for broad-brimmed beaver hats among European aristocracy urged the *coureurs des bois* (runners of the woods) to search Canada's vast hinterland for beaver pelts. The demand continued unabated, and during the next century Montréal grew into one of the fur capitals of the world. The wealthy fur barons of this city zealously protected their holdings from intruders, but a poor German immigrant invaded this coterie to become Americas' first millionaire. This was John Jacob Astor, who began a fortune by buying furs in Montréal, storing them in the warehouse before you, and then selling them in New York, and later, Oregon, at a higher price.

It was Montréal fur merchants who formed the first club on this continent, appropriately named the "Beaver Club." Their dinners were extravagant events held fortnightly during the winter time. Although not a member, John Jacob Astor received a much-coveted invitation to one dinner. This was a special occasion. The club had not met in four years due to the death of their leader, Simon McTavish. The evening began with the old Indian custom of smoking the pipe of peace. During the seven-course meal, large quantities of wine were consumed. A special drink of the evening was the flaming *loup Garou*, or werewolf with a hot foot, which consisted of red wine, rum, and flaming maple sugar. No doubt it stimulated the ceremony of the re-enacting of the scene of the Great Voyage. Using walking sticks, fire pokers, or whatever could be manipulated as a paddle, the fur traders positioned themselves on the floor as though seated in a canoe and imitated the movements of the rowers while bellowing the *voyageur* song,

> . . . row, brothers, row, the stream
> runs fast, the rapids are near, and
> the daylight's past.

The Beaver Club dinner is held annually in the Beaver Club restaurant of the Queen Elizabeth Hotel and is one of Montréal's gayest and most boisterous events.

From the Court House to the Silver Dollar Saloon

Continue along Ste. Thérèse to rue St. Vincent. As you turn left, notice the two little restaurants, Au Vieux Foyer and Le Petit Havre. The latter restaurant has a delightfully obscure location above a gas station and next door to the city morgue. The fortunate few who have climbed the steep stairs selfishly keep the secret that within lies the best eating house in the old quarter.

Looming at the top of Rue St. Vincent, the handsome stone portico of the Old Court House resembles a Greek temple. Built in 1851, seventy-five years prior to the New Court House, around which you just walked, it was designed by John Ostell. Over the years the original design has been altered by an additional storey and a dome which, alas, has caused the loss of much of its original beauty. With the completion of Place de la Justice, the Old Court House will discontinue handling civil cases. By the way, Québec has a different system of civil law from other provinces. It is based upon the 18th-century Napoleonic Code, while the criminal law is based upon the English Common Law – all very intriguing to the visiting lawyer, but confusing to the unprepared litigant.

Heading east along Notre Dame Street, you should know that some of the houses on the other side of the street from the Old Court House were built in the 18th century. As with many of the buildings in the old quarter, the ground floors have been disfigured by artificial stone fronts. However, one of the homes was restored by the La Sauvegarde Insurance Company to provide an art exhibition centre for Québec artists who have not previously sold work through a commercial gallery. The gallery is open every afternoon, and admission is free. Note the solid simplicity of its rough stone exterior, so characteristic of early 18th-century architecture in Montréal. The citizens did not have the time, the means, or the tools to build lavishly. The building next to La Sauvegarde once housed a night club with a girlie show which was so bad that college students referred to it as "the rest home for strippers". The corner building dates back to 1803. At one time it was known as "The Silver Dollar Saloon", because the owner had encrusted three hundred and fifty American silver dollars into the tile floor. The clients used to joke about how they walked on a small fortune.

Monuments of Naval Heroes Beside City Hall

Pause to inspect the two monuments ahead of you. The most conspicuous is the eight-foot statue of Admiral Lord Nelson standing on a tall Doric column. Erected in 1809, it is Montréal's oldest monument and the first such tribute to Lord Nelson in the world. He is dressed in full uniform, his left arm (the other was lost in fighting for his country) resting upon broken rigging. Nelson visited Québec City in his youth and fell in love with the attractive Mary Simpson. He almost ruined his naval career by leaving his ship to marry her. The grey column on which he stands is made of limestone from nearby quarries. Because of the plentiful supply, it was Montréal's favorite building material for over one hundred and fifty years. The panels of the bas-relief represent the principal events of Nelson's naval career, with a description of the events written below. During the last century, the eight upright cannon muzzles outside the base of the monument were used in carrying out public punishments of specific crimes. The culprit was tied to a cannon and lashed thirty-nine times as demanded by British law.

Facing Nelson's column behind a water fountain is the Vauquelin monument. He was a naval captain, honoured by Canadians for his valour against the British at Québec City in 1760. Defeated and fatally wounded, Vauquelin was asked why he did not haul down the flag on his ship. He replied. "My duty is not to strike my flag, but to haul down those of my enemies." The statue depicts the wounded hero leaning against the rigging of his ship.

The area of the fountain and monument is quite historical. In the 17th century it was the site of farm buildings belonging to the Jesuits. Later it became an army barracks, where American prisoners of the 1812 War were shackled and chained in a makeshift prison. It remained a jail until 1836.

The City Hall is situated immediately east of the Vauquelin monument. This ornamented, grey-stone structure is patterned after the City Hall of Paris. Its steep, square roof and high windows are typical of French-Canadian architecture. It was built eighty-seven years ago, but its wood interior was gutted by fire in 1922. The present building was rebuilt within the original walls. Montréal has a bilingual city council composed of forty-eight elected councillors and a mayor. Jean Drapeau, the current mayor, is an energetic man who has stimulated the renaissance that has taken place in Montréal during the last seven years. While rebuilding the heart of the city, he is also responsible for preserving its heritage. For it was he who set up the Jacques Viger Commission to plan and direct restoration of *le Vieux Montréal*. Before his election many historical buildings had been wilfully destroyed. An outstanding example is the destruction of the home of James McGill, who founded McGill University, to make way for the parking lot that you see across the street from the City Hall.

PLACE JACQUES CARTIER

The cobblestoned square running downward toward the harbour from Lord Nelson's monument is called Jacques Cartier Square. It was part of the garden of the Governor's palace during the French regime. Then, after the capitulation of New France to the British, the palace was turned into a school, which was eventually destroyed by fire. Until a few years ago the Square was known chiefly as an open-air vegetable market. Now, the city has enhanced the area with a new park, antique gas lamps, and water fountains. During the summer brightly striped stalls filled with flowers make for a colourful photograph.

Walking down Jacques Cartier Street on the west side of the Square, you will pass the new Le Fournil restaurant and La Clemence Boîte de Chanson. An abrupt turn to the right at the lower end of the street, and you enter a very narrow lane named St. Amable. Of the many streets in the old quarter this one best depicts the Dickensian setting of 19th-century Montréal. The thick-walled buildings crowd the cobblestones and shut out the sun, giving a medieval gloom to the lane. The long, low stone buildings on the left-hand side once contained the storage vaults for the furs of the North West Company. Look up at the walls. Do you see the rusted hooks that once held iron shutters? When they were shut, the whole town seemed a uniform shade of grey. It was believed the shutters were a protection against the city's greatest enemies – fire and disease. In fact they were neither. Time after time fire destroyed hundreds of homes. As for disease, even in 1846 sixty-five per cent of all children died before they were five.

All this changed when Victoria Bridge was built, connecting the island of Montréal to the mainland. Commerce expanded, trade boomed, and people moved to the suburbs.

St. Paul Street—A Cow Track?

At the end of St. Amable turn left. Half a block later you should be standing at the intersection of St. Paul and St. Vincent Streets. From this position look west (to your right) down St. Paul Street. Notice the graceful sweep of the 19th-century buildings as they follow the winding street. This thoroughfare began as an extension of the footpath linking Maisonneuve's Fort to the Jeanne Mance Hospital. Its meandering course would make one think it was probably a cowpath at one time. This isn't too unlikely, as historians claim that many city streets began as cow tracks – the curves developing where the cow stepped aside to munch on a choice bit of grass!

Having looked at the view to the west, continue east down St. Paul Street. The last three houses on the north side of this block have been restored. At one time they were a part of the estate of Denis Benjamin Viger, one-time co-Prime Minister of the Province of Canada before Confederation, and noted publisher. He was a cousin of the first mayor of Montréal. Number 177 was the Viger publishing house. Today it is the Galerie Cartier, with three floors of unusual, beautiful, and expensive Canadiana pieces – certainly worth seeing. The building itself is a typical home of the 18th century. The French government demanded that every house be constructed with a tin roof and a stone fire wall to help prevent fire from spreading. In this case, the pitched tin roof is painted red, with thick fire walls protruding on either side. Take a good look at these chimney-topped walls, for they are the distinguishing feature of *le Vieux Montréal*, mainly because they are not found in the architecture of other cities, and are numerous here. To be completely authentic, the Galerie Cartier should have two ladders attached to the roof, as these were required by the law.

Number 169 was known as the House of the Patriot on account of the wooden sculpture of an *habitant*, in traditional clothes, that once hung in front of the first-floor tobacco shop. The last house on the corner is being restored at the time of writing.

Rasco's Hotel and Bonsecours Market—Montreal's Oldest Landmarks

Continuing along St. Paul Street, the large, shabby building on your left, where the street Marché Bon Secours meets St. Paul, is the Rasco Hotel. If you look closely, you can see the faded letters of its name on the grimy wall between the second- and third-floor windows. Opened in 1836, it was rated by travellers of that time as one of the finest hotels in North America. It was named after its Italian founder, Romeo Rasco, and became the meeting place for the *beau monde*. The highlight of the social season in the 1840's was the January ball at Rasco's. Here all classes of Montréal society gathered, from the wigged and jewelled matron to the feathered and beaded Indian chief. The most popular dance was the waltz, the polka being considered too *avant-garde!* Today, Rosco's rests degraded, ravished by time and the indifference of man, forsaken even by flop-house tenants; the only guests are rats — and perhaps the odd ghost! Luckily the hotel was saved from the wrecker's derrick, and now placidly awaits its restoration to plush and polished beauty.

On the far side of Rasco's is a short lane named after Charles Dickens, who stayed in the hotel and played at the nearby Théâtre Royal. He had been invited to North America by Henry Longfellow and visited Montréal in the spring of 1842.

Across the street from Rasco's sooty black facade is the long, grey structure of the recently restored Bonsecours Market. The thorough face-lifting of this 130-year-old building cost the city two-and-a-half million dollars. It was well worth the expenditure, for it is one of Montréal's most historic landmarks. Built around 1845, it was the central point of activity in the city for seventy-five years. Bonsecours was divided into two portions; the western served as the city hall and the eastern as a concert hall. The old *hôtel de ville* had its most distinguished days in 1849, when it housed the Parliament of Canada for a short time. After the erection of the new City Hall on Jacques Cartier Square eighty-five years ago, the hall functioned humbly as a local market. Vending stalls piled high with meat and vegetables lined its proud old walls. Around the massive Doric columns women sat knitting and children sold flowers. Your ears rang with the sounds of pigs, ducks, roosters, and bargaining housewives. Discarded lettuce leaves and tomatoes stuck to the soles of your shoes. Once considered the most beautiful building in Canada, Bonsecours had become a mid-city farm.

In 1964 the city decided not to demolish this symbol of the past to make another parking lot. Instead, they did a wonderful job of restoring Bonsecours — retaining its original beauty, but making it a functional office building. It was the toughest job of demolition and reconstruction ever done in Montréal. The inside of the building had to be gutted from roof to earth, leaving only the shaky outer shell. Before the walls could be realigned and strengthened, it was necessary to reinforce the foundation with a mat of thirty-six-inch concrete, reinforced with a mesh of steel. Finally the three floors had to be reconstructed, giving 80,000 square feet of floor space to the offices of the City's Planning Department. The finishing touch to the restoration was given by the large copper-sheeted dome. Painted white, it gleams above you, proudly announcing that Bonsecours Market is again the showpiece of Montréal.

Across the street is a row of wooden houses. You will see the weatherbeaten wooded sign identifying a small French restaurant called Le Fournil (see Where to Dine). Above the restaurant is an *avant-garde* boutique with a small but very original collection of women's clothes.

Continuing east, we come to the left-hand corner of St. Paul and Bonsecours Streets, which is the location of another form of activity in *le Vieux Montréal* — a French amateur theatre company known as Les Saltimbanques. This century-old building makes an intriguing backdrop for the *avant-garde* plays of this pocket theatre. Fittingly, it stands opposite the site of the Théâtre Royal, the leading theatre of Montréal for many years. As previously mentioned, this was where Charles Dickens performed in his own plays during his tour of America. Also, this was where Jefferson Davis, the shattered, defeated leader of the Confederacy, stood with tears in his eyes while the crowd saluted him by standing and singing *Dixie*. During the Civil War Montréal's sympathy had been with the South, and Jefferson Davis sought refuge here when the war was over. He lived on Mountain Street.

The Little Church for Sailors— Oldest Church in Montréal

If you stand on the corner of rue Bonsecours directly in front of the eastern wing of Bonsecours Market and look at the roof at the back of the church, you will see a huge statue of the Virgin flanked by two angels. Her arms are outstretched as if to protect the harbour she overlooks. The crown of electric lights above her head was used as a landmark by navigators in guiding their ships into the harbour. However, in recent years the Virgin's aid has been assisted by such technical means as hydrographic maps and navigation buoys. Beneath the statue is a small chapel and observation tower that provide an excellent view of the harbour, the river, and the World Fair site. Another unique feature of the church is the quaint inscription written in French over the front entrance:

> If the love of Mary is graven in your heart
> Do not forget to say a prayer in passing.

The interior of the church is also unique, with an evident nautical atmosphere. Suspended by long chains from the arched roof are eight models of ships, each with masts and funnels. In seven of them the funnels serve as candlesticks for glowing votive lights. The original ships were gifts from sailors who carved them while at sea. Upon their return they presented them to the Bonsecours Virgin in the hope that she would bless them with safe voyages. Now most of the ships are machine-made, as the originals were destroyed by fire.

On the right-hand side of the door as you enter, there is a tile mosaic of Marguerite Bourgeoys, foundress of the original chapel in 1658. On the other side of the door is a similar tile mosaic of Sieur de Maisonneuve, founder of Montréal, who is said to have felled the first tree for the construction of the chapel. The altar is flanked by two large, elaborate lights, gifts of the St. Lawrence River pilots. Generally speaking, the interior is rather plain and cold except for the fluttering colour provided by the small candles. Hidden by warehouses and shipyards, the little church has few parishioners remaining, and it seems forsaken except for sunny-Sunday visitors.

ROOF CHAPEL AND BASEMENT MUSEUM: Two quite unusual chapels are located in the rear of the church. They are worth a visit, if you don't mind climbing a winding staircase of sixty-seven steps. Admission is 25¢ for adults, but for children it is free. The revenue goes to the church, which is one of the poorest in the city. As you climb the narrow staircase, think of the earnest people who have ascended on their knees, step by step, praying continuously, in the hope of having a favour granted to them.

To us the chapel at the top is rather depressing. Everything is covered with a layer of dust, including the altar over which are suspended angels which look like kewpie dolls minus feathers. However, there is a human-interest feature that will soften the critical eye. Behind a glass partition in front of the altar are piled slips of paper. They are prayer notes requesting the help of the Virgin, mostly from children. Their demands range from puppies to the return of dead daddies, but all express an innocent faith that brightens the grey room. Outside the chapel there is another flight of stairs leading to a lookout. Note the old bell dating back to 1771. We think you will agree that the view is worth the climb, especially when it includes a close-up look at the impressive mid-river site of Expo '67.

At the bottom of the stairs in the basement of the church there is another chapel which is dedicated to Marguerite Bourgeoys. The children will be pleased, for it contains a doll museum which traces the life of Marguerite in fifty-eight scenes. Each of these scenes, which line three walls in three tiers, is a miniature stage setting, rich in colour, costume, and detail. It took Sister St. Hélène of the Congregation of Notre Dame two years to reproduce it. The walls of the chapel are the original foundation of the church and are seven-and-a-half feet thick. It is said that Marguerite carried some of the stones herself.

THE MIRACULOUS STATUE: We shall conclude our visit with a capsule history of Notre Dame de Bonsecours. This brief historical digression is necessary because the church's development, Marguerite Bourgeoys and early French Canada are closely associated, and all exemplify the indomitable spirit of the pioneers who founded and built this old part of the city.

Bonsecours Church, in some form or another, has been a place of worship since 1658. It was the plans and labours of a thirty-three-year-old school mistress that brought the first chapel into existence. Marguerite Bourgeoys came to Ville Marie to establish a primary school for girls, but as there were only two hundred and fifty settlers and no school-age children, she spent four years as the housekeeper of the Governor's quarters. During that time she dreamed of building a chapel in honour of Our Lady (Notre Dame) to give courage and faith to the poor colonists whose lives were threatened daily by attacking Iroquois (bonsecours literally translated means "good help"). Hence the name of the church, Notre Dame de Bonsecours. In 1657 her plan was approved, and she solicited aid from people for whom she had done sewing and mending. Unfortunately work was brought to a halt when the authorities claimed the chapel premature since there was as yet no parish church.

When Marguerite had enough children for a class, she was given an old, stone stable to use as a school. Thus was formed the Congregation of Notre Dame, which today is the largest and oldest teaching order in America. It is a secular congregation church, and the members make self-imposed vows like those of the Sulpicians. The immense romanesque building of their Mother House is located in the west end of the city at Atwater Avenue and Sherbrooke Street.

In 1671 Marguerite returned to France to get more helpers. While she was there, she met Baron de Fancamp who owned a tiny statue of the Virgin which was said to have miraculous powers. It was decided that the image would be brought to Ville Marie and a chapel built for it. On her return Marguerite found the material of the original chapel in ruins. Work was resumed, and in 1675 the first church of stone was open for worship. Into a niche of Notre Dame de Bonsecours went the statue de Fancamp had given her. About eighty years later the church burnt to the ground, but among the ruins was found the little eight-inch statue, unharmed. The church you see today was erected in 1771 on the stone foundations of the previous chapel. With its odd-shaped turrets and spire it is like the old provincial churches in France, but in recent years it has been very badly restored.

Somewhere along its three hundred years of history the Bonsecours chapel became known as the Sailor's Church. This was due to the belief that the Virgin statue had the power to aid sailors, and to guide the ships sailing into Montréal. Unfortunately for the visitor, the statue has been removed to the Mother House of the Congregation of Notre Dame for safe keeping. However, the Church of the Sailors remains — growing older, dirtier, poorer, but closer to the hearts of Montrealers.

Pierre du Calvet House

From the front steps of Bonsecours Church you can see, slightly to your right, the thick fire wall or *mur mitoyen* of the most photographed building in the old quarter. It is the Pierre du Calvet house, occupying the northeast corner of St. Paul and Bonsecours Streets. Dating from the early 18th century, it is the only example of a three-storey town house still standing in Old Montréal. The majority are two-storey. Restored by James A. Ogilvy's, a Montréal department store, it has been turned into an historical museum, Bonsecours Historique.

Originally the house was part of the estate of Pierre du Calvet. This notorious Huguenot came to Montréal from southern France and rapidly amassed a forture in the fur trade. After the cession of the city to the British, he won the confidence of the military government, who made him a Justice of the Peace. This placed him in an excellent position to become a triple spy; for the British, for the French, and for the Americans — all at the same time! His treachery was exposed, however, and he served a three-year jail sentence. Several years later he was again accused of treason and was banished from the country. In 1786 he suffered a watery death, shipwrecked on his way from New York to Europe.

When restoration began in the du Calvet house, a secret cellar was found connected to the building by a passageway. For reasons as yet unknown, this part of the old quarter has numerous tunnels under the street. It would make a great setting for a James Bond movie!

A few steps further down St. Paul Street is another restaurant, Les Filles du Roi. Our chapter, *Where to Dine,* has a lot to say about its food, its décor, its history, and its owners. When gathering information for this chapter, we spent many afternoons strolling through these streets, and we could never pass Les Filles du Roi without stopping for coffee and sugar pie. We are sure it was the graciousness of the *maître d'* and the charm of the authentic décor that beckoned us in.

No. 455, further down St. Paul Street, is the restored La Charpente house with an *haute couture* salon in the basement, an *art ventes* operated by Loyola College on the second floor, and remodelled apartments waiting occupancy. It looks as if the entrance to La Boutique Toujours Chic was designed for short people only, but in fact the ground floor and door are half underground because of the build-up of the street over the years. The house dates back to the early 1700's and is very solidly constructed. The field-stone walls are three feet thick, and in the basement you can see the foot-square, hand-hewn pine beams running the length of the house. Even in 1749 it was the focal point of activity. The wife of the Minister to New France wrote in her diary that it was the meeting place for café society. Vincent Morant says that La Charpente was noted for his hospitality as well as for his lavish meals and exquisite wines. When it was built, the Charpente house was considered to be at the outskirts of the fortified city, very close to the gate that opened onto the road to Québec

City. It is also the farthest point east of our walking tour. Now it is necessary to double back the short distance to Bonsecours Street, the centre of the restoration effort.

At the bottom of the sloping hill of Bonsecours Street, it is not hard to detect places where the asphalt has worn off the road, revealing brick-shaped paving stones. The sidewalks of the main streets were usually built of slabs of slate, but for some of the smaller streets short sections of upturned logs were used, slippery in the rain and especially difficult for the women with their long sweeping skirts.

In The Candle Shop and Hochelaga Antiques N'Things (No. 408) on the left-hand side are sold a variety of Victorian objects and also colourful candles. The many unusual, inexpensive items make it an interesting shop for browsing. Being fond of candles, we were impressed by the distinctive designs, the glowing colours, and the economical prices of the ones displayed. What wonderful Christmas gifts!

The Renovation of Three Adjacent Houses

No. 420 is a century-old building which has been reinstated to its original Victorian stateliness. From the outside there is no evidence that this building housed the renowned *haute couture* salon of Marie Paule. Madame Nolin, the owner, has refurnished the entire interior with period furniture costing $100,000. The second floor is her residence. In May, Madame Nolin has a spring fashion show on the roof terrace for her "limousined" clientele.

The neighbouring building (430) has been restored by Fred Lebensold, who is the architect of Place des Arts, Montréal's showpiece centre for the performing arts. This one-time fish market now contains luxurious, high-ceilinged apartments, each with its own patio. If you look closely at the details of the facades of number 420 and 430, you will see they are almost indentical. The reason for this is that Marie Paule could not find documents and drawings to guide her in the restoration, so she used those of Lebensold's building.

Immediately next is a grey building of great historical worth. Dating back to 1750, it was the residence of six generations of the Papineau family. Its most famous member was Louis Joseph Papineau, speaker of the Lower Canada Legislative Assembly, and a gifted orator. He was the leader of the French Canadians in the rebellion *(Les Troubles)* of 1837 and an advocate of the elective system of government. The cause of the movement was a fight for responsible government, as the government ignored the elected representatives, the majority of whom were French Canadian.

The Papineau home is now owned by Eric McLean, the best-known leader in the crusade to preserve *le Vieux Montréal.* When McLean bought the building, it had degenerated to a flophouse. To restore it, he tore down the two brick storeys which had been added in the 19th century and put on the pitched roof and dormer windows. Knock on the facade; you will be surprised to find that it is made of wood. These are the original plankings used by Papineau when he remodelled the house. The walls are four feet thick, and when the interior was restored, nineteen layers of wallpaper were removed.

The last limestone building in this row, on the corner of Notre Dame and Bonsecours Streets, was owned by George Etienne

Cartier, one of the Fathers of Confederation. Before walking left on Notre Dame Street to Château de Ramezay, pause to look directly north. This lower area was once swampland, but as Montréal expanded it was drained and filled. By the way, Au Pierrot Gourmet, slightly west at 425 Notre Dame Street, is an excellent little French restaurant (see *Where to Dine*).

If you look to the left as you are crossing St. Claude Street, you will see Bonsecours Antique Shop, the first and still the largest antique store in this part of Old Montréal.

The Château De Ramezay

The Château de Ramezay, on the corner of St. Claude and Notre Dame Streets is the last stop on our *promenade dans le Vieux Montréal,* and appropriately the most historic building in the country. Classified by the government as a national relic, it is a storehouse of French, English, and American history. This long fieldstone building was built by Claude de Ramezay, the 11th governor of Montréal. Since 1705, governors, Iroquois, fur traders, aristocrats, lawyers, and soldiers have passed through its gates. Its many occupants reflect the history of the city, so let's take a few minutes to highlight the most famous. Governor de Ramezay was a conscientious and honest administrator who, unfortunately, was deeply in debt when he died. This was due partly to the expenses forced upon him by his offices of state, and partly to the expense of bringing up a large family. Out of the sixteen children born to him, only one son lived to perpetuate his name. Incidentally, he was not married until the age of 33 and died at 67.

Claude de Ramezay's wife sold the *château* to the West India Company, and for several years it was the centre of the fur trade. After the cession of Canada to the British it was used as a residence for the British Governors. During the American occupation of Montréal in 1775-1776, it served as the headquarters for the American army under Generals Montgomery and Wooster. General Benedict Arnold stayed at the *château* for a few weeks in 1776, and it was here that he met Benjamin Franklin, who had been sent by the Continental Congress to attempt the difficult job of winning Canada over as the 14th colony of the new English-speaking independent America. Their proposition failed, mainly because of the opposition of the Roman Catholic Church.

It would take too much time to discuss the many transitions of the old *château*, but, if you are interested, they are listed chronologically on a plaque near the front entrance. This building was saved from destruction seventy years ago by the city, who in turn gave it to the Antiquarian and Numismatic Society, who converted it into a museum. There is something for everyone among its unusual collection of relics. The Indian room has arrows, scalping knives, and even a scalp! The Reception Hall, the social centre of the château, contains fine Canadian furniture and paintings from the 18th and 19th centuries. Of special interest to American visitors is the dais and chair on the east wall which General Wooster had installed to give audience at the time of the American occupation.

Don't forget the basement where the main kitchen and bakery are located. Above the great stone fireplace there is a drum which was whirled by a dog inside it, providing the necessary action to turn the spit on which the meat was cooked. Ducking into a passage you will come to a collection of vehicles including Montréal's first fire engine, first gas-driven automobile, and first unicycle. It was the last that particularly intrigued us – just imagine wheeling along the cobblestones to a Sunday afternoon picnic on this precarious machine! The Château de Ramezay is open from 10 a.m. to 5 p.m., Sunday 2 p.m. to 5 p.m., closed on Monday in winter. The admission price is 50 cents for adults and 10 cents for children under 14 years of age.

While we are discussing the architecture of the *château*, step behind the high wrought-iron gates to the more peaceful courtyard. It has been said that this building is one of the finest examples of an early Canadian farmhouse. The general appearance is unchanged from 1706, except for the unharmonious eastern tower added in 1830. The *château* takes its form from the street house which was built as one of a continuous row; we saw examples of this on St. Paul Street. This development into a detached country house is strictly a Canadian innovation.

We chose the Château de Ramezay as the conclusion of the walking tour for its architectural features as much as for its historical significance. It is a pictorial summary of many characteristics pointed out during the walking tour as typical of French-Canadian homes – the thick stone walls, the great end gables carried up to form fire partitions, the pitched tin roof, the dormer windows, and the double chimneys, The overall effect is one of strength and permanence. Although strangled by the octupus called commercial growth, this proud old *château* stands firmly as a guardian of Canada's past.

A Modern Day "Voyage of Discovery"

When you are ready to leave the Château de Ramezay, cross Notre Dame Street and walk down rue Gosford beside the City Hall to Craig Street and the Champ de Mars Station. Take the Métro to Berri-de Montigny, then transfer to the westbound Métro. To get to Dominion Square, get off at the Peel Street stop. If you brought your car you can take the Métro and get off at Place d'Armes, the starting point of our tour. Perhaps, if it is late, you would prefer to have dinner in Old Montréal. Our chapter, *Where to Dine,* describes restaurants in this quarter.

At the beginning of the tour we spoke of *le Vieux Montréal* as the gateway to the West. Many courageous pioneers who discovered and developed America passed through its gates. Today you too have been pioneers — not of new lands but of old. One of the fascinating aspects of Old Montréal is that you are seeing it in the primary stage of restoration. It is not like the tree-lined areas of Williamsburg or Sturbridge with their new-old buildings and modern conveniences. It is not a closed-off area that awaits visitors in best bib and tucker. Rather, it is a functioning part of a busy metropolis. The old buildings are not reconstructed showpieces, but have two hundred years of grime and history stuck to their walls. It demands concentration and perseverance equal to that of our pioneer forefathers to find *le Vieux Montréal* among the warehouses, flophouses, and parking lots. It may not be beautiful, but it is realistic and certainly authentic.

Truly, the old quarter gives the city its charm and historical significance. Without it, Montréal would be similar to any other North American city.

CHRONOLOGY OF MONTREAL

1535 – Indian Village of Hochelaga discovered by Jacques Cartier. He called the mountain Mount Royal.

1611 – Samuel de Champlain visited the site and established the first trading post.

1641 – Hochelaga is consecrated to the Holy Family and christened Ville Marie de Montréal.

1642 – Paul de Chomedy, Sieur de Maisonneuve founded "Ville Marie."

1644 – Jeanne Mance founded Hotel Dieu, the first hospital of Montréal. The site is at the corner of St. Sulpice and St. Paul Streets.

1644 – Maisonneuve defeated the Iroquois at Place d'Armes.

1652 – Lambert Closse defeated the Iroquois near Montréal.

1657 – First school opened by Marguerite Bourgeoys in the loft of a stable.

1659 – First church of Notre Dame de Bonsecours completed.

1660 – Dollard des Ormeaux killed at Long Sault.

1663 – Island of Montréal became the property of the Sulpicians.

1689 – Indian massacre of entire population at Lachine.

1694 – Towers on Sherbrooke Street erected as part of the Montréal Mission.

1701 – Great Indian Peace Treaty signed at Montréal.

1705 – Château de Ramezay built by Claude de Ramezay, the 11th Governor of Montréal.

1722 – Construction of the 18-foot stone fortifications around the city.

1760 – Wolfe defeated Montcalm on the Plains of Abraham at Québec City. The British took possession of Montréal.

1775 – Montréal capitulated to the Americans under General Montgomery.

1776 – Americans under General Arnold departed from Montréal.

1785 – The Beaver Club instituted.

1801 – Beginning of the removal of the walls around Montréal.

1813 – Americans defeated at Chateauguay in an attempt to take Montréal.

1815 – Whale-oil lamps used to provide the first lighting in Montréal.

1821 – Construction of new Lachine Canal commenced.

1832 – City of Montréal incorporated, population 40,000.

1833 – Jacques Viger named first Mayor.

1836 – First railway in Canada.

1837 – Gas used for lighting streets.

1867 – Confederation of Canada.

1879 – First electric street lights.

3.

WHERE TO DINE "BON APPETIT"

Dining out in Montréal is like going to the theatre in London – exciting, relatively inexpensive, but oh so difficult to choose where! It's impossible to walk twenty yards in the central district without a restaurant's beckoning you in. There are four thousand, which in relation to population, puts Montréal neck and neck with San Francisco. As to the quality of the food – if we told you Montréal is the best eating city in North America, you would accuse us of prejudice. So you decide for yourself, and then we can say, "I told you so!" We have already stated that Montréal is an international city. An illustration of this fact is the assortment of cuisines available – Italian, Hungarian, Japanese, German, Indian, Russian, Spanish, Chinese, etc., and, of course, the *prima dona* of the culinary world, French.

You are probably wondering why dining out is the foremost attraction of Montréal. The answer is simple – this is a French-Canadian city! Through their knowledge of preparation and their pride in good service, the French have given Montréal the reputation of being a gastronomical delight. The French have an inherited love of good food, which makes them a very discerning clientele. If its cuisine, its service, and its atmosphere do not meet the high standards, a restaurant will soon close. On the other hand, if it passes the tough entrance exams and enters the inner circle of gourmet "finds", location and paid advertisements matter little, as word-of-mouth will soon create a demand for reservations; because, you see, a growing number of Montrealers have a game (usually played at lunch) called *cherchez le restaurant*. A group of players meet periodically at regular dates to dine. Each member in turn is required to pick out a good eating place to which none of the others have been.

To enjoy to the fullest the pleasures of the palate that await you, it is important to be *au courant* with the dining habits of Montrealers. Here are a few rules of the game.

BREAKFAST

The quickest service probably will be in your hotel. If the restaurant appears crowded, the doorman is sure to know a good coffee shop within walking distance. It is not a Canadian custom to serve your coffee first; so if you are a morning-coffee addict, tell the waitress as soon as you are seated. Surprisingly, French Canadians enjoy substantial breakfasts, similar to Americans, and not the the traditional French *café au lait* and *croissants*. The large choice of menu will always include juice, cereal, toast, and eggs with bacon, ham, or sausage. By the way, do not presume that because the maple leaf is the Canadian emblem you will pour real maple syrup on your pancakes – more frequently it will be corn syrup with maple flavouring. Restaurant breakfast hours are approximately 8 to 9:30 a.m. So, dawdlers, if it is after

10 a.m. and you wish to avoid the cold eye of the waiter trying to set up for lunch, eat in a coffee shop or café. It's quicker and cheaper.

LUNCH

During the morning rush-hour the streets of most North-American cities are crowded with labourers carrying lunch boxes, white-collar workers with brown paper bags, and executives with leather attaché cases. The containers may vary, but the contents are the same – sandwiches!

Not so in Montréal. Here, as in Paris, Madrid, and Rome, the lunch hour is sacrosanct. From 12 noon to 2 p.m. businessmen travel near or far to their favorite eating places. But not always for food alone. Many a pretty secretary has been wooed, many a difficult business deal transacted, and many a hard-boiled employer mellowed by delectable dishes in pleasant surroundings. A large number of restaurants offer a businessman's lunch at a fixed price. Thus you can sample their specialities without paying the more expensive evening prices.

For the visitor who is more interested in sight-seeing than in lingering lunches, look at the restaurants listed in our section on *Budget Restaurants in Central Montréal.* Many of them combine quick service with interesting specialty dishes. Clock-watchers, who just want to grab a sandwich or a hamburger, can choose from the numerous corner cafés and drug stores with luncheon counters. Or, if you are on a shopping spree, most department stores have several luncheon rooms. (See *Shopping Guide.)*

The most economical lunches, for men only, are offered by taverns. Here wholesome, tasty meals cost under a dollar, and a glass of draft beer ten cents. These cool, dark, male retreats dot the downtown area, but the most famous is Le Gobelet in the north end of the city (8405 St. Lawrence).

The outside is a modern office building; the inside is a rustic 19th-century barn. Watch out for the flying budgies while you dine on sumptuous pheasant under glass for only $3.95.

DINNER

Montrealers usually dine between 7 and 9 p.m., although most restaurants are open until midnight. We advise you to reserve a table, and even then be prepared for a twenty-minute wait on busy nights. Dining out is one of the most pleasant forms of entertainment to the Montrealer. It is practised in a leisurely manner, with good conversation just as important a factor as good food and unobtrusive service. Also, most Montrealers dress for dinner – that is, the men wear a shirt, tie, and jacket and the women a dress. At the end of the meal when you receive the bill, the Province of Québec adds a 8% hospital tax. It is customary to leave 15% to 20% *pourboire* (tip). Since many restaurants have their menus only in French, we have included a Menu Translator at the end of this chapter. If you are not sure of the ingredients of a particular dish, ask the waiter – most of them are cool but courteous.

To help you choose places to dine, we have divided the city into three main areas: Central Montréal, with its international specialties; Old Montréal, where individually prepared dishes are eaten in an early French-Canadian setting; and Decarie Boulevard, home of elegant eating in distinctive surroundings. Then comes a short section on "out of the way but worth the trip" restaurants. In each category we have picked out restaurants that we feel give you the most value for your money. Some are high-priced, well-known dineries and other are inexpensive, out of the way "finds". We must emphasize that the restaurants featured at the beginning of each section are not necessarily the most popular or the best dollar value. They simply have some particular feature that we think a visitor would enjoy. Please remember that the prices quoted are subject to change, as restaurateurs inform us there will be up to a 20% increase due to the rising cost of food and the difficulty of finding trained staff. Even so, dining out is less expensive in Montréal than in the majority of American cities. Therefore, without worrisome thoughts about the size of the bill to impair the digestion, you may participate to the full in our finest indoor sport; for we think you'll agree that the pleasures of the table are the most memorable part of a vacation.

To let you know where the restaurants are located, each area is accompanied by a city map. Each number on it corresponds to the number in parenthesis after the name of a restaurant. In addition we have provided the address and phone number of every restaurant mentioned. Last, but most important, please remember that this list is only to guide you. Your own experience in eating may differ from ours – you know the hackneyed saying, "One man's meat is another man's poison."

So *mes amis,* you must decide whether you are in a mood for elegant eating, plain good food, or a gastronomical adventure. Whatever your choice . . . *bon appétit!*

"A MEAL WITHOUT WINE IS LIKE A DAY WITHOUT SUN"

From the time that man stopped swinging from the trees by his tail, intoxicating beverages have been produced. Primitive tribes knew how to start fermentation from sweet potatoes before they knew how to make fire. In the religious cults of the ancient Greeks and Romans "the living blood of the grape" played a leading role – continuing through the centuries as the staple drink of Europe. Unfortunately in America, due to the years of near-Prohibition, wine is often considered a special-occasion drink. Not so in Montréal, where the influx of Europeans since the last World War has furthered the pleasurable habit of wining while dining.

One-quarter of Canada's imported wine is consumed by Montrealers. In the Province of Québec the majority of wine comes from France, and each year the Québec Liquor Board (Q.L.B.) awards coveted contracts to (Régie des Alcools du Québec) wines are various regions of France. Popular R.A.Q. shipped from France in large casks and bottled here. This bulk buying means a good imported wine can be purchased at a reasonable price. Many restaurants use R.A.Q. wines in carafes; thus, for less than a dollar you can enjoy a glass of wine with your meal. Each carafe holds about three glasses.

Montréal restaurateurs are justly proud of their wine cellars. Your preference is a matter of personal taste, but here are a few facts to assist you in choosing a suitable wine to harmonize with the principal dish of the meal. Generally speaking, red wine goes with red meat and highly seasoned dishes, as it enhances the flavour of the meat. For similar reasons white wines are best with light dishes such as chicken, fish, and eggs. Sweet wines are left for dessert.

French wine is the universal standard by which wines are judged; Burgundy and Bordeaux bear its greatest names. Red Burgundy wines are rich, full-bodied and are described as giving you "something to chew on". They should be served with highly flavoured meat, such as lamb and game, or any rich, spicy dish. Two of the finer quality red Burgundy wines available in restaurants are Gavrey Chambertin (about $8.00 a bottle) and a Beaujolais called Moulin-à-Vent (about $5.00).

Red Bordeaux wines (clarets) are drier than the Burgundies with a smaller alcoholic content. They are astringent in their youth, developing their firm, round flavour only after a long period of aging. Enjoy them with beef, vegetables, and cheese. Bordeaux wines available in Montréal restaurants are from the régions of Médoc, Graves, and St. Emilion. If you want a suggestion, try a bottle of Chateau Lagarde from the Graves region (around $5.00).

White Bordeaux wines are dry, spirited, fragrant, and well-balanced – excellent with oysters, fish, sliced cold meats, and poultry. Chablis, a very dry, fresh, white Burgundy, is equally good. Both prices range from $5.00 to $7.00 a bottle. A popular choice with soup or *hors d'oeuvres* is an Alsation wine, such as Reisling (about $6.00).

Most restaurants in our listings have good to excellent wine cellars. Contrary to popular opinion, selecting and enjoying wines does not require skill and experience, but a few basic facts and a spirit of adventure. Discovering your preferences can be fun, especially around so many wine-conscious Québecers.

FEATURED RESTAURANTS IN CENTRAL MONTREAL

A La Crêpe Bretonne . . . A Fantastic Pancake Empire

2080 Mountain St., Phone 842-3481
and 808 St. Catherine E., Phone 842-3485

We begin with a not-to-be-missed experience — eating paper-thin Brittany *crêpes* in either of the two branches of A La Crêpe Bretonne. This is not just another pancake house, but a microscopic Disneyland. Every floor, every room, in fact every corner, is unique. However, the atmosphere stays relaxed and lively, making it a good place to bring children. We often go to the restaurant on Mountain Street for lunch or for a quick supper when shopping Friday nights. Push open a beautifully carved door, and a waitress, prettily attired in Brittany costume and starched lace hat, will show you to a wooden bench and table. From anywhere in the room you can watch the light, crisp 18-inch *crêpes* being made on a large stone hearth. The average price is $1.25. If you are not in the mood for *crêpes,* try the onion soup *au gratin* and chef's salad (one order is enough for two), with perhaps a glass of wine. Such a meal should not exceed $2.10.

On the second floor looms a huge plaster replica of a Brittany fishing vessel. In the dark, quaint atmosphere of its interior you do not mind sharing your bench with a stranger, especially if she's a French model. The menu is the same as downstairs. Crossing in front of the prow of the ship you will enter another room, Chez Grand-mère, a copy of La Mère Poularde in Mont Michel, France. In this Brittany-cottage décor, women in long sweeping skirts beat eggs in front of an open hearth for the forty varieties of omelets that are served. These fluffy, glistening, yellow specialties are served with crunchy French bread and homemade butter.

As you came up the stairs of A La Crêpe Bretonne you will have noticed the lounging, long-haired figures under the red striped awnings of the basement *bistro*. It was named "Chez LouLou les Bacchantes", which roughly translated means "the place of Louis with the moustache", in honour of the owner's famous handlebars. This is the perpetually crowded meeting place of Montréal's would-be bohemians and local intelligentsia who have given a Chelsea atmosphere to this part of Mountain Street. Over a glass of beer and a Camembert-cheese sandwich *en baquette,* you can exchange viewpoints with separatists, painters, poets, expatriates, while watching the *chicerinos* (hip girls) in poor-boy sweaters saunter past. In season, popular delicacies are roasted chestnuts and oysters on the half-shell. At the back of the *bistro* there is a *brasserie*-type restaurant where between 6 and 8 p.m. an exceptionally fine *prix fixe* dinner costs only $2.00 (including a glass of wine).

The only adjective we can think of that describes the décor of the east-end A La Crêpe Bretonne is "out-of-this-world". A heavy oak door opens from St. Catherine into what appears to be a 16th-century abbey hall. From here a cobblestone street winds through a Breton village, ending at a convent courtyard and dining room. Everywhere candles glow dimly on polished oak tables, golden brown *crêpes*, and lively faces. If you want French cuisine, use the St. Hubert Street entrance, just around the corner under the sign "Chez Fanny". The specialties are slightly garlicked dishes, such as *bouillabaisse* (a stew with crab, mussels, red mullet, and octopus) at $4.00, and aioli (boiled codfish with mayonnaise) at $2.75. Every day except Sunday there is a *table d'hôte* menu from noon to 2 p.m. and from 6 to 8 p.m. The choice ranges in price from $2.00 to $5.00 and includes a glass of wine. The décor, as throughout this Disney-styled empire, carries the diner into another *milieu.* Here you enter the titilating, warm atmosphere of a southern-France resort. Louis Tavan, the man responsible for all this, tells us that this is not the end – next year there will be another dining room upstairs. All the restaurants are open daily from 11 a.m. to 2 a.m. Reservations are unnecessary except at Chez Fanny.

Desjardins . . . If Fish Is Your Dish
1175 Mackay Street
Phone 866-9741

In 1892, thirteen-year-old André Desjardins, one of twelve children of a French-Canadian family, arrived in Montréal to learn the English language. He began by cleaning fish at Gatehouse, picking up his English from the Irish who poured into Montréal because of the potato famine in Ireland. With his first earned $50, and a bicycle that he sold for $35, André rented a store. This was the beginning of a restaurant which was to become internationally known, with its own fishing fleet and oyster beds. It is the only restaurant in Canada to be elected to the "Passeport Gastronomique" of Paris. We asked Albert Dejardins, the son of André, how his restaurant has maintainted its excellent reputation for so many years. His answer was, "In any good restaurant the food is well prepared and the service unobtrusive. In addition, I make sure the guest is graciously received in gracious surroundings." The word "gracious" sums up why it is one of our favorite spots. Also we love fish, the *raison d'être* of Desjardins.

The low, white cape-cod cottage restaurant on Mackay Street could double as a museum of North American marine life. A quick perusal of the menu shows Atlantic smelts, Arctic char, Québec salmon, Prince Edward Island oysters, Boston sole, Maryland crabs, Maine clams, Nova Scotia lobster, and Louisiana shrimps. From personal gustatory pleasure we can recommend the live broiled lobster at $5.00 a pound, the Danish *scampi* (some foreign specimens do manage to squeeze in) at $4.50, and any of the *à la newburgs* at $5.00. If you want a suggestion for an *entrée,* try the *crêpes au crabe,* thin *crêpes* stuffed with crab and covered with thick mustard sauce. The Malpeque oysters ($1.00 for half a dozen) are another popular delicacy. Do not miss the restaurant's time-honoured tossed green salad, ceremoniously mixed at your table. One serving at 75¢ is enough for two people. Although Desjardins remains mute about the salad ingredients, it is easy to detect lettuce, tomatoes, hard-boiled egg, olive oil, vinegar, mayonnaise, and crunchy bread that tastefully co-operates to produce the zingy flavour.

Wine and Desjardins go together like a horse and carriage, not only because a good white wine is the *pièce de résistance* of any good seafood dinner, but also Desjardins' wine cellar has more bottles than many Québec Liquor Commission stores. Our preference is Pouilly-Fuissé-Bichot at $3.50 *demi.* If you would like some suggestions, speak to your waiter, or if it is possible, to Monsieur Desjardins himself. He is a connoisseur of French wine and a charming person. Just recently he was presented with a *médaille d'or* for culinary art by L'Association Culinaire Française de Grande Bretagne. Only fourteen of these honours are given in any one country.

Desjardins has four main dining rooms with the same extensive menus and the same expensive prices. The most popular, La Salle Gaspienne, is decorated in an early-Canadian theme with a large portrait of the Gaspé on the wall across from the entrance. On hot summer evenings it's fun to dine under large, gaily coloured umbrellas on the garden terrace named Sous les Etoiles. La Cave Lorraine resembles an old wine cellar with a dark, intimate atmosphere for dining, wining, and dancing. Although prices are high at Desjardins, there is a tremendous dining bargain between 11 a.m. and 7 p.m., when a *table d'hôte* dinner is available ranging from $1.75 to $2.50. After 7 p.m. it is all *à la carte*. Desjardins has free parking and an attendant to watch your car. By the way, this is a Roman Catholic province, so be prepared for a long wait on Fridays – even with a reservation. This goes for all seafood restaurants.

Au 400 . . .

French Cuisine in Classical Elegance
and at Comfortable Prices

630 Dorchester Blvd., Phone 866-9506

The easy-to-find Au 400 is located in the basement of the CIL skyscraper, two blocks east of Dominion Square. The equal fineness of the many better-class French restaurants in Montréal made choosing a favorite impossible. After much deliberation from the visitor's point of view, we decided Au 400 scored the most points. First, it is a large, well-run restaurant, which has served uniformly good food since the turn of the century. Second, there is a dining room for a thick and a thin wallet. Third, it is within walking distance of many downtown hotels. Fourth, while it is a family restaurant catering to a regular local clientele, it easily handles the large groups brought by Casser Tours and Murray Hill.

Having walked down into a spacious foyer you must choose either Chez Lelarge for elegant, leisurely dining, or La Brasserie for less formal, less expensive, and less elaborate meals. There is also a bar, Au Coin de Mer, with music for dancing. If you are interested in Flemish painting, stop to look at the large still life by Abraham Van Bayern in the foyer. It was bought from the Ryksmuseum in Amsterdam. While there is no doubt of its artistic worth and *à propos* theme, Flemish still lifes have never whetted our intellect or our appetite.

The monochromatic décor of the main dining room, Chez Lelarge, is worthy of attention. See how the carpets, the walls, the table linen, the chair coverings, the icons, and even the menus glimmer in shades of gold. The result is a muted elegance, very conducive to good dining and to stimulating conversation. This deliberate understatement of the surroundings is in keeping with the owners' theory that the clientele should create the atmosphere and the food should provide the color. The menu includes both *à la carte* and *la table d'hôte* sections. We strongly recommend you choose from the five alternatives of the daily *table d'hôte*. A lengthy time is spent in the preparation of these specialties, so of course the quality is superior to *à la carte* which, because of its extensive nature, cannot be prepared beforehand. The establishment has three extra-special specialties, one of which will always be on the *table d'hôte*. For a memorable dinner, look for one of these – young capon with wine sauce at $5.50 (a plump, juicy chicken in white or red wine sauce), or young duckling with port wine sauce at $3.75 (orange or olive sauce is equally good), or beef *bourguignon* at $3.75 (delicious stew made from raw beef cooked very slowly in red wine). Remember these prices include the *entrée,* the main dish, two vegetables, dessert, and coffee – an incredibly good value for your dollars! Dessert, if you have an incurable sweet tooth like ours, means the frustration of deciding which melt-in-your-mouth goody to pick from Au 400's renowned pastry cart.

Since La Brasserie is advertised as an informal, quick-service restaurant, we had imagined it as a cafeteria, not as a tastefully decorated dining room with carpets, tablecloths, soft lights, and courteous waiters. Generally speaking the food, the service, and the décor are less elaborate than those of Chez Lelarge. Again we recommend that you choose from seven alternatives of the *table d'hôte,* for the same reason. Do not look for the three extra-special specialties because they are not offered here. The *table d'hôte* prices range from $2.00 for an omelet to $3.75 for a steak, which is about 75¢ cheaper than Chez Lelarge. A carafon of wine is 90¢.

Au 400 is open every day but Sunday. Chez Lelarge is open for lunch and dinner; La Brasserie is open from 11.30 a.m. to 1 a.m. At noon, Au Coin de la Mer has a fixed-price cold buffet with one hot dish at $1.75. Reservations are not essential, except on a Friday or a Saturday night.

As a finishing remark we should mention that we spent a pleasant hour chatting with one of the owners, André Lelarge. This dynamic and handsome French Canadian has a very definite concept of the restaurant business. He mentioned the words, "simple, well-prepared dishes" and "authentic décor" frequently during our conversation as essential to good dining. Just recently André became the consultant of the Québec Pavilion restaurant at Expo '67, and, listening to his ideas, we feel sure it will be as successful as Au 400.

Auberge St. Tropez . . .

Small, Gay, and Oh So French!

1208 Crescent Street

Phone 861-3197

With money anyone can get succulent dishes and famous wines, but courtesy and kindness can never be bought. So goes the gastronomical axiom that seem especially applicable to Auberge St. Tropez. Parting the bead-string curtain you are greeted by a handsome young man with sensual eyes and groomed *doigté*. This is André Guilbert, the one-time Mr. France. Immediately he will make you feel part of the casual *joie de vivre* that permeates the small room. His attire, similar to the waiters' bustling efficiently among the dozen tables, is a bright, silk shirt opened almost to the waist and body-hugging pants. Everything runs as smooth as silk in this crowded, gay restaurant, yet the courteous waiters find time to graciously accept a glass of wine from a customer and to flash that certain smile at a pretty girl.

Since the menu is in French only and the waiters do not speak English, placing your order may prove an adventure in communication. However, equipped with a sense of humour and our menu translation (page 119), you should get by. The cuisine features *provençal* cooking with the special dishes of the towns along the French Riviera. The menu offers a wide selection of *table d'hôte* dinners. For $3.50 you can choose one item without a price after it from each section – ending up with soup, *entrée,* main course, dessert, and beverage. *A la carte* is anything with a price after it. Our recommendations from the *table d'hôte* are *lapin sauté bourguignonne* (sumptuous rabbit stew), *cuisses de grenouille provençale* (tender frog legs in white wine), and *rougets grillés au Fenouil.* For a rich, smooth dessert try the *crème caramel.*

Seated at one of the five tables in the tiny bar at the back of Auberge St. Tropez, we talked with the two charming French owners, André and Serge. Before acquiring their own restaurant, they worked for years as waiter and barman respectively in various Montréal establishments. No doubt this is why they have made the *esprit de corps* of the waiters such an important part of the atmosphere. While the décor is not outstanding, it has a casual intimacy that makes it appear a very "in" spot. The back of the bar is papered with currency brought back from foreign countries by the regular customers. In exchange for each paper note, Serge gives a free drink.

You can make reservations, but still expect to wait during the busy hours. In this relaxed atmosphere people linger over their coffee. Its hours are from noon to 2 a.m. during the week, and from 5 p.m. to midnight on Sunday. Because of the good food, moderate prices, and magnetic personalities of the owners, St. Tropez has rapidly become the first choice of Montréal's young sophisticates.

Le Caveau . . . The Best of the Budgets
2042 Victoria Avenue
Phone 844-0932

It is not easy for us to be objective when discussing this restaurant. When Diane was a student, and later a seventy-dollar-a-week copywriter, the old Le Caveau took the place of Mother's cooking. In one dark corner we made our wedding plans over the $2.95 *plat du jour*. Since then our visits have become less frequent, but, like hearing an old hit tune from a long-gone bachelor summer, we feel sentimental whenever we see their red-checked tablecloths, candles, and baskets of thickly sliced French bread. However, to avoid being accused of being overly romantic, we give you the facts, *à la* Frommer style.

It is a good, inexpensive French restaurant with an informal atmosphere. Originally Le Caveau was located on the other side of the street, but last year it was expropriated by a stick of dynamite to make way for the new subway. While the owner has kept the same menu and the same reasonable prices, he has tripled the seating capacity. Progress must be lauded; still, we miss the good-natured *bonhomie* that oozed from the low ceilings, steep stairs, and cramped dining space of the old place. The present restaurant has retained its décor of a *petite-bourgeoise* inn in France, but the props look new and artificial. Fortunately, the candlelight and relaxed atmosphere mellow the harsh effect.

The key to Le Caveau's increasing popularity? A wide price range, but uniformly good food. Their low-priced daily specials are dining bargains that should not be missed by the budget-minded. Three full-course dinners are offered at $1.20, $1.50, and $2.95. The $2.95 *plat du jour*, a juicy rib of roast beef, is specially priced at $1.50 on Tuesdays. That is cheap even by European standards. While not ambrosial, the $1.20 and the $1.50 specials are thoroughly satisfying. In keeping with the French manner of cooking, these dishes are usually served with a tasty sauce. *Tourtière maison* (meat pie) with tomato sauce, roast loin of pork, and halibut with white wine sauce are the most frequently offered specials.

For more elaborate, but still not expensive, dining choose from the *à la carte* menu. We recommend the onion soup *au gratin* ($1.00) or the half dozen snails ($1.45) as an *entrée*. Until Diane came to Montréal she had never eaten French onion soup; then it was love at first taste! Since it is offered in the majority of restaurants in Québec, you should make a point to try it during your visit. Topped with French bread and Parmesan cheese, this full-flavoured soup makes a filling but delicious *entrée*. A word of warning to prevent burnt fingers and tongues; the *cassolette* comes straight from the oven to your table, so is *très chaude*. As for the main *à la carte* dishes, particular favorites among the regular clientele are *tournedos* Rossini (small thick fillet of beef with *foie gras* and truffles) at $4.50; Dover sole *meunière* (sole fried in butter) at $3.75; brains in browned butter at $2.50, and Lasagne Bolognese style (layers of noodles, meat sauce, and cheese) at $2.10.

Le Caveau also has a popular *table d'hôte* menu for two. There is a choice of ten dinners ranging in price from $6.95 with a carafon of wine, to $15.80 with a half-bottle of wine. Mentioning alcoholic potables, Le Caveau's wine cellar and bar offers a large selection to refresh the spirit without wilting the wallet.

Monsieur McLaughlin, the owner, informs us that his restaurant is open every day from noon to midnight except on Sunday, when it opens at 5 p.m. In case you think it peculiar that an Irishman should own a French restaurant we must inform you that Monsieur McLaughlin is one of many French Canadians with Anglo-Saxon surnames – a by-product of the English acquisition of Québec in 1760.

DELUXE RESTAURANTS IN CENTRAL MONTREAL

The pulse of Montréal, the square mile between University and Guy Streets, has a fantastic number of fine restaurants. After much hair-tearing the following choices were made and listed according to price. We began with the high-priced, high-quality eating houses that average $4.00 for a *table d'hôte* dinner and $7.00 for an *à la carte*. In both cases this price includes an *entrée*, a main course, a dessert, and coffee, but not tax and tip. A super-dooper dinner for two with a good bottle of wine should not exceed $30.00 in any of the mentioned deluxe restaurants. You will find that the majority of high-class dineries in central Montréal are French. This is only natural since Montréal is a French city and *haute cuisine* is fundamentally a Gallic art. Be daring! Try some of the French specialties such as brain, sweetbread, or rabbit. We promise you that you will find it to be a rare adventure in good eating.

Place Ville Marie Restaurants
Place Ville Marie
Dorchester and University St.

On the bustling below-street-level shopping promenade of this modern square, you will find three outstanding restaurants circling an indoor sidewalk café, appropriately called Le Carrefour (Crossroads). This lively complex of food and drink establishments is operated and managed by the Hilton staff of the adjoining Queen Elizabeth Hotel. A visitor looking for the best will find it worth his epicurean while to dine in one of these highly recommended restaurants – Le Carignan, The Bluenose Inn, and The Stampede. The *table d'hôte* and *à la carte* are priced upward from $3.00 for lunch and $4.00 for dinner. Incidentally, reservations are a must. Each restaurant, a page torn from a book on early Canada, exemplifies the policy of the Queen Elizabeth management to use an historically flavoured décor in each of their many restaurants.

This seems to be a suitable spot for a flash bulletin to "martooni-lovers": both the Q.E. and P.V.M. restaurants serve the best martinis in town. We checked with Mr. Legoff, the food and beverage manager, to find out why. It seems the secret is to always use a cold glass, the best imported gin, and a small amount of good vermouth. The result is a very dry, very good, very potent, four-ounce drink for $1.50.

Thinking of martinis makes us think of Le Carrefour, which makes us think of pretty girls. If you are wondering where all those dashing executives and *chic* secretaries that you see in Place Ville Marie go after work, try to get a table in Le Carrefour between 5 and 7 p.m. This unique underground *rendezvous* offers potables and light snacks. During the cocktail hour, a boy circulates among the tables with a tray of free *hors d'oeuvres,* and at your request, a wandering trio will play your favorite song. Located in the midst of the restaurants, which we are about to describe, Le Carrefour makes a pleasant prologue to dining.

Le Carignan . . . French Canadian
Phone 861-3511
Local 2436

Le Carignan was named after the French infantrymen who arrived in 1665 to defend the struggling colony of Ville Marie de Montréal from the attacking Iroquois. When the regiment disbanded, four hundred men remained in Canada as farmers, soldiers, and *voyageurs*. A mural of these ancient soldiers dominates the far wall of the plush blue-and-gold dining room. The colourful outfits of the waiters are copied from the original Carignan uniforms, but are slightly shorter to allow for more freedom of movement. The restaurant features French-Canadian cuisine of the highest quality. Even the gold-and-brown plates, on which your food is artfully arranged, are made of bone china. Celebrated specialties include the *tourtière québecoise* and the rack of lamb, *sur commande du Colonel*. Menu is *table d'hôte* and *à la carte*. Le Carignan is open seven days a week. Lunch is served from noon to 3 p.m., and diner from 6 p.m. to 1 a.m. There is music and dancing from Monday to Saturday.

Bluenose Inn . . . Seafood
Phone 861-3511
Local 2435

The centre restaurant of the trio leading off Le Carrefour received its title from the humorous nickname applied to the Nova Scotia fishermen. "Bluenose" is one of the few strictly English-Canadian terms to become part of the language of Canada. It is also the name of the Nova Scotia fishing schooner that gained world fame by winning five international racing trophies. Look in your pocket for a Canadian dime; our nation has honoured the *bluenose* by putting her impress on every ten-cent piece. The decidedly nautical atmosphere of the restaurant is evoked by the clever use of detail—the mural of Lunenburg schooners, the huge anchor, the fishnets, the merchant-marine-styled uniforms of the waiters, and the burlap and fishnet menus. Of course, the colour blue reigns supreme, from the carpets to the seaweed of their special Maritime Clambake (baby lobster baked on seaweed and garnished by clams and shrimps), priced at $6.50. Whatever your main dish, do not miss a side order of fiddleheads (cooked fern sprouts). These delicious green delicacies are available in any of the P.V.M. restaurants, which are open Monday to Saturday from noon to 3 p.m. for lunch, and from 6 p.m. to 11 p.m. for dinner.

The Stampede . . . Steaks
Phone 861-3511
Local 2434

This is the last of the restaurants off the shopping concourse to be discussed. A westerner will feel at home in the Stampede, with its ranch-house décor and cowboy waiters. However, anyone who likes steaks and chops will enjoy eating here. If you wish, step up to the Butcher counter, choose your own cut, and brand it well done, medium, or rare. While waiting for your sizzling steak you can order your liquor cowboy style, which is a man's-size, two-ounce drink (the normal Q.E.and P.V.M. shot is one-and-a-quarter ounces), or else "call for your bottle on the bar". This is the old western tradition of serving your favourite brand in a full bottle. You drink what you want and pay only the amount of liquor consumed. Open daily except Sunday. Lunch is served from noon to 3 p.m.; dinner 6 p.m. to 11 p.m.

Altitude 737 . . . Buffet
Phone 861-3511
Local 2447

From the subterranean town of Place Ville Marie we spring upward at the speed of 42 floors in 30 seconds to the highest restaurant in the British Commonwealth. If you are looking for the ultimate in glamorous eating and spectacular surroundings, reserve a table in this glass-encased penthouse, perched on the 45th floor of the P.V.M.'s Royal Bank Building. Dining becomes a many-splendoured thing when you hang suspended between the earth and the stars (a position previously accorded to lovers only). Unfortunately, the prices are as high as the altitude; so try to wangle an invitation from a rich relation, or put it on your company's expense account. The restaurant specializes in an elaborate hot and cold buffet at both lunch ($4.50) and dinner ($6.50). After 9 p.m. it's *à la carte* with a $3.00 minimum. If you are more interested in romance than in food, there is a very nice bar, and a quartet for dancing after 9.30 p.m. The restaurant and bar are open daily from 11 a.m., which leads to the suggestion that you come up during the day for a panoramic view stretching as far as the Laurentian foothills and the mountains of Vermont and New York. This way you avoid the nightly minimum charge.

The naming of this pie-in-the-sky restaurant is a rather interesting story. When the Queen Elizabeth Hotel opened in 1958, there were many complaints from French-speaking Montrealers who thought it should have a more patriotic French-Canadian title. So with the opening of the new dining show-piece in 1964, the management decided to have a "name the restaurant" contest. The winning name, Altitude 737, was completely bilingual and also accurately descriptive as the restaurant is 737 feet above sea level.

La Vieille Porte . . . Continental
Place Victoria
Stock Exchange Bldg.
Phone 866-3057

. . . Roast beef by the site of Récollect Gate, the 18th-century western entrance to walled Montréal. This historical fact is reflected in the restaurant's twenty-one early-Canadian doors artistically arranged into a most unusual wall mural. According to Mario, the *maître d'*, this salute to Québec woodcarvers is valued at $20,000. Although the mural is the outstanding feature, the hand-hewn brick walls, the delicate wrought-iron dividers, the modern handsome chairs and thick carpets make an impressive combination of 20th-century comfort and early-Canadian surroundings. La Vieille Porte proudly advertises that it won an award from *Institutions Magazine* for superlative achievement in interior design; so when we say "impressive", we have the real meaning of an overused adjective in mind. The food is continental, with the accent on roast prime ribs of beef and such titivated fish dishes as giant Chinese shrimp *sauté provençale* served on Fiesta rice, and jumbo shrimps stuffed with crabmeat and oven baked in garlic butter. Open Monday through Friday from 11:30 a.m. to 1 a.m.; Saturday 5 p.m. to 1 a.m.; Sunday 5 p.m. to midnight. As the evening wears on and the crowds thin out, this air-conditioned restaurant becomes chilly; so, ladies, bring a sweater. We suggest you make reservations, as within a few months of its opening La Vieille Porte became a favorite. There is a car park underneath Place Victoria off St. James street. Ask the attendant to show you the elevator to the Shopping Concord, then turn left and ask the first passerby where the restaurant is located.

Les Deux Cultures . . . French
2055 Mansfield
Phone 288-8227

Only a few years old, Les Deux Cultures has already climbed into the elite circle of Montréal's great French restaurants. As the name implies, it is a clever blending of Gallic elegance and Anglo-Saxon tradition. You first enter an old English pub, The Pillars, where the dark oak panelling, Tudor-type beams, and heavy walnut chairs are caught in the soft glow of amber lanterns. This makes an exciting prologue to the pale elegance of the main dining room. Here you enjoy classical French cuisine, surrounded by graceful Directoire-styled furniture and crystal chandeliers that reflect the delicate green-gold colour scheme. *Table d'hôte* specialties include Brome Lake duckling and roast beef. Every *à la carte* dish is individually prepared, which means that if you prefer steak *bordelais* to the listed pepper steak, just ask for it. The restaurant encourages the guest to question them on the preparation of their dishes and the sauces used. This is simplified as only the captain or *maitre d'* takes the orders. Open daily from 11:45 a.m. to 1:00 a.m.; Sunday from 5:00 p.m. to midnight. The wine list is excellent, and light music is provided by a string trio. A doorman will park your car without charge.

Café Martin . . . French
2175 Mountain St.
Phone 849-7525

When Montrealers argue as to which restaurant has the finest *haute cuisine,* Café Martin's name is always in the running. One of the country's most famous French restaurants, it's the place where visiting dignitaries are taken to sample Montréal's cuisine. For the past forty years Café Martin's has been housed in the same stately mansion — smack in the middle of what is today the hip section of the town. Aloof, but not pretentious, its popularity remains constant. We strongly advise reservations in any of its three dining rooms—the tiny below-street-level Seafood Bar, the main dining room, and the elaborate second-floor Flaminco room. The extensive *table d'hôte* menu is surprisingly inexpensive, ranging from $2.50 to $4.50. It is offered every day until 9:30 p.m. in the main restaurant. The *à la carte* spécialties include chicken Café Martin, frogs' legs *à la provençale, filet-mignon provençale,* and lobster Thermidor. Sauces, the basis of French cooking, are excellent here. As you would expect, their wine list is lengthy and thorough. Leo Dandurand, the proprietor's father, who founded the restaurant, at one time gained a spotlight in the sport world by owning both the Canadien hockey team and the Alouette football team.

Chez Stein . . . French
2149 Mackay St.
Phone 842-9139

Chez Stein is another great French restaurant that has proved its worth over the last half-century. The décor of this one-time Victorian home is nondescript, but the two small dining rooms reek of refined traditionalism. The leisurely service gives the guest time to examine the Canadian masterpieces hanging on the walls. The menu, in the spirit of true French cooking, lists from the simplest dishes to the most elaborate imaginable. The conventional *table d'hôte* runs from $3.25 for half a roast chicken to $13.50 for *Chateaubriand* with trimmings for two people. However, if you want to join the "French cooking is the best in the world" fraternity, order from the specialty section. You will be right, whatever you choose! It is particularly recommended that you try the delicate, chestnut-flavoured *crêpes Suzette* for dessert. Also the restaurant has a *table d'hôte* lunch at $1.75. The hours are from 11:30 a.m. to 10 p.m.; closed on Sunday. There is a doorman who will park your car. So for a memorable dinner in a quiet, cultured atmosphere, remember the name, Chez Stein, justly coined the dean (*le doyen*) of French restaurants in Montréal.

MODERATE RESTAURANTS IN CENTRAL MONTREAL

Now we turn to restaurants that have the flair that turns a simple meal into a memorable feast, but in a moderate price range. We also pick out a few that serve plain good food in relaxing surroundings. In these restaurants an average *table d'hôte* dinner runs about $2.50 to $3.00. If you are ordering from the middle price range of the *à la carte* menu, an *entrée,* main course, and dessert will be around $5.00. May we again remind you that these figures are only guidelines; you could readily halve or double the quoted amounts. We have not considered wine or gratuities in the prices given, but all the mentioned places have wine cellars, and a carafe costs less than $1.00. Internationalism is the key word to our moderately priced restaurants. Montréal, being a seaport, has attracted a multitude of races. Over the years restaurants sprang up to meet the needs of these various world tastes. As a result of all this, Montréal can claim a vast variety of international dineries. Come with us in the next few pages while we discuss mouth-watering dishes from around the world, always remaining within walking distance of Dominion Square.

Osteria dei Panzoni . . . Italian
2070 Metcalfe
Phone 249-7183

For a year we daily walked past a modest, white, stucco building with a brown-and-white sign reading "Osteria dei Panzoni". Since in Italy most *osterias* are cheap places where you go to drink wine, play cards, and gab, we foggily connected it with the Italian students at McGill University (just a block away). One warm spring evening, lonely for old Rome, we decided to find out what was inside. *Mama Mia!* An authentic Italian *trattoria.* We would like to think of it as our own personal find, but it had been discovered already by Montréal's Italian set. The final stamp of approval was given by the Verdi Opera Company from Florence. They found the Osteria their second day in town, and throughout their sonorous sojourn, arguments and arias bounced from the grey stucco walls until four in the morning. The word *trattoria* implies that it is a small neighbourhood restaurant in which "you eat well and pay little"—as the Italian expression goes. With its bright, clean surroundings, efficient, friendly waiters and first-rate food, the Osteria dei Panzoni compares favourably with any of its Mediterranean-Boot counterparts that we have visited. Order any of the *à la carte* dishes marked with an asterisk and you are sure of a superlative dinner. As an *entrée,* share a serving of cannelloni. It is a giant noodle stuffed with meat delicacies and drenched with a creamy cheese sauce. On Saturday and Sunday from 5 to 1 p.m. the restaurant has a special *table d'hôte* menu which offers the house specialties at approximately $1.50 savings per person. Try to sit in the main dining room rather than upstairs. It seems more Italian, with an open kitchen in which you can see the chefs preparing their specialties over charcoal fires. Since most restaurants in Italy allow you to bring your dog along, the final touch of authenticity would be to fall over a few sleeping pooches as you manoeuvre your way to a table.

Tokay . . . Hungarian
2022 Stanley St.
Phone 844-4844

Stanley Street is microcosmic proof of Montréal's claim to international cuisine; within two short blocks, electric signs blink out the names of German, Hungarian, Italian, and French restaurants. The Tokay, named after the Hungarian grape which is pressed into a raisin-flavoured wine, is an intimate but sophisticated supper club. Do not glance in the window and be nonplussed, for the front is a coffee house; the main dining room is in the rear. Besides various kinds of coffee, the budget section offers full-course meals for about $1.50. An inexpensive way to sample Hungarian cuisine, it has become a very popular luncheon spot. Although we have never been to Hungary, it seems safe to say that the food is authentic, since so many Hungarian immigrants patronize the place. For a dining treat, don't stay in the front part but follow the tender, shrill wails of the gypsy violins to the rear of the restaurant, hang up your *kulac* (wine bag used by Hungarian horsemen), and order the *fatanyeros.* A gourmet's daydream, this sumptuous mixed grill consists of artistically arranged portions of veal, *filet mignon,* pork chops, sausages, bacon, cabbage, tomatoes, and French fries. Amazingly enough, the price is only $7.00 for two persons. If you are in a "hang the expense" mood, try a glass of the abominably expensive but velvety-mellow Tokaji Assu, a Hungarian wine costing $1.35 a glass. The Tokay's *ludlab,* a heavenly concoction of unsweetened chocolate and cherries, is a marvelous conclusion to a meal. To describe it as chocolate pie would be truthful but an outrage to its exquisite taste. The restaurant also has an excellent *table d'hôte* menu swinging from $2.95 to $4.50 in the evening, to $1.50 to $2.50 at lunch. Open seven days a week, and the wandering gypsy minstrels perform every night. Reservations are strongly recommended, because the dining room is very small.

The Continental . . . Continental
2114 Mountain Street
Phone 849-6391

What better location for an intriguing hodgepodge of "around-the-world" delicacies than the block-long swingers' strip on Mountain Street. Smack in the middle, the colourful Continental offers from Acapulco, baked avocado and lobster *au gratin;* from Italy, *scallopini parmigiana;* from Paris, *canard à l'orange;* from Sweden, grilled scampi with garlic butter; and from Venezuela, *biftek tomatado*—to name-drop a few of the more exotic dishes. The pitfalls of offering such a varied menu and yet serving a high quality of food are easily overcome by the diversified owner-chef George Mede. Having plied his trade in many countries, he has learned to keep one foot in the kitchen and the other in the dining room. As the motivating force of the restaurant, he gives suggestions to the customers, samples the wine, supervises the musicians, and prepares "George's Specials". Everything on the menu is *à la carte,* ranging in price from shish-kebab at $2.50 to *Chateaubriand bouquetière* for two at $9.75. We offer no suggestions, because George says, "Every dish has its own special charm." By the way, the spices in the Mexican and South American specialties have been reduced to suit our uninitiated taste buds. The discreet red glow of the table candles gives a mellow, warm touch to the contemporary luxury of the surroundings. A pianist plays in the background, and over all hovers the jovial, rotund figure of George. Open 11 a.m. to 2 a.m. daily, except Sundays.

If you want the same international cuisine, prepared in the same kitchen but at less expensive prices, go to La Soupière in the basement of the Continental. The cozy, informal atmosphere is relaxing, and the jet-setter crowd fun to watch. Although the menu is not as varied as upstairs, there is an ample choice of savoury viands. Many

Montrealers think that La Soupière serves the best onion soup in town.

Martin's . . . English
980 St. Antoine St.
Phone 866-3461

As a small child Chris always considered it a big occasion when his family of nine went out to dine. Twenty years ago the popular family restaurants were Desjardin's, Drury's (since torn down), Café Martin, and Martin's. Founded in 1861 as the New Carleton Hotel, Martin's is Montréal's oldest restaurant. The hotel with its five dining rooms was managed by the Martins and their five sons. During the First World War this hospitable establishment gained the affection of the Canadian soldiers. Before going out on the town they would deposit their money with Mrs. Martin for safekeeping, picking it up again the next morning. They called their kindly banker "Mother Martin"; the name caught on, and to this day every Montrealer speaks of going to "Mother Martin's" for dinner, even though many of the post-war generation do not know the story behind the name. In fact, "Mother Martin" died many years ago, and the restaurant was sold to another Martin family in 1960.

In 1965 Martin's moved to their present location, bringing their long marble-and-mahogany bar, their wood chandeliers, and their collection of oil paintings. For over half a century a favorite sport of the dining clientele has been to try and find the nude in the mind of the elderly gentleman who sits with his pipe and newspaper in the controversial painting over the bar. By keeping the old familiar props, Martin's has also kept the relaxed and convivial atmosphere that made the original restaurant so popular. The new place features the same excellent English cooking; roast beef, steaks, chops, seafood, with great pies, tarts, and puddings for dessert. There are three large dining rooms which seat four hundred people. Downstairs in the Carleton Club something new has been started in the way of satirical revues. Martin's is open daily from 10 a.m. to 1 p.m.; Sunday, 5 p.m. to midnight. Free parking available.

Heidelburg House . . . German
1498 Stanley St.
Phone 844-3914

Kassler rippenspeer mit sauerkraut and *jägerschnitzel mit späten,* two specialties as exciting as their gutteral names. The Heidelburg is noted for good German cooking, schmaltzy atmosphere, and buxom barmaids. Here the props of Germany's many *Ratskellers* have been rolled into one—beer-barrel tables, wood beams, stucco ceiling, tuxedoed waiters, checkered tablecloths, and a lively German band. For a full evening's entertainment go "aperitif-ing" in the bar section, dining in the restaurant section, and dancing in the candlelit Troubador Club. There is both an *à la carte* and a daily *table d'hôte*. At noon the daily menu is about 50¢ cheaper than in the evening. However, to sample true German cooking, choose from the *à la carte* house specialties. From personal experience may we suggest the delicious *wiener schnitzel* at $2.25 or the heavy but delectable stuffed-beef *rouladen* at the same price. Open 11:30 a.m. to 2 a.m. daily; Sunday, 4:30 p.m. to midnight.

Metcalfe Street Steak Houses . . .

Prices range from $2.65 to $3.75
(including baked potato)

Metcalfe Street, in the heart of our metropolis, has gained renown as the place for a steak. Shoulder to shoulder stand four restaurants specializing in beef. All serve uniformly good, red-brand meat. The price varies slightly depending upon the décor and service.

Au Pied de Cochon . . . French
1449A Metcalfe Street
Phone 849-2195

Cozy, quiet dining on checker-clothed tables under softly lit coach lamps. Besides steaks, the restaurant features French specialties such as frogs' legs *provençale* and pigs' feet stew *au Cognac*. Open daily from noon to 2 a.m.; Sunday 5 p.m. to midnight.

Curly Joe's Steak House . . . American
1453 Metcalfe Street
Phone 845-7603

What this restaurant lacks in atmosphere it makes up in well-prepared steaks. It offers high-quality, individually prepared steaks at very low prices. By the way, menus of these restaurants are posted in their windows, so you can compare prices before entering. At Curly Joe's you sit in booths and eat off arborite tables. The service is speedy.

The Upstairs . . . Slick Hayloft
1455 Metcalfe Street
Phone 845-6552

A combination of good steaks and pleasant surroundings. The stable effect is created by brown beams, stucco walls, and straw embedded in the mortar of the ceiling. Although The Upstairs has the same owners as Curly Joe's, prices are about 15¢ to 20¢ higher per steak. Highly recommended is the prime rib of roast beef, so tender and tasty it reminded us of choice cuts at the Durgin Park Restaurant in Boston. The beef, including baked potato and sour cream, is reasonably priced at $2.75 or $3.75 for a larger portion. Unless you are extremely hungry you will find the $2.75 plate quite sufficient.

Joe's . . . American
1459 Metcalfe Street
Phone 842-4638

Recently renovated and enlarged, this popular steak house now has an additional dining room and Hideaway Lounge downstairs. The large, juicy steaks are served on wooden platters. The service is quick and efficient, with a continual flow of enthusiastic customers. Open from 1130 a.m. to 2 a.m. daily, Sunday from 11:30 a.m. to 1 a.m.

"Let's go to Joe's for steaks," is a frequently heard suggestion among Montréal's steak-lovers. It could mean Joe's, or it could mean Curly Joe's. The two rivals have been battling for years. Which beef is tastier? It's like asking which wash is whiter, Tide's or Oxydol's!

BUDGET RESTAURANTS IN CENTRAL MONTREAL

Here we are out to prove that inexpensive restaurants can serve exceptionally good food. Many are small, family-run establishments with personable and relaxing atmosphere. Just the place for the foot-weary sightseer who wants a tasty meal without all the furbelow of a top-drawer restaurant. You can come in casual attire (but please no shorts!) and, unless stated, reservations are pointless. Most popular-priced restaurants have a mimeographed sheet of daily *table d'hôte* specials that will give you top eating value with little dent to your pocketbook. For about $1.50 you can choose a full-course meal, including soup, the main course, dessert (not always), and coffee. Ordering a 3-course *à la carte* dinner will run upward from $2.50. Unlike most big cities, where you must be told which budget eateries have passable cuisine, in Montréal even stand-up lunch counters of the 5-and-10¢ stores serve delicious food. With hundreds of worthy restaurants to choose from, we decided to single out some that are particularly popular with Montrealers and that may be harder for the visitor to locate.

Café des Artistes . . . French
1473 Dorchester Blvd. West
Phone 933-0529

Interested in the local hang-out of the radio and television crowd? This is the place, probably partly because of its off-beat atmosphere and partly because the C.B.C. building is across the street. Café des Artistes, squeezed into an unconverted old home, is a labyrinth of small, odd-shaped dining rooms which exude an effortless *bonhomie.* The rolling floors, the cartoons on the walls, the narrow hallways are in keeping with its peculiar character. Over the flower boxes of the ten-tabled outdoor café you can watch the pedestrians and the drivers play cat-and-mouse during the 5:30 rush hour. It's a restaurant where artists, romantics, and young-at-heart linger over the good basic French cuisine, while the candles burn down on the red-checkered tablecloths. The popular choices are *coq-au-vin* (delicious sauce), *ris de veau,* and *au poivre*. There is a daily *table d'hôte* as well as an *à la carte* menu. Open from 11 a.m. to midnight daily, Sunday 4 p.m. to midnight.

At night the sounds of the latest recorded music waft from the upstairs discothèque. It's a good spot to catch a performance of the latest dance steps—the later the hour, the greater the crowds.

The Stable . . . American
1429 Crescent Street
Phone 842-9445

This answers the question of where to dine if you are travelling with children. The atmosphere is as serene and homey as Sunday night dinner at nanna's. In fact many of the regular clientele are attractive, silver-haired pensioners, or earnest, young students who read while they eat. Even the middle-aged (or older) waitresses, with their patient faces and black-and-white uniforms, make us think of nurses pushing prams in the park. The good food is unbelievably low-priced. A complete dinner ranges from $1.35 for a salad plate to $2.75 for a sirloin steak. The soup and rolls are homemade. The small dining room is at the back of the old house, and to get to it you must walk through the large foyer and past the kitchen. Do peek in, for you will be delighted at its cleanliness. We wish we could say our kitchen were as clean. The Stable is open only at mealtimes, so check the following hours carefully to avoid disappointment. Lunch is served from 11 a.m. to 2 p.m.; tea (60¢ for shortcake; 40¢ for tea and toast) from 3 p.m. to 5 p.m.;

dinner from 5 p.m. to 7:45 p.m. The restaurant is open every day except Sunday. In July and August it is closed both Saturday and Sunday. Although there is no children's menu, a reduction is made in price in proportion to the serving. No liquor is served.

Chez Constant . . . Swiss
1463 Metcalfe Street
Phone 288-3791

A small, quiet restaurant reputed to have excellent French and Swiss cuisine at reasonable prices. By ordering from the daily menu you can get a full meal for about $2.00. A *table d'hôte* dinner, with a main course of a small, tender filet mignon and a carafon of wine, comes to only $3.00. Typical Swiss specialties from the *à la carte* section are cheese fondue at $3.50 and fondue *bourguignonne* at $4.25. The street-level dining room has a rather dingy appearance, so take our advice and head directly to the upstairs Tell Bar, which has the same menu. It's quite delightful, with dark beams, carved woodwork, and stucco walls on which hang Swiss murals. Notice the long, curved alpenhorn above the bar and the century-old crossbow. Open daily from 12:30 to 9 p.m.

Pam-Pam . . . Hungarian
1425 Stanley Street
Phone 288-3090

When the Pam-Pam opened its doors eleven years ago it was Canada's only espresso restaurant, serving fourteen brands of coffee. The menu offers a wide array of continental dishes, but Hungarian food is the specialty. Mr. Gotlieb, the owner, informed us that Hungarian mixed grill was the favorite of his regular clientele. We checked the price – $5.60 for two people, which is cheaper than the more luxurious Tokay down the street (see Deluxe section). Unfortunately we have never eaten the Pam-Pam's mixed grill, so we cannot compare the quality. However, we have ordered often from the daily menu and have always been satisfied. A typical *table d'hôte* menu runs from $1.00 for wieners to $2.20 for sirloin steak garnished with green peppers and mushrooms. Roast duckling at $1.50 is a popular *à la carte* choice. You can see from the above prices that the meals are extremely reasonable. Undoubtedly this accounts, in part, for the crowds of college students one sees here. It seems that students always nose out the dining bargains! The décor is simple, with small tables shoved close together. It's a happy, casual place, open daily from 7:30 a.m. to 1 a.m.; Saturday 1:30 p.m. to 1 a.m.; Sunday 12:30 p.m. to 12:30 a.m.

The Coffee Mill . . . Continental
2046 Mountain Street
Phone 288-3546

Here's another pleasant, clean espresso restaurant in the most colourful section of the city. The specialties of the house include roast pork, paprika chicken, and Hungarian goulash. You can choose from the *à la carte* main courses, starting at 70¢, or from the daily specials which offer well-prepared if not distinctive dishes. The tiny few-steps-below-the-street outdoor cafe is a fun spot to sit. After an afternoon of browsing through the boutiques and art galleries in this area we can never resist stopping for *capuccino* (35¢) and *ludlub* cake (35¢). They have a large assortment of mouth-watering but calorie-loaded goodies. The one that looks like a strawberry jellyroll is divine! The Coffee Mill is open from 7 a.m. to 11 p.m., closed all day Sunday – an excellent choice for people on a tight budget.

Chalet Lucerne . . . Chicken Bar-B-Q
1631 St. Catherine West
Phone 935-4513

Bring the kids! In the privacy of the tall, roomy booths they can throw chicken bones at each other without disturbing the fellow at the next table. The only item on the menu is chicken – tasty, tender, juicy chicken. One quarter for 80¢, a large quarter 90¢, half for $1.35, and large half for $1.60. It comes with a separate dish of hot Bar-B-Q gravy and rolls. The large quarter makes an average adult portion. Top this off with their delicious Swiss chocolate roll (35¢), and you have a kingly meal at plebeian prices. The service is very fast. Hours 11 a.m. to 5 a.m. daily.

Ben's Delicatessen . . . Delicatessen
1001 Burnside Ave.
Phone 844-1000

Like Molson's Brewery, St. Joseph's Oratory, and Les Canadiens, Ben's Delicatessen has grown into a local institution. In a sightseeing checklist you would find that Ben's for smoked meat at four in the morning is our city's equivalent of Paris' onion soup at the 4 a.m. opening of Les Halles market. In both you'll be surrounded by an exciting, sad-funny potpourri of humanity that is the gut of a cosmopolitan city. For fifty years Ben's has been "the" place to go after high school proms, college stags, Place des Arts concerts, and nights on the town. It is one huge, barren, intensely lit room, but nobody minds. Its tables are often sticky and its chairs uncomfortable, but nobody notices. One wall is papered with yellowed, autographed pictures of its famous patrons, but nobody looks. What accounts for its long, successful life? We might hazard a guess that it has something to do with the delicious smoked meat sandwiches. It's not all they serve, for we are willing to bet they have the longest menu you have ever seen—more than a hundred and eighty items. Count them! The service is quick and the crowds are thick from 7 a.m. to its closing at 5 a.m. If you are not around in the small hours of the morning, try Ben's at lunchtime. Complete meals from $1.50. Charcoal-broiled steaks and spaghetti with unsmoked meat are two popular choices.

Murray's Restaurant . . . American

Open seven days a week, this chain of clean, large, efficiently run establishments offers good basic food at budget prices. Of the nine restaurants, four are located in central Montréal—three on St. Catherine Street (640, 962, and 1504) between Morgan's Department Store and Guy Street, two on Dorchester Blvd., and one in the Laurentian Hotel. Recommended for breakfast, for afternoon tea, and for people with children. Incidentally they have very clean, well-equipped washrooms. Murray's can be described as a cross between the American Howard Johnson and the London tearoom. They have convenient locations, quick, neat waitresses, and thoroughly acceptable food. But like their English counterpart the functional, colourless décor exudes a stuffy, middle-class propriety. There is both an *à la carte* and daily *table d'hôte* menu with the usual American viands. Sirloin steak is the most expensive thing on the menu—$2.85 *à la carte* or $3.50 as a full dinner. Murray's hours are from 7 a.m. (8 a.m. on Sunday) until midnight.

HOTEL DINING IN CENTRAL MONTREAL

From the spectacular, new-fledged Château Champlain to the plush, patriarchal Ritz Carlton, hotel dining means great dining. A sweeping statement perhaps, but a true one. Hotel restaurants have always competed with local restaurants for a place in the gourmet circle. Although Montréal has always been known for its international eating, up until ten years ago most of the specialty restaurants were small family operations catering to a specific clientèle. Due to T.V. documentaries, foreign movies, and lower travel fares, the city's outlook grew more cosmopolitan and the need arose for large, first-class restaurants. This need was partially filled when the Queen Elizabeth opened their international rooms in 1964. The other big hotels realized that they must add an international zip to their excellent but conventional restaurants if they wanted to keep guests registering and to attract the growing number of sophisticated taste-buds. The result, as previously stated, is that hotels now house many of Montréal's greatest restaurants. Here are few to whet your interest. All are deluxe; all advise reservations.

Beaver Club . . . Queen Elizabeth Hotel
900 Dorchester
Phone 861-3511

The Beaver Club, off the main lobby of Hilton's Q.E. Hotel, appropriately honours the most famed feast of Montréal history (see Old Montreal, page 31). The illustrious members of the original Beaver Club would find the ritual of their sumptuous dinners changed but not the quality of the food and drink.

The early Canadian décor—snowshoes, beaver pelts, muskets, oak panels, period uniforms of the staff—provides a picturesque setting for the bustling Hilton-trained waiters. Look on the back of the parchment-coloured menu to find the story of the Beaver Club. Two specialties that our gourmet ancestors would rave about — Oka pheasant baked in clay at $6.25 and "the members' treat", which is tender, marinated beef in red wine sauce at $3.75. Hilton's nothing-but-the-best *modus operandi* has gained the Beaver Club an excellent reputation with both Montrealers and visitors. Open every day; lunch from noon to 3:00 p.m.; dinner from 6:00 p.m. to 11:00 p.m.

Café de Paris . . .
Ritz Garden . . . Ritz Carlton Hotel
1228 Sherbrooke W.
Phone VI. 2-4212

The Ritz Carlton restaurants are the couth hangout of debutantes, dowagers, dilettantes, dazzling damsels, and other assorted *beau monde*. Pierre Demers, who has supervised the kitchens for the last 20 years, was the first French-Canadian to become a chef for a large hotel. Another feather in his cap—Air France was so impressed with his food preparation that they now have the Ritz Carlton cater to all their flights out of Montréal. Entering by way of a small foyer with a marble floor and four cherub statues, you will pass through a quiet, spacious cocktail lounge. The blue-and-gold dining room seeps timeless tradition that even fresh paint can't hide. Its stolid, indestructable gentility provides a secure retreat in this rapidly changing city. We could no more imagine the Ritz Carlton with a newfangled décor than we could imagine Queen Elizabeth with her skirts six inches above her knees. The *à la carte* menu offers superlative French cuisine, with a small but daily changing list of specialties ranging from $3.75 to $5.00.

In the summer the Ritz Garden, opening off the Café de Paris, is a verdant oasis amidst the confusion, noise, and dirt of the downtown area. The patio on which you dine curves around a small garden with a duck pond (yes! real ducks), lush grass, fountain, and waterfall. This delightful spot is a luncheon favourite of the middle-aged women of dignity" segment of society. The menu is the same as that of the Café de Paris. Hours, Café de Paris: 6:00 p.m. to 10:30 p.m. Hours, Ritz Garden: noon to 3:00 p.m. and 6:00 p.m. to 10:30 p.m.

La Réserve . . . The Windsor Hotel
Dominion Square
Phone 866-9611

Another hotel restaurant whose excellent French cuisine is a firmly established fact. The large, modern dining room is turned into an intimate Riviera resort by clever decorating devices — stone-vaulted arches, stucco-and-brick walls, and attractive murals cunningly flanked by green shutters so as to appear like windows looking onto sun-baked landscapes. The gay Mediterranean mood is enhanced by a Spanish trio, whose lilting tunes will sooner or later entice you onto the dance floor. The menu is both *à la carte* and *table d'hôte* with sirloin steak *bouquetière* for two ($11) and Dover sole ($3.50) being two of the most popular choices according to the *maître d'*. The cold, silky-smooth vichyssoise (the last "s" is pronounced) is a superb way to begin a meal. Many in-the-know Montrealers (including the manager of a rival hotel) claim it's the best in town. We think so highly of this potato-leek soup that "La Réserve for vichyssoise" has become our after-theatre ritual. Open from 11:00 a.m. to 1:00 a.m.; closed Sunday.

Le Neufchâtel . . .

Le Château Champlain Hotel

Place du Canada

Phone 878-1688

Here's a flyer on a restaurant that's just in the paper stage at the time of this writing. It's located on the main lobby floor of Montréal's newest, most deluxe hotel. As the Canadian Pacific Railway operate both the Château Champlain and the Château Frontenac in Québec City, they were able to steal the chef from the renowned Château Frontenac and install him here. Even before the doors are open there is a buzz around town that Le Neufchâtel will be the place to dine. The décor will be reminiscent of the classical splendor of the 18th century. Le Jardin, an extension of the main dining room, will be a luxurious garden restaurant overlooking Dominion Square and Mont-Royal. How about the quality of the food? Well, we must wait and see, but if it's as good as Québec City's Château Frontenac, Montréal can add another great restaurant to its gourmet list.

Kon-Tiki . . . Sheraton Mount-Royal Hotel

Peel and Burnside
Phone 842-7777

It would be unforgivable to conclude this section without mentioning one of our city's most unique restaurants. The two huge wooden Tiki gods at the entrance to the dining room will give you a hint as to its décor. Once inside, you will be instantly transplanted to the exotic South Sea Islands. Wherever you look there are totem poles, waterfalls, tropical gardens, and canoes hanging from the ceiling. Too many props, perhaps, but certainly an eye-catching interpretation of a Pacific island hut. Incidentally the Kon-Tiki was named after the flimsy raft on which a small band of adventurous Norwegians floated 5,000 miles from Peru to Polynesia, proving it was possible for the South American Incas to have settled in Polynesia. The food is Polynesian, and the menu offers both *table d'hôte* and *à la carte* with prices for a full meal ranging from about $5.00 to $8.00. If you want suggestions try the tomato beef Kon-Tiki and the breast of chicken long hut. For a scene-stealing dessert, order the delicious Kon-Tiki *flambé* (a flaming cocoanut shell filled with rum ice cream) at $1.35. At noon the restaurant offers a smorgasbord at $2.00 per person, a great dining bargain discovered by many businessmen. Open daily from noon to 2:00 a.m.; Sunday, 5:00 p.m. to 11 p.m. Free parking after 6:00 p.m.

THE SUNSET STRIP ON DECARIE BOULEVARD

Having attempted to unscramble central Montréal's restaurant menagerie, we hope you are left with pangs of hunger, parched tongues, and wild thoughts of extending your holiday for the sole purpose of sampling more Québec cuisine. Hold on! Don't quibble over choices yet – that was only our first stop! Now we zoom northwest, with the speed of Batman, to the 3-mile-long, 12 lane-wide expressway called Decarie Boulevard. Suddenly you become part of a modern American city with flashing neon signs, drive-in-restaurants, hot-dog stands, cloverleafs, and high-rise apartment blocks. Keep on the outside service lane (heading north) of this newly widened expressway if you want to go to the big, brassy, expensive restaurants which over the years have earned this segment of Decarie the title "Sunset Strip". The key word is quality – in food, service, and décor. All are slickly operated, major investments.

It all began with the small restaurants that mushroomed around the Blue Bonnet racetrack. Gambling was their main profit, but food was served to hold the dice hand steady. Mentioning no names, but one of the old-time gambling establishments has become Canada's biggest, most successful restaurant. This is a little off the theme, but when the Boulevard was the only road to the Laurentians, Montrealers will remember the huge circus tent filled with canvas lawn-chairs and camping equipment. However, not many know that the tent was sold to the Stratford Festival in Ontario and used for their first Shakespearean performances.

This year the top restaurant owners, along with businessmen on The Strip, have formed an organization called The Decarie Promenade. They hope to safeguard the high standards of their establishments and advertise jointly. Certainly if you're looking for first-class, American-style dining, you can't beat these restaurants. Dinner runs upward from $5.00 per. Most of these dineries provide lounges with entertainment and dancing. In recent years The Strip has become an increasingly popular dining spot with Montrealers, mainly because of its reputation for consistently good food with a minimum of waiting. Also the downtown problem of where to leave the car is solved by large, free parking lots. We now begin a comment on five of Decarie Boulevard's top restaurants. Two of them, Ruby Foo's and Tokyo Sukiyaki, rank with America's culinary greats.

Ruby Foo's . . . Canada's no. 1 restaurant
7815 Decarie Blvd.
Phone 737-6533

Did you know that Montrealers arrange to have Ruby Foo's frozen food flown to them while vacationing in Miami? Would you believe that folks from other towns have been known to fly to Montréal airport, hire a taxi, drive to Ruby Foo's, eat dinner, then catch a later plane home? Are you impressed that Zsa Zsa Gabor, Bobby Vinton, Walter Pidgeon, Judy Garland, Mayor Drapeau, Jan Pierce, Miream Makeba, and Judy LaMarsh make it a point to dine at Ruby Foo's when in town? These are just a few facts from its phenomenal history. Sounds like a Hollywood fairytale doesn't it? But there are staggering statistics to back up the statement that it's Canada's largest and most successful restaurant.

The Sunset Strip on Décarie Boulevard.

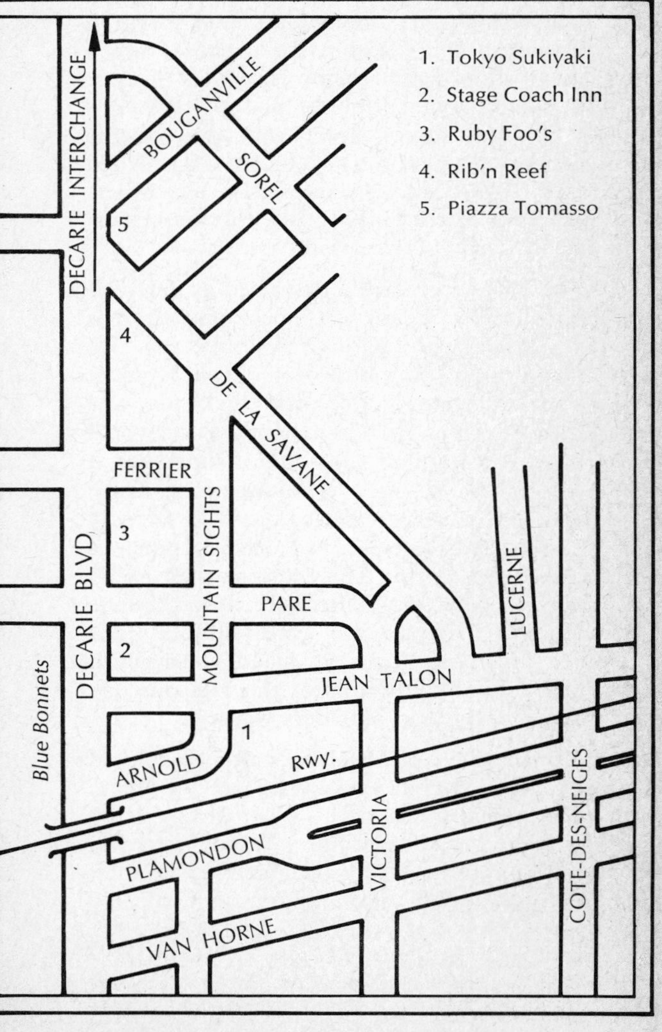

To begin, it was the only individual Canadian restaurant listed on the Canadian Stock Exchange (shares almost doubled between 1960 and 1965). It seats 1,100 people at one time; feeds three-quarters of a million customers annually; grossed four million dollars last year; employs 90 chefs and 375 restaurant staff. Within the premises are a pastry shop, butcher shop (five tons of meat consumed a year), lobster pound, as well as a 118-unit motor hotel with one of the highest occupancy rates in the city. Now, having rolled off these impressive figures lets get down to the "nitty-gritty" of any restaurant – décor, service, food.

The décor could be described as a Hollywood interpretation of Chinese palace; or is it a Mandarin pagoda? Anyway the five dining rooms, two lounges and eight banquet salons are contrived, colorful, luxurious, and befitting. Upon arrival at Ruby Foo's you'll be given a number, and after a short wait it will be called over a loudspeaker. Once you are seated in the dining room the friendly red-jacketed waiters provide efficient gracious service. When we commented on their excellence to Mrs. Korchof, Ruby Foo's Public Relations Director, we were told that each morning there is a staff meeting, at which time any misdemeanors of the previous day are discussed and offenders warned.

In the days of Montreal's orange-colored streetcars, Ruby Foo's was an ice-cream diner called Gallagher's. When it could not obtain the Howard Johnson franchise, it was sold and turned into a Chinese restaurant. As its clientele developed more educated taste-buds, Ruby Foo's added French, American, and fish dishes to the menu. The result is a fantastic array of tantalizing items (ask the waiter for suggestions if your eyes tire from reading). The restaurant is noted for overly abundant portion – a good thing to remember if you're ordering Chinese food. For instance, the famed Pu Pu platter ($4.25), consisting of egg rolls, chicken wings, breaded shrimps, spare ribs, and dry won ton, is for two people but will easily serve four if you order a bowl of rice with it. Another highly recommended specialty, the whole rib of roast beef ($5.25) covers the entire plate and is garnished with Yorkshire pudding, baked potato Monte Carlo, and French green peas. For dessert, if you can still lift a fork, try one of the delicious goodies from the pastry wagon. After dinner, relax and do a little people-watching over your coffee. This remarkable dining mecca attracts as many social levels as Mont-Royal park on a hot Sunday evening. Open daily from 11:00 a.m. to 2:00 a.m. and Sunday from 11:00 a.m. to 1:00 a.m. Dancing to a trio in the Black Sheep Lounge.

Tokyo Sukiyaki . . .

Exquisite Dining in a Japanese Garden
7365 Mountain Sights
Phone 731-8651

This unique restaurant is well worth the extra time it will take to find it. If you are taking your car, follow our map and watch for an ordinary, small office building marked only by one bright lantern. Don't be dismayed by the exterior. Push open the door, remove your shoes, and slip into another world. Padding along in your grass sandals behind the rustling silk kimono of the Japanese hostess, you pass rock gardens, tinkling brooks, waterfalls, little bridges, and finally stop before your own dining cell *(sukiya)*. In Japanese tradition you remove your sandals at the entrance and sit on cushions on the floor. In the serene privacy of this simple, clean hut you are served as authentically and ceremoniously as if you were guests in a Japanese home.

Since no-one in our party had eaten Japanese food, the waitress described each dish in great detail and demonstrated with endless patience the use of chopsticks (the only implements you are given). The menu lists eight choices, ranging from $3.50 to $5.50. We strongly urge you to try the Sukiyaki Special, since its six courses allow you to taste most of the restaurant's best dishes. By the way, the men are always served first and according to Japanese etiquette they do not wait for the others, but start eating immediately. Each course is a gourmet's daydream, beginning with the *hors d'oeuvres* (small pieces of halibut, octopus, and tiny dried raw fish) and ending with the *sukiyaki* prepared in front of you on a little charcoal stove. After all these exotic flavours, the delicately flavoured fresh melon makes a perfect dessert.

Whatever you eat, it's a must to order a carafon of warmed *saké* at $1.50. This bland rice wine sipped from thimble-sized porcelain cups appears impotent, but after the fifth mouthful, watch out! We asked our dainty Japanese waitress what she thought of *saké*. With a flutter of her kimono she replied, "Never touch the stuff. All I drink is rum." After dinner lounge on your pillow, sip green tea, and bask in the tranquil atmosphere which is broken only by sounds of trickling water, and from a distant cubicle an occasional male voice calling, "More *saké*". Although we have never dined in San Francisco's famed Yamato restaurant, a friend who has eaten in both claims Tokyo Sukiyaki's food superior. A high compliment, as she is a dyed-in-the-wool native of this rival eating-city. Open every day from 5:00 p.m., Tokyo Sukiyaki should be doubly underlined by adventurous eaters.

Stage Coach Inn . . . Steak and Fish
7385 Décarie Blvd.
Phone 731-7771

The crackling log fire, the overstuffed leather chairs, and the dark panelling make the Stage Coach Inn an ideal dining spot during cold Canadian winters. But good food is not seasonal, so this restaurant is a year 'round choice for many gourmets.

The glamorous, Old West décor of the foyer is carried through to the spacious red-boothed dining room. The menu, offering both *à la carte* and *table d'hôte* dinners, lists a surprising number of international specialties. Just picture this scrumptious feast for $4.95! Begin with delicately flavored clam chowder; then order succulent veal tenderloin stuffed with Swiss cheese and Virginia ham; conclude with hot, freshly baked apple pie. If you are a member of the "apple pie without cheese is like a kiss without a squeeze" school of thought, then be sure to order a wedge of zingy Canadian Oka cheese. The final touch to the dining masterpiece is a full-bodied red Bordeau wine such as St-Emilion at $3.25 a half bottle. By the way, the Stage Coach Inn has an excellent businessmen's lunch for about $2.00. Open daily for lunch 11:30 a.m. to 3:30 p.m.; and for dinner 5:00 p.m. to 10:30 p.m.

Rib'N Reef . . . Steak and Fish
8105 Décarie Blvd.
Phone 735-1601

Here's another tastefully designed modern restaurant specializing in beef and lobster. However, two features set it apart from its rivals. First, the management serves only scientifically fed beef imported from Boston. It seems eastern Canada does not have the climate to grow the corn that is essential to the very best beef breeding. Although the prices are a little high, the roast prime rib of beef ($5.50 *à la carte*) ranks with that of the town's best restaurants. The second feature is the Monday and Friday night lobster party which the Rib'N Reef instigated. For $6.50 they will serve all the live broiled lobsters and scampies you can eat. This isn't just a come-on either! The waitress will urge you back for a second, third, and even fourth plates. So, seafood lovers, fast all day and then gorge. (P.S. The bicarbonate of soda is not included in the price of the dinner). Both the rather small, American colonial-styled dining rooms are comfortably elegant. Open daily: lunch from 11:00 a.m. to 2:00 p.m.; dinner from 5:30 p.m. to 2:00 a.m.

Piazza Tomasso . . . Italian
8205 Décarie Blvd.
Phone 739-6331

It began back in 1934 with Mamma Tomasso cooking chili con carne for their newly acquired forty-seat restaurant. The gross profit of the first day came to $10.20. When this dish proved to be a flop, Mamma turned to spaghetti, an overnight hit, and thirty-three years later, still the restaurant's star attraction. Judging by the number of Italian personalities that eat here, success has not spoiled Mamma Tomasso's cooking. Included in their list of stars are Gina Lollobrigida, Liberace, and Tony Bennett. As you enter the front door Mamma Tomasso's beaming portrait greets you. There is a choice of downstairs dining room or the more interesting upstairs Boot Room and La Strada Terrace Bar. Curb service is also available. We still laugh thinking of the look on a young man's face as he and three small children tried to eat heaping plates of spaghetti in a Volkswagen! Even the rear-view mirror had spaghetti strands dangling from it. If you are just snacking try the Tomasso pizza-plus at $2.75 — there's enough for four people. The *à la carte* menu ranges from spaghetti with meat sauce for $1.25 to lobster at $4.00. The Roman buffet in the upstairs Boot Room is great for people who like "a bit of everything". The buffet costs $4.00 per person and $2.25 at noon. It features dozens of cold dishes (antipastos, cold cuts, and salads) and two hot pasta dishes. Open from 7:30 a.m. to 1:00 a.m. daily. Weekends 11:00 a.m. to 1:00 a.m., the Boot Room is closed Monday.

RESTAURANTS IN OLD MONTREAL

From ultra-sophisticated dining along the twelve-lane Strip, we suddenly find ourselves looking for rustic French-Canadian restaurants half hidden in the narrow winding streets of Old Montréal. These ancient buildings with their thick beams, rough stone walls, and low ceilings convert beautifully into picturesque dining rooms. Add waitresses in period costumes and tasty French-Canadian dishes. *Voilà!* a memorable dinner. With the restoration of vintage buildings and the growth of public interest, eating in Old Montréal has become the "in" thing; people flock to the small quaint restaurants with their excellent prepared dishes and authentic décor. Unfortunately, most owners are more interested in expanding their seating capacity than in enlarging their kitchen and storage space. Thus the quality of the food has suffered in some cases. Over the past year we have taken six out-of-town guests down to Old Montréal to dine. Three times the food was superb, twice we were disappointed, and once actually embarassed as our onion soup had no onions and our steaks arrived in a pool of hot fat. As a general rule we would stay away from Old Montréal restaurants on busy weekend evenings. It seems to work in a direct ratio that the thicker the crowds, the poorer the food. However, in any of the following restaurants we have always been satisfied, and often delighted, with the food from Monday to Thursday. Although we have not been entirely complimentary, please don't cross off Old Montréal dining. It would be a shame to miss the opportunity of sampling early Québec cuisine in such history-steeped surroundings. Since the menus are written only in French, you'll need our menu translation. Most restaurants offer moderate priced *à la carte* dishes, going from 50¢ to $1.50 for the *entrée,* and from $2.00 to $5.00 for the main dish.

Les Filles Du Roi . . .

Memories are made of this!

415 St. Paul East

Phone 849-6556

The restoration of this dilapidated 18th-century house into an exquisite restaurant is a magnificent attribute to Old Montréal. The owners, Jean-Jacques and Gertrude Trottier and their seven sons, spent two years studying Canadian history and searching

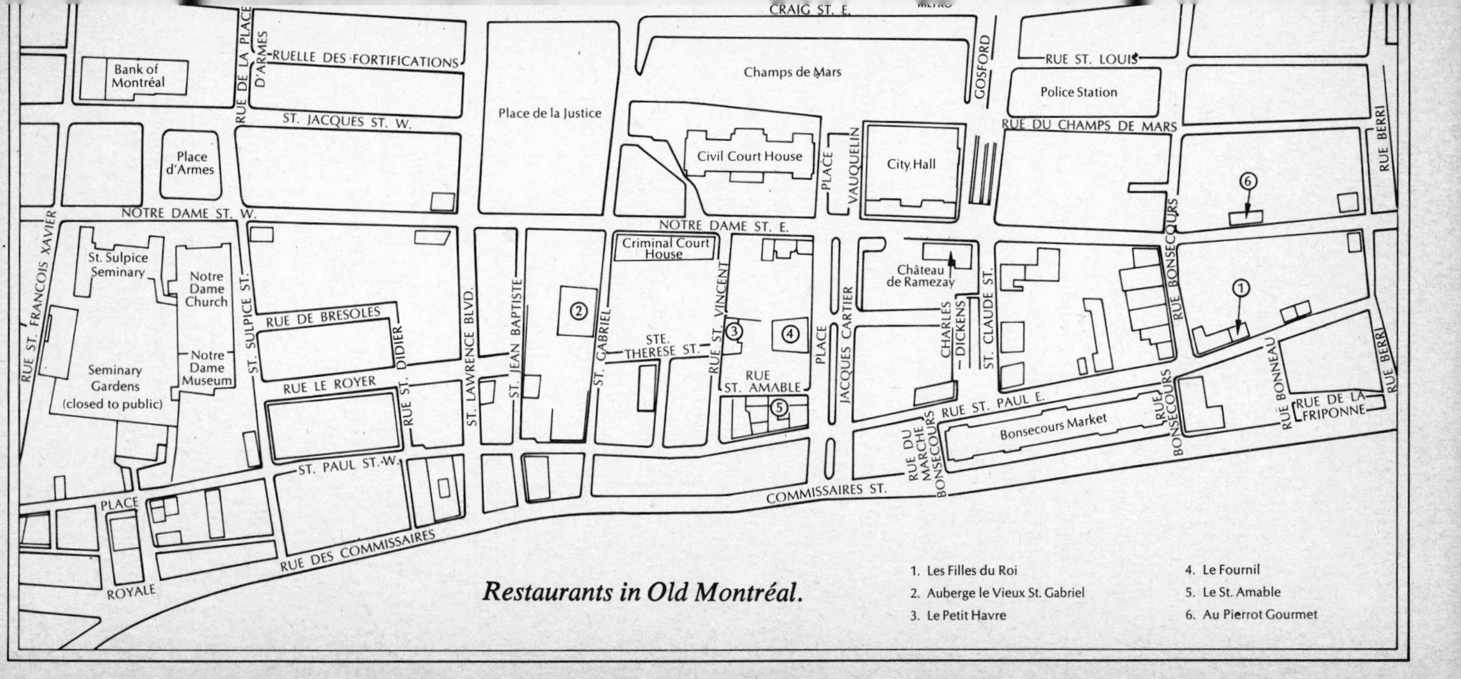

Restaurants in Old Montréal.

1. Les Filles du Roi
2. Auberge le Vieux St. Gabriel
3. Le Petit Havre
4. Le Fournil
5. Le St. Amable
6. Au Pierrot Gourmet

Québec for authentic materials. As a team they renovated, decorated, and now operate Les Filles du Roi. What excites us most are the relics of Canada's past, which are not just decorative objects but have been discreetly modernized to become a functional part of the dining room. For storage, an armoire carved with a penknife by Madame Trottier's grandfather; for heating your coffee and tea, a unique four-tiered stove; for drinking water, a huge, black iron pump. Note how the early Québec pine chairs on which you sit have been altered for comfort. Since this generation is considerably taller than the previous, pieces have been added to the bottoms of the legs to make the chairs higher. Also the uncomfortable rawhide seats have been covered by patchwork cushions made by Madame Trottier from the old pants of her five sons. Even the waitresses sew their own costumes!

The menu offers French-Canadian specialties and the usual American dishes (roast beef at $4.50 and filet mignon at $4.75). For those of you who have never tasted authentic early Québec cuisine, we recommend the *assiette canadienne,* at $2.50. It includes large helpings of three specialties of the house *(tourtière, ragout de boulette, ragout de cochon).* The homemade pickled beets and tomatoes are a perfect complement. If you are still game for dessert after such a heavy, hearty main course, we again call your attention to the French Canadian specialties. All are sweet, rich, and yummy. For example the *pain cuit dans le sirop* is made of crusty french bread dunked in maple syrup and topped with heavy cream, and the *tarte à la farlouche* is pie with a molasses and raisin filling.

Even the name of the restaurant has been taken from a very interesting part of Québec history. In the latter part of the 17th century the leaders of New France realized that, to increase the population and to keep the men from running off with Indian girls, they would have to import marriagable women. When the boatloads of *les filles du roi* or wards of the king landed, the eligible men were given two weeks to marry. Often there would be as many as thirty weddings in one day.

Les Filles du Roi is open every day from 11 a.m. to midnight. If you are browsing in Old Montréal, the restaurant offers excellent *table d'hôte* lunches ranging from $1.24 to $2.50. Certainly Les Filles du Roi and the charming Trottier family will give you warm memories of *la Belle Province*.

The oldest, largest, best-known restaurant in the old quarter, AUBERGE LE VIEUX ST-GABRIEL at 422 St-Gabriel St., has a huge following. Even with a reservation (861-2044) expect to wait. Established as a hotel in 1754, the restaurant still uses some of the original props. We discussed the history of "St. Gab" in the walking tour of Old Montréal. The main dining room is a happy combination of genuine antiques and modern reproductions. The star attraction is the massive stone fireplace transported block by block from the old place. Depending upon our financial state at the time of arrival, we either order the 14 oz. rib steak at $2.50 (baked potato and salad included), or *le canard à l'orange* at $2.75, or for a big splurge, *médaillon bouquetière flambé au cognac* — beef garnished with vegetables and flamed in cognac — at $4.75. A half bottle of *Moulin à Vent* goes beautifully with each of these dishes. Open daily, closed all day Sunday.

One block east of Auberge St. Gabriel, just off Notre Dame Street, a small, unobtrusive sign announces LE PETIT HAVRE. Perched above an Esso Station and beside the city morgue, this deceptively small restaurant is located at 437 St. Vincent St. Like any good dining hideaway it is dark, intimate, and relaxed with a checkered cloth and candle on every table. It used to be rated as Old Montréal's best by those who live in the quarter. Now that it has been "discovered" by Montrealers, the question whispered among its regulars is, "Will Success Spoil Le Petit Havre?" We usually begin with *les escargots* (the chef has a heavy hand with the garlic), then *le tournedos,* and for dessert, *les oranges au cointreau.* It's delicious for only $5.00, excluding wine and tip. Closed Sunday. Reservations: phone 861-4108.

Another intimate little spot serving good French-Canadian food is LE FOURNIL. Presently situated across from the Bonsecours Market, it will be moved to 438 Place Jacques Cartier by the time you read this book. Yvon Deschamps, the owner, told us he would use the same early Québec decor that made his original place so picturesque. Le Fournil is popular, partly because of its reasonable prices and partly because of its casual, homespun atmosphere. Here you can get pigs' feet at $1.60, beef stew at $1.90, or meat pie at $1.50. The most expensive item on the menu is *le steak au poivre* at $4.50. Upstairs Yvon is trying something new with a *boîte à chansons* — sounds intriguing! Open daily. Phone 878-4401 for reservations.

Yvon also owns LE ST. AMABLE on St. Amable Street — natural stone walls, exposed pine beams, and antique Canadian furniture, with, of course, traditional French-Canadian food. Phone 878-3066 for reservations.

Our last stop in Old Montréal, AU PIERROT GOURMET, is a most unusual place. Climbing up a flight of creaking stairs, you'll enter what appears to be the home of a middle-class French-Canadian family, with a television in one corner, and a huge fridge in another. No matter when you go, there'll always be men talking and drinking wine around a big table. Certainly this is not the type of restaurant you would expect to be written up in *Glamour* magazine, or to be visited by the Governor-General of Canada. But it is! And it's all because of the patron-cook, Jean-Louis Larre. His forceful character and famed cooking has made this unattractive neon-lit room a gathering place of gourmets — be they gangsters or ambassadors. We wouldn't think of suggesting a particular dish. Eat whatever *le patron* has specially prepared for the day and you will have something to write home about! We should add that Jean-Louis takes it as a personal insult if you don't order what he suggests. Please note that Au Pierrot Gourmet is shut down during the summer months. Open daily in the winter, except for Sundays.

OUT OF THE WAY RESTAURANTS

Regardless of the ominous letters from our publisher asking, "Where is the restaurant section?" and in spite of the ten pounds Chris has gained since the beginning of this chapter, our gourmet conscience will not allow us to entirely overlook Montréal's many "out of the way but worth the trip" restaurants. So here goes — with the speed of a radio announcer describing a touchdown in the last seconds of a football game.

Located in north Montréal at 3961 St. Lawrence, MOISHE's has been the city's undisputed steak palace since 1938. The quality of the meat is assured by Mr. Moishe's going to the packing house every dawn to stamp his name on the best available beef. Rib steak at $4.75 and filet mignon at $5.00 are most popular. Loads of little services to make you feel welcome — free parking, special children's price, no checkroom tipping, and bowser bags. Open daily. Phone 845-3509.

Much further north and harder to find, CHEZ BARDET at 591 Henri-Bourassa East is reputed to be the most authentic French restaurant in the country. The B.P. Guide gives it two stars – the only other Montréal restaurants to rate this honor are Chez Stein and Café Martin (see our Deluxe Central). Superb food, running well over $5.00 for a complete dinner. Closed Sunday. Phone 381-1777. If you take the Métro get off at Henri-Bourassa.

Do you want to go to Madrid for an evening? Grab a cab and head for 368 Mount Royal East. Here in the colorful, crowded CHATEAU MADRID you get the best *paella* and Spanish guitar in town. Sipping your soup *(gazpacho anduluz* at 60¢) to the intense foot-tapping flamenco dancing, you will soon be shouting *"Olé"* with the habitués. A wide variety of Hispanic specialties beginning about $3.00. Phone 845-2843. Open daily; no entertainment Mondays.

LA GRENOUILLE ET LE BOEUF at 3459 St. Denis, just above Sherbrooke, is a little-known offbeat place with the menu painted on the walls. When you enter the small, black-lit room fluorescent frogs and bulls jump out at you from one wall and the butcher, the baker, and the candlestick maker from another. Only steaks and frogs' legs are served, but at remarkably low prices. The most expensive item, a huge Boston steak, costs $3.50. The delectable tender frogs' legs are the best we've ever eaten. Open daily. The kids will love it!

Let's make a quick switch to the top-drawer AU LUTIN QUI BOUFFE at the corner of St. Grégoire and St. Hubert (phone 271-1188). Inside this medieval inn you'll find an art gallery (with artist at work), a live piglet (with photographer to take your picture feeding it), and singing waiters (who might easily break out with the farewell aria from *La Bohème* while serving your Rock Cornish game hen). Complete dinners soar upwards from $6.00. The restaurant reeks of atmosphere, which accounts for the great number of tourists that have sampled their excellent French cuisine.

The last of our restaurants to be discussed and perhaps the most distinguished, the city-operated HELENE DE CHAMPLAIN is fantastically located in the middle of the Expo '67 site on St. Helen's Island. Unfortunately, during Expo it will be open only to visiting dignitaries. This elegant old stone building provides a marvellous view of the south shore and the entrance to the St. Lawrence Seaway. Dinner on the outdoor flagstone terrace, a delightful summer treat, hovers around $5.00. This does not include wine — a must, since you are sitting on the finest wine cellar in the country.

Whoa there! It's not the end yet! We forgot CHINATOWN, the cheapest eating area in Montréal. The little that's left is found between the downtown district and Old Montréal. Specifically Clarke and the cross street La Gauchetière. Don't wander into just any restaurant — some of the worst look the best. If you want Chinese food in posh surrounding go out to Ruby Foo's or Bill Wong's on The Strip. In Chinatown, it's the greasy-spoon styled cafés that offer the best, most authentic Cantonese food, at rock-bottom prices. Here are two, chosen because their regular clientele consists of Chinese Montrealers. The KWONG CHOW café at 1095 Clarke is open daily until 3:00 a.m. with booths in the front and a larger, more pleasant dining room in the rear. Depending upon your hunger, a full-course meal for two people ranges from $3.00 to $6.00. If you have a party of four or more, be sure to try the Kwong Chow Appetizer at $3.25. A few steps down the street at 1023 Clarke the SUN SUN LUNCH also serves delectable Cantonese food in drab surroundings. A five-course meal for one (enough for two) costs $1.75. The "game hen upper arms stuffed with bamboo shoots, chopped meat, water chestnuts and oyster sauce" makes our mouths water just writing it down. Costs only $2.00. Open daily until 5:00 a.m. — what better way to end a night on the town?

Well, that's it folks! You are now in the know as to Montréal's cuisine. A few dinners around town and we feel sure you'll join us in a loud *oui* (pronounced "we") of approval with the old cliché, "An Englishman eats to live and a Frenchman lives to eat."

FRENCH		ENGLISH
à la bourguignonne	:	large cuts of braised meat with a sauce of red wine, mushrooms, and onions
à la carte	:	a stated price for each dish
agneau	:	lamb
bordelaise	:	cooked in white wine
bouillabaisse	:	a celebrated fish stew
boulette	:	meatball
brut	:	unsweetened
canard	:	duck
cervelle	:	brain usually of veal, lamb, pork, or beef
champignons	:	mushrooms
chapponeau	:	a young capon
châteaubriand	:	a thick piece of tenderly cooked filet of steak
chou-fleur	:	cauliflower
confiture	:	jam
citron	:	lemon
cochon	:	pig
coquille	:	shell
côte	:	rib
côtelette	:	cutlet
crème glacée	:	ice cream
crème de riz	:	cream rice soup
crêpes	:	French pancakes
crevette	:	shrimp
croissant	:	fancy bread in crescent form
croûtons	:	small pieces of crusty bread fried in butter and added to soups
déjeuner	:	breakfast

doré	:	dripped in beaten egg yolks
entrecôte	:	sirloin steak
entrée	:	hot or cold first course
épinard	:	spinach
escargots	:	snails
fèves	:	beans
foie	:	liver
fondue	:	hot melted cheese
fraise	:	strawberry
framboise	:	raspberry
fricandeau	:	veal stew
frit	:	fried
fromage	:	cheese
gâteau	:	cake
gibelotte	:	rabbit stew
grenouille	:	frog
haricot	:	bean
homard	:	lobster
hors d'oeuvre	:	a variety of small dishes served before the meal
huîtres	:	oysters
jambon	:	ham
lait	:	milk
laitue	:	lettuce
légumes	:	vegetables
lyonnaise	:	shredded fried onion has been added
meunière	:	butter and lemon added
nouilles	:	noodles
oeufs à la coque	:	boiled eggs
oeufs à la poêle	:	fried eggs
oeufs brouillés	:	scrambled eggs
oeufs durs	:	hard-cooked eggs

oignon	onion
pain	bread
pamplemousse	grapefruit
pieds de cochon	pigs' feet
poire	pear
pois	peas
pomme	apple
pomme de terre	potato
potage du jour	soup of the day
pot-pourri	stew
poulet	chicken
provençale	garlic or onion and olive oil have been used
purée	mashed
ragoût	meat stew with plenty of gravy
ris d'agneau	sweetbread of lamb
riz	rice
rognon	kidney
rôti	roast
saignant	rare
saumon	salmon
sauté	quick pan cooked in butter
soufflé	light baked pudding
table d'hôte	a meal of several courses for a fixed price
tarte	pie
tournedos	small filet steak
truite	trout
veau	veal
viande	meat
vin	wine
volaille	poultry

4.

SHOPPING IN MONTREAL

It's both thrilling and exasperating to shop in a strange city. It's thrilling because you can discover articles you would never see at home, but exasperating because you don't know the city and are usually short of time. If the length of your Montréal holiday is less than a week don't attempt a shopping *sortie* without some careful strategy planning. Of course, the first thing is to read over this chapter and decide whether you'll be window browsing, bargain hunting, souvenir collecting, or following a shopping list. Don't forget to count your money! If you have many specific items to buy, it's wise to start by purchasing the standard ones in the department stores. Then go on to the more specialized shops for the more unusual things.

Montréal is a shopping hound's paradise. The golden rectangle, a tightly packed mile framed by Guy, Sherbrooke, University, and Dorchester Streets is bursting with tourist-worthy stores. Here you can wander at will, dropping in and out of glamorous, gilt-walled boutiques, tiny, offbeat artisan workshops, towering department stores and vast, futuristic shopping complexes. If you want to go farther afield there is neon-lit St. Hubert Street in north Montréal. However, we don't know why a visitor would want to go there since, with the exception of St. Hubert Plaza, it's just like New York's 34th Street, London's Oxford Street, or any city's budget shopping district, where the items cost less but offer little novelty or character. In this chapter we've stuck closely to the downtown area, and even then many excellent stores haven't been mentioned simply because of limited space.

Throughout the Province of Québec and especially in Montréal, the visiting shopper is offered good values in a wide range of merchandise, including many appealing conversation pieces. This includes both imported items and the products of local crafts. Since Canada is a member of the British Commonwealth, non-Canadians will find some saving in such imports as bone china, woolens, linens, and yard goods. Whether your taste, or should we say the bulge in your wallet, leans towards fabulous $25,000 furs or fuzzy $4.50 Ookpiks (Eskimo owls), once you know where to look and what to look for, it's fun and most rewarding to shop in Montréal. The following regulations and suggestions are given to aid you in planning a successful and enjoyable shopping expedition.

REGULATIONS AND SUGGESTIONS

According to U.S. custom regulations, each individual is allowed to return with $100 worth of duty-free purchases for personal use once every 31 days. If you don't live in a dry state and are 21 years of age, you can carry home one quart of liquor. Of course both these rules apply only to U.S. citizens who have remained in Canada 48 hours or more.

A gift sent to thank your next-door neighbor for watering your plants is duty-free too, provided the enclosed bill of sale doesn't exceed $10 and is marked "gift". Of course, the reason for and destination of your gift is immaterial.

In Québec the sales tax is 6%, except for children's clothes and food. A complicated way to avoid the tax is to have the article sent to your plane or train or a U.S. address, but check to make sure the shipping charges are not more than the sales tax. Many department stores do not charge to ship, but smaller shops can't afford this service.

Most stores in downtown Montréal close at 6 p.m. from Monday to Wednesday, and 9 a.m. Thursday and Friday. On Saturday the department stores are open all day, but many boutiques are closed during the summer months. All stores are closed on national holidays.

A word of warning: On the last stroke of five o'clock, pandemonium begins its temporary reign of the city. Suddenly there are no available taxis, queues for buses stretch a block or more, Métro stations are packed, and cars crawl bumper-to-bumper. Knowing this, Montréal shoppers head for home at 4:30 p.m. We urge you to do the same.

It is also wise to try to avoid shopping between noon and 2 p.m. Since the salesperson's lunch hour corresponds with that of the office worker, the stores are often crowded and understaffed.

The salespeople are all bilingual, but unfortunately not all are courteous. This happens more frequently in smaller shops, where the staff sells on a commission and may try to give you a hard line. If you know a dress is a size too large, don't be intimidated by a condescending voice saying, "But

Madame, that's the latest style this season." Simply find someone else to serve you, or else look for a similar item in another shop.

DEPARTMENT STORES

We've begun with these large emporiums because they are primers to a successful shopping expedition in a strange city. Not only do they set the price norm 99% of the time, but also, if the purchased item is not to your liking it can be returned without fuss or bother – provided of course, that you kept the sales slip.

The north side of downtown St. Catherine Street is the easy-to-find demarcation line for the major department stores. Four are within walking distance of one another; the fifth, Dupuis Frères, is on the other side of St. Lawrence Blvd. Like all large stores each has a distinctive personality and special charm. In our coverage of them we've begun with the traditionally English Ogilvy's and moved eastward.

Ogilvy's . . .

Corner of Mountain and St. Catherine

A sophisticated 70-department specialty shop with a reputation for hand-picked, often whimsical, merchandise and window displays that have become a St. Catherine Street tradition. It is all part of Brigadier Nesbitt's rather odd merchandising policy, in which he declares that as long as an item is a pleasure to have, who cares whether it's a big commercial success. This makes Ogilvy's an Aladdin's lamp for the *aficionado* of the new and unusual. By the way, if you meet a costumed Scot parading through the main floor playing the pipes, you'll know it's closing time.

Starting on the top floor, there's an excellent collection of antiques in perfect condition. The magnificent old Chinese rugs (one pillar rug has been there for years) are rare enough to merit space in a museum. The glass and china department on the fourth floor has a sprinkling of unique gift ideas, but you need a discerning eye, as the merchandise isn't well displayed. The last time we browsed through, we picked up a zoidic glass as a birthday present for "an in-law who has everything"; and being an inveterate bargain hunter, Diane was overjoyed at finding plates by Fornasetti marked at half price. Nine of them are now hanging on our kitchen wall. The Tartan Room, which adjoins the gift shop, is a pleasant spot for afternoon tea.

If you usually buy imported *haute couture* in the U.S., don't leave Ogilvy's without visiting the second floor. Suits by much designers as Patou, Chanel, and Molyneux are much cheaper here than in Paris, but of course they are not made exclusively for you. If Ogilvy's advertises a fashion show it's a good idea to go – not to the show but to the store a few days later, when the modelled clothes are offered at such fantastic reductions that customers fly in from New York especially for the sale.

Simpson's . . .

Corner of Metcalfe and St. Catherine

A friendly, functional shopping place with a wide price range and an enormous stock of day-in, day-out items. In general there's nothing exorbitantly expensive; even the sixth-floor gift shop hasn't a hint of a pitch to the rich. The modern, neon-lit departments and the orderly arrangement of the merchandise (everything of a kind in one section) are guaranteed preventatives to frayed tempers and blistered feet. It also partly accounts for Simpson's popularity with middle-income families. A mother with one child by the hand, another in her arm, and a third on the way, can't search through three departments for one article. The store's image has also been built around its gigantic discount sales. By the way, don't think that articles flamboyantly advertised as "Specials" are necessarily reduced in selling price. It could be a method of getting your attention.

The basement often harbours some real bargains (seconds, overstocks, and discontinued lines) if you have the time to hunt them out. The men's furnishing department on the second floor has racks and racks of ready-to-wear English wool suits. There's also a large choice of Aquascutum coats (material from London and made up here) that retail for $90 – about 15% cheaper than in the United States. Simpson's Fur Salon with the exclusive Jacques Heim collection is another highly regarded department. A Canadian Majestic mink stole priced at $600 is a very popular item with Americans. We don't know why, since there's no dollar saving and still the sticky problem of getting it over the border. Perhaps because of Canada's notoriously long, cold winter it's wrongly assumed that our mink have a thicker, more luxurious coat.

Eaton's of Canada . . .

Corner of University and St. Catherine

Like Topsy, Eaton's just grew and *grew* from an obscure drygoods shop in Toronto to Canada's biggest retail organization, with outlets from coast to coast. Montréal's largest department store, it occupies a complete city block and is still expanding. At the time of this writting the mechanical armadillos of construction are crawling into battle position at the rear of the store. By 1970 Eaton's will have developed into a magnificent, ultra-modern shopping complex with underpasses, overpasses, squares, and fountains.

Part of the reason for Eaton's dynamic growth is its zealously guarded image of honesty and reliability. "Goods satisfactory or your money refunded" was instigated by Timothy Eaton in 1859 and completely revolutionized retail merchandising. Today the policy has become so firmly established that a customer can even phone and have the unwanted item picked up. But what we like best about Eaton's is the scrupulously honest and genuinely courteous salespeople. Take, for example, the last time Diane was in the Young Montréaler Shop; a bottom-heavy matron was contemplating the purchase of burgundy hipster pants and striped sweater until a salesgirl discreetly persuaded her that culottes and matching blouse were more becoming.

Eaton's nine vast floors have a panoramic variety of everything from chocolate-coated ants to racing yachts. The Fine Food Shop at the back of the first floor will delight the gourmet – a hundred varieties of cheese, truffles, quail eggs, and Eaton's own fabulous Blue Ribbon ice cream. The ready-to-wear floors (2nd, 3rd, 4th) are punctuated with high-fashion boutiques for men, women, and teenagers. Eaton's is also well known for its yard goods (beautiful British wools in the fall), for its clearly marked counters of cosmetics, for its *avant-garde* college shop, and for its ninth-floor dining room. If you are interested in Eskimo arts and crafts, visit L'Igloo on the seventh floor.

Extremely service and promotion minded, Eaton's places interpreters, interior decorators, hospitality hostesses, a shopping service, and a tourist information bureau at your service. Its gigantic Santa Claus parades, held in every major city and broadcast on both radio and television, have become part of the Canadian way of life.

Henry Morgan and Company . . .

St. Catherine Street opposite
Phillips Square

Owned by the illustrious Hudson's Bay Company, this dignified, Victorian-styled emporium exudes solid quality. Shopping is usually serene here, since there are few huge discount sales to attract bargain seekers. The ladies' department on the second floor has an excellent selection of Canadian-manufactured coats and suits, with a sprinkling of exciting imports. In the sportswear section the Kul-E-Tuk jackets and the Hudson's Bay Blanket jackets will be of special interest to the visitor, as also will be the china department, renowned for the largest selection of Wedgewood in Canada. Often so-called bargain basements are cluttered catch-alls for undesirable items from the rest of the store. But not Morgan's basement! This newly completed Bon Marche has streets of shops which display everything from go-go clothes to pastries – all low-priced, all good quality. It's a bargain mart all right, but with a dash of imagination. Morgan's Regency Room makes a relaxing luncheon spot, or for lunch-on-the-wing, La Soupière serves delicious soups and desserts.

Dupuis Frères . . . 865 St. Catherine E.

If you wonder what an "authentically French" department store looks like, hop on the Métro heading east to Dupuis Frères. For the last 99 years they have catered primarily to a French clientèle, but don't worry, all the salespersons are bilingual. The fashion-conscious woman will enjoy shopping here — fur coats in lynx, mouton, and rabbit; traditional saris in gold silk; and daytime ensembles by French couturiers Jacques Heim and Louis Feraud. Although the store is a firm supporter of Canadian merchandise, most departments are spiced with items from around the globe. You'll forget that the Maisonneuve restaurant is a department store dining room with your first mouthful of its superb cusine. Incidentally, it's the only store restaurant in Canada with a wine and beer license.

SHOPPING COMPLEXES

By 1972 a shopper will stalk the stores of central Montréal during a fierce rainstorm without wetting the soles of his shoes. How? By the "three-dimensional" theory of town planner Vincent Carlos which will establish a system of pedestrian underground and overpass connections linking office complexes, hotels, railway stations, restaurants, department stores, and hundreds of small shops. The core of Montréal will be a 100-acre showpiece unequalled anywhere else in the world, but more of this in the chapter on places of interest. Now we are concerned only with shopping in the vast, newborn complexes that are actually cities-within-a-city.

Place Ville Marie

Situated on Dorchester Blvd. between Manfield and University, the P.V.M. has become a symbol of the downtown renaissance. It includes a shimmering aluminum skyscraper bank, an open-air square larger than New York's Rockefeller Plaza, and a 7-acre subterranean shopping promenade with 64 stores and 2 theatres as well as numerous restaurants, bars, and coffee shops. With 80,000 people passing through daily and 20,000 working there, the small glass-walled shops do a booming business. The shopping promenade is rather like a recumbent department store with a separate entrance and owner for each department; but unfortunately, since a certain area has not been alloted for each specific kind of shop, you may find the hodgepodge appearance disconcerting on your first visit.

If you become confused, stop at the circular Information Centre in the middle of the concourse. Besides giving information about Place Ville Marie (P.V.M. to Montrealers), it sells souvenirs, 7 city guidebooks, and Expo '67 Passports. A few steps away the ALBERT GILLES COPPER SHOP displays an outstanding selection of beautifully crafted copper art. Each item, from the popular $2.00 ashtrays to the magnificent $700 console and mirror, is created in the Gilles seven-man workshop just outside Québec City.

If you want proof that men are becoming as fashion conscious as women, glance in the P.V.M. Barber Shop. This large, dashing salon, staffed with replicas of Perry Como, specializes in styling men's hair. Although we like to think of ourselves as "with it", it was a slight shock the first time we caught a glimpse of a friend with his head wrapped in a hairnet! An ordinary haircut costs $1.75, while a cut, shampoo and styling come to $4.50. Ask for Giovanni. His deftness with the scissors and innate Italian diplomacy are well known about town.

Next door THE SKI SHOP, owned and managed by U.S. and Canadian Olympic skiers, Les Streeter and Jimmy Quarles respectively, is staffed entirely with experienced sportsmen. Shop here if you want the best in active or spectator sportswear with such labels as Sport Craft, White Stag, and Bogner. Their extensive collection of imported ski sweaters includes handsome Norwegian handknits. This is the place where sports-minded teen-agers spend their carefully saved allowances, where older and wealthier Montrealers shop as a matter of habit, and where ski buffs drop in with the first frost. During the summer The Ski Shop sells high-priced, co-ordinated sportswear – very similar to that sold by the famous Bermuda Shop in New York. Incidentally, upstairs on the plaza Streeter and Quarles have opened another shop that will outfit you for any sport from deep-sea diving to mountain climbing.

The BELLEFEUILLE gift shop displays a small but tasteful collection of articles which are fine examples of Canadian handicraft and Eskimo art. Across the promenade the TOY WORLD offers playthings of unusual quality from around the globe, while the nearby CASA BELLA has many intriguing Spanish imports in wrought iron and carved oak.

If you're a bibliophile or just footweary, don't miss CLASSICS on the lobby level. Here, in the tranquil atmosphere of one of Canada's finest bookstores, you can browse through rows of well-displayed books, sink into a comfortable chair, light a cigarette, and peruse, contemplate, or just cat nap.

One more thing! P.V.M. makes an excellent, albeit somewhat crowded, lunchtime spot. The trio of Carrefour restaurants are discussed in our dining chapter. For a quick lunch the speedy Hilton-run St. Lawrence Cafeteria has a wide choice of hot and cold dishes, and the food is better than many first-class restaurants in the United States. Beer and wine are served also. Between noon and 1:30 p.m. the Instant Theatre provides unique lunchtime entertainment, with three half-hour performances of one-act plays by such well-known playrights as G. B. Shaw, Chekhov, Noel Coward, and Edward Albee. This P.V.M. pocket theatre only holds ninety people, so it's wise to get your tickets in advance. Sandwiches and coffee are sold at the door.

Place Victoria

Walking down Beaver Hall Hill from Dorchester Blvd. you will come upon Place Victoria at the edge of the city's *le vieux quartier*. Look for a soaring, sleek-lined structure wrapped in glass, with four startling white columns as corners. Currently the tallest of the Canadian skyscraper family, its statistics, tenants, and tours will be discussed in another chapter. The subterranean shopping arcade, similar to P.V.M.'s in composition, appearance, and size, has a double level rather than one large promenade. In the middle of the concourse an enormous kaleisdoscopic chandelier stretches through a three-storey staircase, and the luminous flash of its 3,000 glass pieces dominates each floor. The first level features a variety of ready-to-wear fashion shops for women and men. Many are branch outlets of stores found in other shopping complexes. The nearby FRENCH SHOES has enjoyed a long popularity. Almost all the shoes are designed in Spain with American lasts. The latest fashion are always here, not in a few display samples but in a wide range of colours, styles, and sizes. Best of all the price hovers around $20. FLORSHEIM'S, known across America for their excellent men's shoes, have an impressive selection in their display window a few yards away.

The lower shopping promenade contains a post office, liquor store, cinema, delicatessen, bookstore, art gallery, and handicraft shop. The last mentioned, MAYNARD'S CANADIAN COLLECTION, has a small display of articles representing almost every craft native to this country. An examination of their display is a speedy way of finding out what is available along this line. For expensive dining there's LA VIEILLE PORTE with its award-winning French-Canadian décor (see Restaurant chapter), and for snacks there are cafeterias on both levels.

Place Bonaventure

At the time of this writing the opening of Place Bonaventure in April 1967 is a few months away. Don't think this is "just another commercial venture" in Montréal's construction boom. As one of the most complete trade centres existing anywhere today, Place Bonaventure is destined to revolutionize the character and quality of retail merchandising in this country. The functions, facilities, and statistics of this mammoth $75,000,000 project are enough to boggle the imagination. With a strategic location just behind the Queen Elizabeth Hotel and with all transportation systems passing near or through its great central shopping mall, P.B. is slated to become the Mecca of the future city.

At the hub of this complex, in the massive shopping reception area, daily average traffic of 200,000 pedestrians (double that of Place Ville Marie) is expected. It's no wonder that the rents of its 100 shops will be the highest in Canada! Gus Dubinsky, the manager, has not released the names of the retail companies that will lease the 350,000-square-foot, double-level space, but he did say that they will be merchants offering quality goods and personal service. Some shops will be completely new to Montréal; others will be branches of large chains. The upper promenade or fashion floor has a magnificent boulevard 300 feet long and 50 feet wide, with stores of a specific type grouped in one allotted area. Even the store fronts are being closely controlled so that the overall aesthetic expression will not be adversely affected by individual tastes, All in all, Place Bonaventure's shopping plaza, to be known as Les Galleries, promises to be a thrilling place for shoppers, browsers, people-watchers, and just about everybody.

So much for the large department emporiums, both horizontal and vertical. Following is an alphabetical mélange of some specialty shops that we think you'll enjoy. Again, we remain within the "golden mile" of central Montréal.

CHINA, GLASS, AND GIFTS

Montréal department stores are noted for their excellent selection of these items. However, here are four more that deserve recognition.

The tall, courtly, red-brass doors of HENRY BIRKS AND SONS on Phillips Square reflect the inimitable reputation it has gained over the last four generations. From simple Montréal beginnings, it has developed into a national organization with quantities of quality merchandise. The famous Birks "blue box" has become a Canadian institution. Many girls receive a "blue box" with a sterling spoon inside at birth; next their engagement ring comes in a small velvet "blue box", followed by wedding gifts in "blue boxes" of all shapes and sizes; then it starts all over again with the next generation. Besides imported goods such as English bone china, Irish crystal, French leather, and Swiss watches, Birks have their own silver and jewellery workshops where highly skilled artisans create outstanding items at reasonable prices. On the upper level there's an entire room for china alone. However, we refuse to be drawn into the controversial subject of how much money an American saves by purchasing English bone china in Canada. A preferential tariff must make a difference, but you'll have to browse around yourself to find the exact answer. Salespersons automatically say 30%, but in-the-know friends claim the saving isn't enough to pay the cost of shipping it over the border.

The connoisseur of home accessories will be delighted by FERRONI at 2145 Crescent. Every nook and cranny of this shop displays items of an unsual nature, such as the large, crystal swan with silver-plated wings and matching salt cellars. There are chafing dishes, cannister sets, wastepaper baskets, copperware from around the globe; but in keeping with its name, Ferroni leans toward Italian imports.

Around the corner at 1446 Sherbrooke, BETTY MCDOUGALL stocks a fascinating array of highly imaginative knickknacks. The affluent aficionado of conversation pieces will love the delicately worked toothbrush holder shaped like an incense burner, or the scotch-tape dispenser concealed in a diminutive ticker-tape machine, or the stapler that looks like an ancient telegraph key.

And around still another corner the two tiny below-ground rooms of LEOPOLDINE (2138 Mountain) are alive with fragile, floating mobiles and sleek-line Scandinavian accessories, Tucked away in one corner is the outstanding hand-decorated thistle stoneware by Buchan of Scotland. It sells for $8.50 a place setting – a real "find". In the back room there's a rack of cotton dresses by the Finnish designer Mari Mekko. These soft-toned originals are silk-screened, hand-painted, washable, and cost from $40 to $50.

HANDICRAFTS

It was only six years ago that Canadian craftsmen were recognized officially as artists and became eligible for grants from the Canada Council. Since then shops have sprouted like mushrooms after a rain, stimulating the production and raising the standard of crafted works. Central Montréal is sprinkled with small and large, good and not-so-good craft boutiques. Unless you're a craft dilettante, many of the displayed articles will be unfamiliar, making it difficult for you to judge their artistic worth. As an orientation we suggest a visit to one of the major handicraft concerns listed here. Each is fundamentally interested in high quality, not profit, so offers a discriminating outlet which is of benefit both to the public and to the craftsmen. From these displays you'll see that the French Canadians have gradually evolved a distinctive style, making their fabric, woodcarving, and pottery – especially their pottery – second to none.

Just north of the Mount Royal Hotel at 2025 Peel is located the national headquarters of the CANADIAN HANDICRAFT GUILD, a non-profit organization which sells and exhibits the best work currently being done in all craft fields. Downstairs there are pine furniture, hooked and braided rugs, original ceramics, tufted coverlets, handwoven bags and unusual Christmas cards by Eskimo artists (from 15¢ to 40¢ for each card.) Upstairs you'll find the best selection of Eskimo sculpture in Montréal, artistically displayed. From the $2.00 souvenirs to the $300 *objets d'art*, these unique abstract carvings depict a starkly realistic picture of the Eskimo way of life. Until two decades ago the inhabitants of the Arctic were considered to be a nomadic mongoloid race who paddled kayaks, built igloos, dried cariboo, and wore animal skins sewn together with fishbone needles. Their fascinating carvings and skin sewings, which are products of skills practised since history dawned, were virtually unknown until the Guild sent a representative to make a sample purchase of their crafts in 1948. Gradually it was realized that 80% of the Eastern Eskimos were able to produce artistic works, making them the oldest art group in North America. With the help of the Canadian government, their art has gained international appeal, especially the soapstone carvings. It's no wonder! Whoever sees them remains enthralled. The figures seem to burst, so to speak, out of cold, grey stone, their primitive shapes exuding a static vitality which, at its best, has some similarity to Michelangelo's Unfinished Prisoners in Florence.

A word of warning: Before you buy Eskimo art in any store, look for the symbol of original art authorized by the department of Northern Affairs – a black igloo on a white label.

At the rear of the room an entrance opens to the Galeries des Artisans, where craftmen exhibit to an increasingly enthusiastic public.

The CENTRALE D'ARTISANAT DU QUEBEC, a non-profit organization under the jurisdiction of the provincial government, has its headquarters at 1450 St. Denis and a retail store in the lobby of the Queen Elizabeth Hotel. The former is next to the Berri-Demontigny Métro station and offers a wide choice of Québec crafts. The rustic pine carvings depicting French-Canadian scenes ($3.00 and up) and the sturdy onion soup bowls ($3.00) are distinctly Québec and make wonderful gifts. For only $8.00 you can pick up a square yard of unusual, brightly colored, handwoven fabric that looks great hanging on the wall of a foyer or den. Of course there's Eskimo art, traditional and modern jewellery, functional ceramics, and way-out iron sculptures, the price range is as wide as the selection. Incidentally, they also have maps and information about other handicraft shops in the province.

In the tableau of Mountain Street shops, the TOURNESOL stands in the limelight – original in conception, design, and content. For the first time in history a group of craftsmen linked talents for the sole purpose of opening an ideal craft outlet as visualized by the artisans themselves. Here, in a shop designed like an art gallery, only Canadian crafts which have met strict aesthetic and technical standards are sold. They have an exceptional selection of ceramic vases, cups, bowls, and decanter sets, displayed with thought and imagination. The prices of the glowing enamelled copper plates begin at $60, but we didn't dare ask the price of their magnificent batik wall hangings. Veronique Arseneau, one of the founders, shows her handwoven ties in a rainbow of muted colors priced at a low $3.50. Generally speaking the goods in this unique shop are expensive but worth every penny, because you are assured of getting the best.

FOOD FOR THE EPICURE

Most people are aware of Montréal's reputation for fine international dining, but few realize that a great variety of gourmet foods are available in shops, supermarkets, and department stores. We have discussed Eaton's Blue Ribbon section with its 'round-the-world delicacies. Steinbergs, our major grocery chain, have expanded their gourmet sections until they have become almost separate shops. Even the number of small epicurean shops scattered across the city has increased as more and more people travel.

MAGNANI FRERES (9245 Lajeunesse) import and manufacture Italian specialties. Gourmet cooks will love the weird and wonderful shapes of their pastas. The attached Chez Magnani restaurant probably serves the most authentic North Italian cuisine in town. (*Don't* see our restaurant section because we have just "discovered" it.)

In downtown Montréal AUX DELICES, at the southeast corner of St. Catherine and Drummond, has a large pastry shop with yummy goodies that you can eat there or take out. DIONNE ET FILS, across St. Catherine on the northwest corner, has been specializing in table delicacies since 1870. Customers come in droves at Christmas for their *pâté de foie gras* and elegant fruit baskets.

At noon and at 5 p.m. people stand in line for the delicious cakes, cookies, and pastries at COUSIN in Place Ville Marie and Place Victoria. Their instant gourmet dinners, including frozen *coq au vin,* beef *bourguignon,* and *ragoût de pattes,* are snatched up by working wives. Scattered through these complexes there are also several outlets for the well-known "made in

Canada" LAURA SECORD chocolate and candies.

For thirty years the CHEESE SHOPPE at 2054 Union near McGill University has stood its ground while bigger and better buildings fell under the scythe named Progress. Although the Scottish proprietor, Robert MacConnache, carries caviar, truffles, imported tea, and fad food such as chocolate-coated ants, he prides himself, and rightly so, on his tremendous selection of cheeses. Whatever you name he has, or will get and deliver for you.

Have you ever wanted to make your own wine but lacked the knowledge and equipment? If so, see Mr. Franck at the WINEMAKERS' CELLAR (1197 Mackay). Before coming to Canada he worked in a winery for twenty years in Czechoslovakia. In his one small shop you can buy everything from the recipe book to the sealing wax. A bottle of homemade wine costs about 25¢, but unfortunately the quality leaves much to be desired.

JEWELLERY FOR THE DISCRIMINATING

If you are in the market for a three-carat diamond or a conventional leaf-and-flower spray brooch, anyone can point out a reputable firm, but if you are looking for something extraordinary, something beautiful, art that is wearable, then search out our city's jewellery designers. We have some of the world's foremost. Take, for example, MAURICE BRAULT, who shook his head at an invitation to join Tiffany's in New York. His work includes a brooch for the Queen Mother and a ring for Cardinal Léger. In an old, high-ceilinged atelier at 1546 McGregor Street, he creates modern, often free-form jewellery in silver, gold, and platinum. Every piece is custom made.

In his tiny whitewashed shop at 1184 Mackay, HANS GEHRIG meticulously executes contemporary jewellery. His clean, strong, architectural designs produce a total effect of simple elegance that is never out of style. He prefers to design but keeps a fairly large selection of rings, brooches, and pendants in stock. The prices of his rings begin at $35 in silver and $100 in gold. LE DOLMEN, the adjoining room, displays ceramics by Québec craftsmen which Hans sells at very reasonable prices – well-turned cups for $2.50, decanter with 6 glasses for $17, and ashtrays up from $2.50.

To jewellery connoisseurs, finding WALTER SCHLUP's atelier at 1482 St. Catherine Street, near Mackay, is like finding the pot of gold at the end of the rainbow. Believe me, you'll need that gold to buy his creations! And rightly so, since each is an *objet d'art* illustrating the parallel between sculpture and jewellery. On the walls of his tiny shop hang photographs of objects that look like abstract sculptures but which are really his jewellery enlarged 20 to 30 times. While his designs vary greatly, the lines are always fluid, graceful, and unexpected; the craftsmanship topnotch. He often mixes silver and gold, rough and smooth textures for a striking effect. His gems and precious stones aren't conventionally "set" in the metal but "grow" out of it as naturally as a flower on a stem. The prices of his earrings and cuff links begin at about $35 and his rings at $60.

BOUTIQUE STROLLING

In reaction to mass production and *prêt-à-porter* fashion, more and more people are eclectic shopping; that is, they are turning to many diverse shops for unusual one-of-a-kind merchandise. To answer this need small specialty shops are popping up everywhere, even within large department stores. Montréal, because of her cosmopolitan nature and international artisans, has an especially fascinating array of these boutiques. Since most of them are clustered in specific easy-to-reach areas, we have outlined some short strolls which we think you'll enjoy—as a shopper, a browser, or a sightseer.

LE VIEUX MONTREAL

The history and restoration of our oldest quarter was discussed elsewhere in the book. We are now concerned with the picturesque shops that occupy the restored century-old buildings. Wandering down narrow streets, under scaffolds, and over rubble, you'll unearth an intriguing potpourri of articles at all price levels.

Place d'Armes, easily reached by Métro, bus, or car (see Chapter 2 for directions) is a good starting point. Walking a few hundred feet west along Notre Dame you'll pass WOLFE'S DISCOUNT SHOES, where famous names are about $4.00 cheaper than downtown. Turning left down St. François Xavier, you enter a little pocket of outstanding antique importers, appraisers, and auctioneers—JACOBY'S at 480 St. François, FYFE-MCGREGOR at 204 St. Sacrament. WILLIAM P. WOLFE at 222 de l'Hôpital specializes in rare books, prints, and manuscripts.

The next cross street is St. Paul, the oldest thoroughfare in the city. Just after turning left you'll pass a small, well-stocked art gallery named JASON TEFF. Next comes Place Royale, the cradle of Montréal and historically the most important square in Montréal. It was here that settlers landed in 1642 and Maisonneuve erected his fort and chapel. Nothing remains but a thirty-foot obelisk to mark the spot.

The windows at 361 Place Royale display the most delightful and unusual children's clothes we've ever seen. It's called ANNA BELLE *pour les enfants*. Anne Pritchard, the designer-owner, thinks of her shop as a studio-laboratory for the development of pacesetting fashion ideas for children. Prices range from $10 for overalls to $75 for a coat and dress ensemble. Across the street at 151 St. Paul, Pierre Leduc's GALERIES PLACE ROYALE has a reasonably priced collection of Canadiana, glass, copper, lamps, and handicrafts, Eskimo carvings, and an art gallery upstairs. The beige handwoven purses with the wood button fastenings seem a good buy at only $7.95, as do the typically Québec *catalognes* (rag carpets) at $4.95 a yard. A little further east at 134 St. Paul there's another antique shop, CHARLES DE CHARTRES, stuffed with fascinating but impractical articles such as snuff boxes, moustache cups, and 19th-century bedroom slippers.

That takes care of the shops in the eastern sector of *le Vieux Montréal*. If you wish you can continue walking down St. Paul for about a mile with little to be seen between there and the restoration of the western part, or you can walk up to Notre Dame Street, hop on the first bus heading east and get off at Place Jacques Cartier. For the shops around this area turn to our chapter on a foot tour of Old Montréal. There's much more activity in the western section with churches, theatres, restaurants, hotels, art galleries, and museums to visit. Be sure to

La Guinguette, sidewalk café in downtown Montréal.

Fashion Shop in Le Drug.

poke about in BONSECOURS ANTIQUES at 441 St. Claude Street, right beside the Château de Ramesay. Three rooms and a basement are crowded with Canadiana. The choice is wide, the quality good, and the prices fit a less loaded budget. After a two-hour car drive to the Eastern Townships just for an old wine jug to convert into a lamp base, we found the same quality jug in Bonsecours Antiques for the same price. For zippy *avant-garde* dresses ($40 and up) and for Québec handwoven souvenirs (aprons, towels, ties, etc.), look up the BOUTIQUE BONSECOURS at 363 St. Paul East, across from the market.

CENTRAL MONTREAL

While the principal shopping artery is St. Catherine Street, the sophisticated specialty shops dwell in the dignified old houses of Sherbrooke Street. A coat of paint, a few bright awnings, a beckoning sign and presto, the doddering Victorian *grandes dames* regain their girlish charm. The smaller streets cutting these two main thoroughfares grow more alluring daily as colourful boutiques blossom haphazardly along their sides—treasure troves to the wandering shopping hounds. Here's a quick tour of its core to give you an impetus to poke about for yourself.

The Cheese Shoppe, founded 31 years ago.

The carriage trade begins its swing up Sherbrooke Street from the corner of Guy, so we will do the same. Sauntering east along the south side you will encounter art in all its varied aspects, from Canadian contemporary paintings at the Waddington Galleries to imported antique furniture at John L. Russel and Palestine glass pieces dating from pre-Christ times at Petit Musée. After four blocks turn right at Crescent Street, coined Montréal's Fifth Avenue; it's a gay short block of adjoining 19th-century mansions whose basements, drawing rooms and attics are now home to tiny, vital boutiques. Here is a rundown of some of the high-fashion boutiques. For the *dernier cri* visit ELLE (No. 2115), directly affiliated with the famous Parisian magazine by the same name. Its clothes and accessories are shipped from France once a month. Well-established IRENE WILSON (No. 2155) caters to the more conventional women who want beautiful tailoring above all else. RAYMONDE (No. 2134) on the other side of Crescent is a spanking new basement boutique whose friendly French-Canadian owner designs all the clothes you see. Street dresses cost about $65 and cocktail dresses about $90. Unfortunately, there aren't many dresses on display, since most of her clothes are custom made. LA BOUTIQUE FANTASQUE likes you to browse through their attic rooms containing slightly used and one-of-a-kind new outfits. On the other side of Burnside Street JOHN WARDEN, a Canadian fashion designer, who has had meteoric rise to local fame, has recently opened an off-beat polka-dot boutique (No. 1409) with "different" clothes for the younger set. Samantha Eggar visited the shop on her last visit to Montréal, choosing many of his outfits for her wardrobe.

Flowers in Dominion Square.

Let's move from fashion to art. If your taste runs to the contemporary, don't miss the superb exhibition of Canadian painters and sculptors at the GALERIE LIBRE (No. 2100). Georges Delrue, the proprietor, designs his superbly original jewellery in the upstairs atelier (ring to enter). Many discriminating Montrealers claim that for quality and prices you can't beat MICHEL BOURDA'S ANTIQUES (No. 2137). All this is a mere sampling of what's happening on one compact little street!

Horse racing attracts huge crowds

Now, for those of you who are on the look out for inexpensive, imported knick-knacks such as a Chinese adding machine or a bark drawing, turn right on St. Catherine Street and you will find within a few feet two stores packed with oriental and bamboo gift ideas, THE CHINA PAGODA (1383 St. Catherine) and next door LA MAISON BAMBOO.

Continuing one block west along St. Catherine Street and turning right at Bishop, you'll come to number 1431, one of the best dress boutiques in this area—at least to our mind. BOUTIC FRANGINE and the tiny adjoining craft shop are owned by two very charming and very young French-Canadian girls. Although only open one year, the shop has done extremely well and it's easy to see why. Their large (in relation to other boutiques), well-made collection of clothes is reasonably priced and artistically displayed. The one-of-a-kind dresses range from $25 for a simple wool to $80 for a cocktail gown. Simple floor-length crepe gowns cost only $60, which is certainly not much for such taste and talent! If you spy something you like but it's the wrong size and color, Micheline will, for an additional $5.00, make one up especially for you and ship it to your home address.

On your way back along St. Catherine Street you'll pass the world's largest assortment of paper-bound books at CLASSICS (No. 1327). If you're interested in Québec's current political problems here's your chance to pick up a few inexpensive paperbacks such as *Québec States Her Case* by Frank Scott and Michael Oliver, or *The State of Québec* by Peter Desbarats.

Mountain, the street on the east side of Ogilvy's entertaining windows, is the most colourful of all the streets running between the mountain and the harbour. At the top sit the stolid mansions of the wealthy; at the bottom cringe the drab tourist and boarding houses; while squeezed in the middle are a miscellany of sights, sounds, and smells to rival Noah's Ark during the 150 days of the flood. To the visitor the lively slice of Carnaby Street between Burnside and Sherbrooke is the most intriguing. Since many of these shops and restaurants have been mentioned before, we'll leave you to poke about as you wish. But don't forget the imaginative gifts at LE CHENET, or the antiques piled seven storeys high in H. BARON, or CATY'S in the Le Drug, or HEANEY'S Irish linens. And, of course, there's the renowned HOLT RENFREW at the corner of Sherbrooke and Mountain with three floors of exclusive boutiques.

By this time even the steps of the most eager shopper will have faltered, so why not pop into the nearby Coffee Mill (2046 Mountain) for capuccino or Le Colbert of La Crêpe Bretonne (2080 Mountain) for a glass of wine and a *crêpe*.

5.

NIGHT LIFE

Montréal never sleeps! More than any other North American city, she thrives on the switch from day life to night life. During the day, Montréal goes about the business at hand. Then at the first glimmering of dusk, her pulse quickens. St. Catherine Street casts aside her prim business dress for a glittering, lavishly lit evening dress. By nine o'clock the city sparkles vivaciously with a myriad of entertainment. The choice is yours!

Advertised to American visitors as Petit Paris or Paris of the North, Montréal's nocturnal charm isn't limited to its French character, but rather reflects its multi-cultural background. For the culture hound with a yen for sophisticated places, there's magnificent Place des Arts for concerts, where svelte, diamong-ringed women sip vichy water during intermission. For the swinger there are the action-packed discothèques (the biggest in North America), where tense young bodies in the latest "in" gear cavort on a highly polished steel dance floor. For those searching out "typical French-Canadian" entertainment, there's the warmth and magnetism of the *chansonnier* singing to an enrapt audience in a smoky café. For the man's night on the town, there are shiny, sensual bodies gyrating to the throbbing beat of burlesque music. For those who just want a relaxing drink before sleeping, most hotels and motels have a softly lit cocktail lounge with unobtrusive entertainment.

Whatever entertainment draws you out when the moon is high, Montréal has it, and an evening will cost you less than in other North American cities. Best of all, Montréal after dark erupts with an unself-conscious, exciting personality that's exclusively her own, and totally unlike any place else on the continent.

TIPS FOR THE NIGHT ON THE TOWN

1. Reserve in advance at nightclubs, supper clubs, and theatres.
2. Montréal is normally quieter from Monday to Wednesday than during the rest of the week.
3. Jacket and tie for men and a dress for women are *de rigueur* in the evening.
4. Canadian liquor is of lower proof (alcoholic content) than American.
5. There's no law specifying the amount of liquor to be served in drinks in Québec, and establishments vary considerably.
6. Canadian beer and ale is popular with U.S. tourists, as it is heavier and richer than the American equivalent.
7. If you buy the unattached lady in a burlesque house a drink (it's probably cold tea), pay for it immediately. A running bill can zoom up to hundreds of dollars in a very short time.
8. Montréal's night life is late awakening. Since dinner doesn't begin until after 7 p.m., discothèques, lounges, clubs aren't busy until after 10 p.m.

Les Feux-Follets.

La Place des Arts.

Ancient church spire in Old Montréal.

Place des Arts . . .
175 St. Catherine Street W.
Phone 842-2141

Although the performing arts always enjoyed a rich and varied life in Montréal, the spectacular new Place des Arts complex intensified every facet of cultural activity. By the summer of 1967, this lavish $40 million centre will include a 1,300-seat theatre, an 800-seat recital hall, a 3,000-seat concert hall, shops, lounges, and a three-level underground parking area.

Salle Wilfrid Pelletier, the first and biggest to be opened, has been called one of the finest combination concert hall-opera houses in the western hemisphere. This boldly futuristic structure houses an exceptionally comfortable and glamorous auditorium. None of the seats are more than 135 feet from the stage, but all the rows are set further apart for added leg room. The acoustics nudge perfection. Some of the world's greatest entertainers say it it the best they have ever seen. The stage, 100 feet wide and 55 deep, can handle the most complicated productions and can be transformed into an orchestra shell within minutes. Just push a button and it rises out of the floor!

The sumptuous main lobby symbolizing grand living of the 20th century parallels that of Milan's La Scala or the Paris Opéra. It features an outstanding collection of Canadian works of art. Even if you don't attend a performance, it's well worth a guided tour. They are held daily during the summer from 10 a.m. to 4 p.m. weekdays, and from 1 to 4 p.m. Sundays. Adults 50¢, children 25¢.

For information about performances and reservations, phone the Place des Arts box office.

Here's a tip. If you attend an evening event, take the Métro, which has direct access to Place des Arts. With parking facilities for 800 vehicles and a total seating capacity of 5,100, you can imagine the traffic tie-up whenever the three halls are in use. By riding the Métro to Place des Arts, you will have the opportunity to see the two crowning laurels that have helped our city to take its place alongside London, New York, Paris, Tokyo, and San Francisco.

THEATRE

As previously mentioned, the superb Place des Arts is greatly responsible for the intensified theatrical activity in Montréal. Unfortunately for the English-speaking visitor, there are two drawbacks. First, since Montréal is a French city, it follows that most of the plays are presented in French. Second, similar to Europe, the majority of local companies close or go on tour during the summer months. To find out what is playing, consult the weekly *Current Events* magazine or the daily newspaper.

French Theatre

There are approximately a dozen professional or semi-professional French companies that have made Montréal a hotbed of *avant garde* acting and stage techniques. The reason is due in part to the cultural inclinations

Ballet and opera, two highlights of the Montréal Festival.

of the French and in part to the "quiet revolution" that has made the French Canadian prone to new and unusual ideas. Following are listed some of Montréal's best known and most highly regarded companies, who offer consistently good plays with top-notch artists.

Le Théâtre du Nouveau Monde . . .
Orpheum Theatre
525 St. Catherine Street W.
Phone 845-7149

A French-language company that enjoys an international fame, thanks to successful tours of Europe and North America.

Le Théâtre du Rideau Vert . . .
Stella Theatre
4664 St. Denis Street
Phone 844-1793

Another excellent French-language theatrical company that has gained a reputation for consistently good productions.

The Montréal International Theatre . . .
La Poudrière
St. Helen's Island
Phone 526-0821

This should be listed among the "must-sees" for anyone who enjoys a good play in a unique setting. This company specializes in staging plays in their original language, including English, French, Spanish, German, and Italian. And you're in luck! English is the most popular language. Can you imagine seeing such rib-tickling Broadway hits as

Montreal's night life vibrates with joie de vivre.

Who's Afraid of Virginia Woolf? and *Mary, Mary* in a history-steeped converted powder magazine dating back to 1812? A delightful experience! Performances take place between March and November.

English Theatre

Generally speaking, there's been a dearth of English-language theatre in Montréal in the last few years. Part of it is due to the proximity of the large theatrical centres of New York and Toronto. Today English theatre is struggling to get back on its feet.

Instant Theatre . . .
Shopping Promenade, Place Ville Marie
Phone 878-2589

Already discussed in our chapter on shopping, this highly successful company performs thirty-minute plays in English to a lunchtime audience that packs the ninety-seat theatre daily.

The Barrel Theatre . . .
1191 Mountain Street
Phone 861-7902

This is a new group that has a cozy, pocket-sized theatre in the hub of Montréal. Currently live performances alternate with foreign movies. Perhaps in the near future this schedule will change, as the relaxed and congenial atmosphere is attracting a regular theatregoing audience.

La Comédie Canadienne . . .
84 St. Catherine Street W.
Phone 861-3338

This is a modern, air-conditioned theatre that presents the plays of its own company as well as travelling companies. In 1967 it began a new and successful venture with an instantaneous translating machine that allowed the English monolinguist to enjoy French productions.

INTERNATIONAL FILM FESTIVAL

Inaugurated in 1960, the International Film Festival each summer offers some of the best films produced in about fifteen countries. The program always includes North American premières, as well as award winners from the important European film festivals. The Festival also shows prize-winning short films and special educational and scientific productions. Matinees are usually devoted to high-quality children's movies. For details call Montréal International Film Festival, 306 Sherbrooke Street E., 842-8931.

MOTION PICTURE THEATRES

There are over seventy cinema houses in Montréal. These show American, European movies in English or French, and some in other languages. Theatres are generally open seven days a week. Reservations are necessary for shows at the Alouette, Imperial, and Seville theatres. There are no drive-in movies.

The only Cinerama theatre is the Imperial, at 1430 Bleury Street.

Children under the age of ten are not allowed in Québec's movie houses, and between ages ten and sixteen, they are admitted only at theatres authorized for this purpose for special films. Posters are placed at the wickets of authorized theatres. Children under sixteen must leave the theatre by 6 p.m.

MUSIC AND DANCING

The Montréal Festival . . .
Phone 849-1182

Unfortunately for the summer traveller, July and August are traditionally poor months for the performing arts. But in Montréal, this is not true. The entire month of August is devoted to the Montréal Festival's presentation of opera, ballet, symphony, theatre, and jazz concerts. While famed international performers are imported for star billing, the society's main purpose is the encouragement of Canadian artists—and it has done just that, ever since its founding back in 1936. Many of its "discoveries" are now starring on the leading stages of London, Paris, and New York.

Montréal Symphony Orchestra . . .
Phone 844-2867

The Montréal Symphony performs at Salle Wilfrid Pelletier of Place des Arts during its main season from October to May. Under the brilliant direction of its past conductor, Zubin Mehta, the orchestra has won national and international acclaim.

During the summer months, the same orchestra presents open-air concerts at the chalet on top of Mount Royal. A promise of good music, a spectacular view, and a cool evening breeze brings throngs of people. Every seat is sold—even the encircling grass is strewn with the blankets of students, who can romance to the strains of a classical concert without paying admission.

Les Grands Ballets Canadiens . . .
Phone 861-1808

Montréal's leading ballet company has won national and international praise. It performs during the fall and winter season at Place des Arts, but still finds time to tour the country and make numerous television appearances.

Les Feux-Follets . . .

Folk dancing has always been popular in French Canada, so it is not surprising that Montréal has organized one of the world's best companies. Les Feux-Follets was assembled as part of the Montréal Parks Department Summer Festivals Program. Its director, Michel Cartier, travelled long distances to gather folklore, original songs, traditional dances, and authentic costumes of Canada's cultural groups. In 1965 the company made its professional debut with *A Canadian Mosaic* in ten scenes, including an Eskimo walrus hunt, a jazz suite reflecting today's urban youth, and an ancient Indian betrothal ceremony. Instantly successful, Les Feux-Follets toured Mexico, South America, Europe, and the United States the following year. Representing Canada in the Canadian Pavilion at Expo, this young company (average age of the performers is 20) has won international fame as the dancing ambassadors of Canada. Don't miss them!

MONTREAL'S BRIGHT LIGHTS

In keeping with her reputation as a lively international city, Montréal's cabaret entertainment swings the pendulum from large, lavish floorshows to intimate after-hours jazz soloists. There's such a profusion of night spots scattered throughout the city that any listing short enough to fit into this chapter would be full of unforgivable omissions.

So instead we're giving you a taste of what's available by breaking down the bright lights into four categories—supper clubs, discothèques, *boîtes à chansons,* and burlesque houses. The places mentioned are centrally located, many within walking distance of the downtown hotels. All enjoy a respectable reputation among Montrealers for good dollar value. We have deliberately left out the after-dark establishments, regardless of how unique or interesting, that are situated along the once-notorious St. Lawrence Blvd. This area is safe since Mayor Drapeau polished its tarnished reputation, but generally speaking, the "dives" are poor dollar value.

SUPPER CLUBS

Follies Royale . . .
Empress Hotel
5560 Sherbrooke Street W.

This plush nightclub, with one of the most spectacular stage shows to be found anywhere, is housed in the Empress Hotel. But don't be fooled. It's not a hotel, but rather a converted movie theatre. Currently the admittance charge is $2.00 per person. Dinner costs from $3.50.

For as little as $5.50 per person, you can watch a live show of Ed Sullivan's varied scope and Le Lido's evocative lushness. Les Follies Royale comprises a chorus of dazzling, long-legged beauties whose professional dancing and fabulous costumes hold a top notch on the nightclub circuit. This is the main feature, but the show offers numerous acts, including acrobats, trick cyclists, very clever cinematography, and big-name singers.

La Salle Bonaventure . . .
Queen Elizabeth Hotel

This posh supper club (the emphasis is as much on "supper" as on "club") is situated just off the main lobby of the hotel. It's the mainspring of the Montreal night-life scene. Just recently La Salle Bonaventure adopted a policy of bringing in big-name entertainment while continuing their superb menu and impeccable service. For such a top-drawer club, the cover charge of $4.00 per person ($5.00 Saturdays) does not seem unreasonable.

La Salle Bonaventure has become an "in" spot for Montréal's café society. Here you'll find this city's most glamorous gowns and biggest diamonds twirling around the dance floor to the mellow tones of a full orchestra.

Casa Loma . . .

94 St. Catherine Street E.

Less expensive, less plush, but still top quality for your money, the Casa Loma offers an international stage show of comedy, variety, vocalists, and of course, that all-time favourite, girls, girls, and more girls (scantily clad dancers rather than strippers). That's downstairs. Upstairs there's a huge hall with a large, raised dance floor as the central attraction. This is the go-go palace for people who like their discothèques without frills and cover charges. The music is solid, loud, live, and continuous. There's lots of space for the frenetic contortions of the young of all ages, and they come either stag or in couples. In the supper club the admission charge is $1.50, with mixed drinks the same price. Upstairs there's no entrance fee except on Saturday nights, when it's 50¢.

Le Café-Concert . . .

Le Château Champlain

Place du Canada

At the time of writing, this plush-lined hideaway is not yet open, but by the look of the plans, it should be one of the most fascinating supper clubs in North America. The rich red, gold, and purple "Moulin Rouge" décor will feature at one end a full-sized stage for continuous entertainment in the French music-hall tradition. Down one side and across the other end will be two tiers of balcony boxes with padded velvet on the railings and stair-rails. The fourth wall will be covered with huge 19th century paintings in heavy gilt frames. With its wide, winding stairs, Victorian wall brackets, and balcony carvings, this *chic* fun spot is uniquely reminiscent of an Edwardian theatre.

DISCOTHEQUES

Discothèques have sprung up in every cosmopolitan city the world over—and Montréal is no exception. The heart of the city throbs with the beat of its music. You'll find go-go dancers gyrating in the second-storey windows at the corner of St. Catherine and Drummond, providing five o'clock entertainment for the bus queue across the street. Montréal has not only the largest discothèque in North America, but also the most unique and, we are convinced, the most crowded on a Friday night. This is the recognized stag night, when the *bon vivant* atmosphere bubbles at its highest. Many of the discothèques offer good, reasonably priced dinners, but the real atmosphere begins later (after 9 p.m.) with the pounding music and tightly packed crowds. There's no admission charge, no cover charge, and no minimum. Single girls are ensured of a very warm welcome from the men packed three deep around the bar.

Le Drug Hot . . .
2130 Mountain Street

This wildly popular, kookie drugstore, with its food, fashion, and art boutiques, deserves a special trip, even if it's just to see its weird steel rod and chain-mail store front.

The discothèque is located in a noisy, low-ceilinged basement. It's reached from the outside through a separate door with a buzzer and slot that permits the doorman to look over the customer before allowing admittance. The way-out décor in purples, blues, and oranges is almost as loud as the pounding canned music and as turned-on as the frenzied movements on the tiny dance floor. It's considered very "in" by the jet-setters. Gourmethèque food (whatever that means) is served at lunch and dinner.

Mousse Spacteque . . .
1467 Crescent Street

The uninformed would never guess that the ordinary-looking building on the corner of Crescent and Burnside harbours one of the world's most fantastic discothèques. Its space-age atmosphere is projected through total sense stimulation. Dancers twist on a polished stainless steel floor, while colours flash faster and faster on the encircling alabaster mannequins; three projectors toss rapidly changing slides around the room; wild, exotic perfume fills the air. Suddenly the mood changes. The music softens, the beat slows, the lights dim to blue; the perfume changes to lavender, and the dancers cling fiercely to each other, barely moving. Mousseau, the creator of this global environment, has nudged Montrealers one step further towards Huxley's Brave New World.

La Licorne . . .
1432 Mackay Street

The prima donna of discothèques, La Licorne was the first of its kind in Montréal. Many still claim it's the best. It was modelled after its Paris counterpart, and the international set throngs this dark, intimate *cave* every night of the week. There's always lots of action—and not just on the dance floor. An excellent lunch and dinner are served at very reasonable prices.

Cave Don Juan . . .
2022 Stanley Street

Another similar *cave* that zoomed to popularity, proving true the owner's philosophy of, "Bring in the models and the rest will follow." It attracts Montréal's young sophisticates and would-be jet setters. There's nothing outstanding about the Spanish décor, the canned music, or the tiny dance floor. Also, beer is served only on Sunday. Then why the long line-up to get in every night? Because Montréal's most eligible male and female bachelor's are rumoured to hang out here. So, swingers, the next move is yours.

Chez Pierre Le Grand . . .
1200 St. Catherine Street W.

The biggest discothèque in North America is conveniently located at the corner of Drummond and St. Catherine. You can learn the latest *yé-yé* movements by watching the shapely go-go dancers gyrating in cages—then try it yourself on a large, raised dance floor crowded with enthusiastic swingers of all ages. The rustic décor, reminiscent of an old *auberge*, is in keeping with the informal atmosphere.

LES BOITES A CHANSON

For a taste of French Canada's newest art form, listen to the intense singing of a French *chansonnier*—a person who writes the words and music and performs them himself. The *chansons* are usually sad, proud songs pertaining to folklore or topical politics. The *chansonnier* can be compared to the Portuguese *fado* singer and the American folk singer. In fact, Gilles Vigneault has been called the Bob Dylan of Canada. He is a talented, magnetic French-Canadian singer who has taken the French-speaking world by storm. Being a passionate nationalist, he writes songs that are profoundly Québec. His most successful, *Mon Pays*, won first prize at two international songfests and vibrantly reflects the attitude of those who feel apart from the rest of Canada.

CHEZ CLAIRETTE, conveniently located at 1456 Mountain Street, is a popular *boîte à chansons*. After climbing a steep flight of stairs, you enter a dark room lit only by candles on the red-checkered tablecloths. Between shows it's noisy and crowded, but as soon as Clairette or her guest steps on the stage, silence reigns. It's impossible not to respond with fervent enthusiasm to such stirring, intense music, even if you don't understand a word of French.

LE PATRIOTE at 1474 St. Catherine E. is another *boîte à chansons* with a dedicated following. It's a huge, barren hall with wooden tables and chairs and a stage at one end. Since it serves only cider, it caters to a younger crowd.

GIRLS! GIRLS! GIRLS!

Since curvaceous ladies who shed their clothes on stage are prevented from performing their art in many U.S. cities, American visitors are usually interested in hearing that Montréal abounds in burlesque houses. Most shows consist of a number of costumed strippers who come out one at a time and over a period of twenty minutes go through their act of undressing. There is sometimes a comedian, a singer, or an acrobat between the acts.

CHAMPS SHOW BAR at 1220 Crescent Street is one of the better burlesque houses. Out of twenty-five dancers who appear nightly, there are usually at least a couple of outstanding strippers. The cover charge is $1.00 per show. Mixed drinks cost $1.50.

The ALL AMERICAN CAFE at 1234 Dorchester Boulevard is less crowded and slightly more sophisticated than Champs. It has the same type of show on a smaller stage, with no cover charge, no minimum, and no admission. The prices for drinks are about the same.

If you're in an international mood, you'll find a good black and tan revue, with comedy, song, and dance, at ROCKHEADS (1252 St. Antoine). There are three shows nightly from Monday to Saturday, one show Sunday. For belly dancing admirers, the CASA DEL SOL at 2025 Drummond has shows from 2 p.m. to 3 a.m., with $1.00 cover charge. The exotic Middle Eastern décor of the Kismet Room is in keeping with this voluptutous dancing, which depends more on movements than on nudity for effect. Close by, there's another belly dance show at the CLUB SAHARA, 1177 Mountain Street. It's advertised as an "authentic Arabic Club", since its star, Fawzia Amir, was the one-time favourite of the late King Farouk of Egypt. You pay $1.50 cover charge at the table, but none at the bar.

The recently opened CHEZ PAREE at 1258

Stanley offers a better-class strip show with a bevy of exotic girls from around the world. This club also contains a couple of intimate bars and an orchestra for dancing. The only cover charge is $1.00 for the floor show.

Although CASINO DE PARIS is located a long way east at 312 St. Catherine, we mention it because it features entertainment with female impersonators. If you go in for this sort of thing, you'll get a kick out of the show. Weekend cover charge is $1.00.

Last of all, for the rock and roll buffs, drop into the ESQUIRE SHOW BAR at 2245 Stanley. It has loud, continuous entertainment until 3 p.m. Check the daily papers or *Current Events* to find out who's starring. They often import such all-time greats as Chubby Checker and Fats Domino.

At 2 p.m. when Montréal bright lights are beginning to fade, there are a couple of small, off-beat coffee houses that are just awakening. These small, intimate spots offer strong coffee and good jazz until dawn. BLACK BOTTOM at 1350 St. Antoine also serves chicken wings to the hungry. LE OP at 3545 Park Avenue sticks to jazz, coffee, and quiet conversation.

This has been a sampling of what goes on in a city that never sleeps. Night spots in Montréal are exciting, highly diversified, and not that expensive. It can be fun, sophisticated, boisterous—whatever you want. It's up to you!

6.

ACCOMMODATIONS

Within the last decade tourist accommodation in Montréal has almost doubled. Previously there were a few good hostelries that were adequate enough for the steady tourist trade and small conventions. Then the current building boom and its catalyst, Expo '67, changed the scene. All of a sudden, construction workers in their yellow safety helmets took over, causing one bewildered visitor to write home that Montrealers practised civil defense every day. It seems that every year of the 1960's has brought a new deluxe hotel and the visitors to fill it. The result has been a slightly unbalanced hotel situation and a rash of ultramodern accommodations, but few older, moderately priced rooms.

Generally speaking the hotels crowd the hub of the city; the motels flank the incoming highways; and the tourist homes are scattered throughout the downtown area. Altogether there are approximately 11,000 rooms at prices starting as low as $7.00 a day. The remarkable thing about Montréal's hotels and some of her motels is their distinctive personalities. There are swish aristocratic ones catering to high society, functional businesslike ones catering to conventions, and still others, old and picturesque, that are frequented by the press. This individuality in the realm of hospitality helps to make your Montréal stay a memorable experience.

The following is by no means a complete list of living accommodations, but merely a recommendation of some lodgings that we know to be clean, satisfactorily serviced, and of good repute. For specific information concerning rooms during Expo '67, refer to the last chapter in the book.

PRICES

Even though the rising costs of labour, food, and taxes have pushed up room rates across America, Montréal has managed to keep her prices a few notches below comparable hostelries in other big cities, especially those in the moderate and inexpensive categories. The year 1967, however, is a horse of another colour. Undoubtedly Expo '67 and the flurry of redecoration in the hotels will unsettle the price situation. At the time of this writing, the prices are fluctuating daily, some lodgings setting outrageously high rates, others claiming only nominal increases. It is expected that very shortly the government will step in to categorize lodgings and to fix maximum prices. Probably rates will jump about $3.00 and stay there for 1968.

To simplify your choice we have broken our listing for 1967 into four categories. Each price range refers to double or twin with bath and without meals. Please remember that this is only a guide!

Deluxe	$25.00 to $40.00
Expensive	$15.50 to $30.00
Moderate	$12.50 to $15.50
Inexpensive	$ 7.00 to $14.00

Just recently the government passed a law that all lodgings must post their rates in each room. Note that the prices are subject to a 8% provincial tax, which shouldn't bother the American visitor since his dollar is worth about 7% more.

You would be wise to make reservations in advance during the summer months, especially during the six months of Expo '67. To arrive in a strange city and to spend fruitless hours searching for accommodations can be very frustrating. If you don't have a reservation, your wisest move is to go directly to the information kiosk in Dominion Square. The staff there can tell you which lodgings have vacancies.

HOTELS

In the following pages we have chosen ten large hotels and motor hotels from the centre of the city. All are close to the department stores, fashionable boutiques, theatres, restaurants, train and Métro stations. Most are within walking distance of Dominion Square, a mecca to visitors because of the regularly departing sightseeing buses and the proximity of Cook's and American Express.

The order of the hotels has nothing to do with our preference. We simply began with the most expensive and worked down. All can claim a hundred or more rooms and a well-established reputation among both visitors and Montrealers. Each has its own characteristics and atmosphere. This list includes the older commercial hotels, the modern motor-inns with swimming pools, and the newer "showpieces" with the ultimate in service, décor, and comfort.

The Ritz Carlton . . . Deluxe
1228 Sherbrooke West
Phone 842-4212

This indisputable *grande dame* of Montréal's hotels gives a touch of Old World elegance to sophisticated Sherbrooke Street. Centrally located on the corner of Drummond, it is surrounded by some of the most *chic* shops in Canada. Open since 1912, the hotel has retained its unhurried but efficient charm. The gracious staff, from the manager, Mr. Conolly, to the bustling bellboys, know many of the frequent visitors by name and can anticipate their wishes. After a lengthy stay one celebrity is quoted as saying, "There are very few hotels like this left in the world today. They are all glorified motels now." All the 300 rooms and the 50 suites combine practical comforts with lavish extras — carved mahogany furniture, drapes and matching bedspreads hand sewn on the premises, special lighting on the dressing table, television, radio, a maid to turn down your sheets each night, and bedside buttons to summon members of the staff. The high ceilinged rooms are generally quiet, except those located on the Drummond Street side.

In 1964 a cool million dollars was spent in a major face-lifting, but the Ritz held onto its hushed elegance. The plush, dim-lit lobby is still the traditional rendezvous of Montrealers. Last year the hotel gained international repute as the place where Elizabeth Taylor and Richard Burton spent their wedding night.

Designed and operated in the great manner of the Cézar Ritz chain, its wine cellar is the largest in Canada, with a special selection from the reserved stock of George V Hotel in Paris. Off the lobby there's the

Lounge for cocktails and the deluxe Café de Paris for scrumptious French cuisine. (See Where to Dine). The adjoining patio offers lunch and afternoon tea while overfed ducks quack and cavort in the courtyard pool. Downstairs the Maritime Bar and the Ritz Café serve meals, the latter until 8:30 p.m., at which time the lights go down and the prices up.

Garage parking and additional cots for children are not included in their already high rates. Sixty per cent of the rooms are air-conditioned, and all have private bathrooms, another first in Canada for the Ritz.

Hotel Bonaventure . . . Expensive
Mansfield and St. Antoine
Phone 878-2332

Under sumptuous hostelries we swing from the city's oldest to its newest, so new that it is still under construction at this writing. This unique luxury hotel is perched on the top three storeys of the 17-storey Place Bonaventure, which is the largest convention mart in the world, with a gigantic shopping complex (see Shopping in Montréal), Métro and train stations on the lower floors. Guests arriving by car can drive to an express elevator that will take them to the rooftop lobby. The lobby is linked to the four guest room wings by glass-enclosed bridges spanning a two-and-a-half acre garden.

There are 45 bedroom arrangements in this hotel of 400 air-conditioned rooms. Each is equipped with coloured television, electric blankets, and direct dial telephone with message-writing service. The large bay windows of the outside rooms give a panoramic view of the city, whereas the inside rooms face the garden landscaped with trees, lagoons, fountains, waterfalls, and a year-round swimming pool. During the winter the water of the fountains will freeze and coloured lights will play on its ice formations. Beside the swimming pool there will be a skating rink. A few quick turns around the sheet of ice, and then splash, into the pool! Unique—but remember to take off your skates first.

Apart from its 1,500-seat capacity ballroom, the Bonaventure is fully equipped with a kosher kitchen, a main dining room in a *château* décor of stone and old wood, a coffee shop designed to resemble a trading post and a spectacular entertainment lounge. It promises to be the ultimate in modern elegance. Centrally located too! Hotel Bonaventure belongs to the Western chain. Free parking.

Le Château Champlain . . . Expensive
Place du Canada
Phone 878-1688

This gleaming $35 million hotel dominates the new exciting complex, Place du Canada, at the foot of Dominion Square. Built and operated by the Canadian Pacific Railway Company, which owns hotels from coast to coast, it is Montréal's first skyscraper hostelry. Its curved contours and arched windows contrast sharply with the severe rectangular shapes of the other high-rise buildings.

The architect designed Le Château Champlain to be contemporary but also to blend with its historic neighbors, the turrets of Windsor Station, the Gothic St. George's Church, the huge dome of St. Mary's Cathedral, and even the monuments of Dominion Square. As a point of interest, it was the arch over John A. Macdonald's monument that gave the architect the idea of choosing the distinctive arch-shaped windows for the hotel.

Planners of Le Château Champlain decreed that every guest must feel he is in one of the world's finest hotels. To ensure this they hired top-flight men in the decorating field. The décor does not reflect one overall theme, just uniform good taste. Each functional space has its own personality, with common traits of elegance and graciousness expressed in the vibrant colours, the dark wood, the glimmering chandeliers, and the interesting *objets d'art.*

Regality rules the main lobby in vaulted gold-leafed ceilings, a winding marble staircase, and luxurious tapestries. All 640 guest rooms are U-shaped with large bow windows set in the curve, affording a breathtaking view of the city. To make the visitor feel at home in the room, the designers left it uncluttered by luggage racks. Instead a mirrored dressing room adjacent to the bathroom holds the suitcases and clothes. Even the bath is sumptuous, with imported Portuguese marble in place of tile.

Each floor contains only 20 rooms, and the 34th and the 35th floors are devoted exclusively to a variety of suites, ranging from two rooms to six rooms. The two deluxe suites include a sitting room, dining room, library, master living room, marble bath-dressing room with sunken tub and, oh yes, a bedroom! Le Château Champlain boasts of seven restaurants and cocktail lounges in a variety of locations, from plaza level to rooftop, and a variety of types, from an artist's outdoor café to an opulent, 850-seat supper club, built like an Edwardian theatre with a full-size stage for continuous entertainment in the French music-hall tradition.

As soon as the first pre-cast concrete wall was heaved into place, that awesome group, the Sidewalk Superintendents of Montréal, claimed this was "not just another hotel". Word travelled fast, and a year before it opened reservations were already booked as far ahead as 1970.

As a result of the C.P.R.'s determination "to create a hotel which would reflect its sophisticated setting in the heart of Montréal", this city has been presented with a most magnificent expression of hospitality. Of course, Le Château Champlain provided every facility imaginable, from AM-FM radio to five levels of underground parking.

Queen Elizabeth Hotel . . . Expensive
900 Dorchester Blvd. West
Phone 861-3511

Since it is Hilton managed and C.N.R. owned, you might say that the Queen E was born with a silver spoon in its mouth. When this massive, streamlined complex opened in 1959 it revolutionized the Montréal hotel industry, for here was a huge complex organization that ran like clockwork but still had time for such personal touches as the morning paper delivered daily to each room.

Nothing is forgotten in this city-within-a-city! In fact, a guest need never step outdoors to satisfy his needs. Occupying one entire city block in the hub of Montréal, its location is as well known as Trafalgar Square in London. The hotel complex is linked by a tunnel to the C.N.R. Central Station and to the wonderful world of shops in Place Ville Marie (see Shopping in Montréal). But the mainspring of its operation lies in the huge, high-ceilinged front lobby, which throbs with activity twenty-four hours a day. Although encompassing shops, information booths, reservation desks, restaurants, nightclubs, and hordes of people, it exudes a luxurious yet business-like personality.

The guest rooms and suites have been redecorated for 1967. Of course all have air conditioning (individually controlled), TV-radio sets, and wall-to-wall carpets. Some of the rooms have been planned especially for women patrons, with such thoughtful boutique items as hat boxes, bath oil, foot massager, iron and board, candles, and bathroom scales (party-poopers).

Some of the best and most expensive eating in Montréal can be found in the Queen E (see our restaurant guide). Most of the dining rooms open off the main lobby, with the notable exception of the Panorama Room on the 21st floor. Here, between the stars and Montréal's skyline, you can wine, dine (light snacks), dance, and romance with no minimum or cover charge. Other facilities include baby-sitting services, men's health club, full secretarial services, and free parking. There is no charge for children sharing their parents' room.

The Queen Elizabeth has become the overwhelming favorite of conventioneers. In fact, of just about anyone who wants readily accessible facilities, dependable service, and fine dining.

The Windsor Hotel . . . Expensive
1160 Windsor Street
Phone 866-9661

This sedate octogenarian, which once hosted this city's greatest gala events, succumbed with head held high to being sliced in half to make way for a steel and glass skyscraper. In the remaining 300-room north wing, the hotel's Victorian dignity rests intact. It's been totally redecorated, but none of its original splendor has been lost. The 5-room royal suite, once occupied by visiting kings, queens, and princes, still overlooks Dominion Square with a regal eye. If you get a chance, poke your head in the historic Versailles Ballroom, considered by many to be still the most elegant in Canada.

The hotel's 275 rooms are mostly air conditioned, with TV and private bath. The huge windows draped with velvet and the high ceilings decorated with crystal and gilt are reminiscent of the days of its youth.

The excellent array of restaurants range from the sophisticated La Réserve with nightly dining and dancing (see Where to Dine) to the comfortable, oak-panelled La Lanterne, a bar for men only until 3 p.m., after which it opens its doors to the ladies. The Windsor is a favorite haunt of people who enjoy a good meal in a quiet, refined atmosphere and plush, spacious surroundings.

Le Martinique Motor Inn . . . Expensive
1005 Guy Street (below Dorchester Blvd.)
Phone 866-4611

Situated just few minutes drive, or a fifteen minute walk, from Dominion Square, Le Martinique caters to people who enjoy being spoiled. Your welcome begins with their exclusive, in-hotel parking and drive-in registration (you can almost park your car in your room). All 211 units are air-conditioned and have individual thermostat controls, direct dial telephones, T.V., radio, and background music. The décor is coolly elegant in pale blue and green upholstered French Provincial. Some luxurious suites are equipped with open fireplaces and private bars.

The spacious lobby reflects the dual personality of Le Martinique – the warmth of the Old World in the intricate wrought-iron chandeliers and wood-burning fireplace, and the efficiency of the new world in the newsstand, smoke shops, colour television, and even a tiny art gallery.

There's a choice of dining facilities to satisfy every guest. Les 4 Saisons restaurant offers international dishes in an elegant setting. The Coffee Shop provides moderately priced meals, and during the summer the terrace is a pleasant place to dine. In the secluded courtyard, reminiscent of a Roman garden, you can swim in a heated pool or just soak up the sun from a deck chair. At night there's the Petite Boîte for dancing and entertainment.

The Seaway Motor Inn . . . Expensive
1155 Guy Street (above Dorchester Blvd.)
Phone 932-1411

Another member of the young generation that caters to the motorist. This ultramodern, service-minded motor inn has 160 rooms and suites decorated in either Spanish or French Provincial or in Chinese. All are tastefully executed with all those important extras you expect to find in a first-rate lodging establishment.

When the Seaway was built, Montrealers were enthralled with its circular, futuristic dining room that seems to sprout from a single-stemmed base. Appropriately called La Ronde, it has gained local renown for its charcoal-broiled steaks. The Seaway's cocktail lounge, Le Village Africain, has also caught on in Montréal. Its darkly lit, jungle atmosphere is very conducive to dancing and romancing.

For the keep-fit enthusiasts there is

an indoor swimming pool, a Finnish sauna bath, and a health club. For imbibers there's the Pyrenées Terrace. The Seaway operates her own licenced 3-hour sightseeing bus tours of the city. Parking is free.

The Sheraton Mt. Royal . . . Moderate
1455 Peel Street
Phone 842-7777

This is the business man's darling, partly because it's one of the largest and most centrally located hotels, partly because it has six distinctive cocktail lounges, and partly because its huge, pulsating lobby plays a leading role in Montréal's way of life. People-watching from one of its overstuffed chairs is a prime sport. If you sit long enough, you're sure to meet someone you know.

The 1,000 air-conditioned rooms are fully equipped with private bath or shower, television, and radio. The contemporary furnishings are beginning to show signs of age (the hotel was built forty years ago), but generally the rooms exude a cheerful, homey amosphere.

The myriad of restaurants and lounges are a feature attraction for most guests. The most obvious of these is the Rendez-Vous Lounge, which is smack in the middle of the bustling lobby. Its gay, candy-striped carousel awning gives a frivolous, feminine touch to the lounge. The small secluded Bon Vivant has a warm, English-club atmosphere for man-to-man discussions until 5 p.m. After that they roll in the Roast Beef Wagon for delicious meals. If you don't go anywhere else, do drop in to the Picadilly Lounge, which is an internationally known meeting place frequented by individuals from every walk of life. Every Montrealer, at some time or other, has arranged to meet someone in the Picadilly Lounge. As for dining, it's hard to beat the Kon-Tiki with its South Pacific drinks and Polynesian food (see our restaurant chapter).

Being a commercial hotel, Sheraton Mt. Royal offers many facilities—shops, drug stores, parking and all the extras that conventions demand. Free parking. No charge for children sharing parents' room.

The Laurentian Hotel . . . Moderate
1130 Windsor Street
(at the corner of Dorchester Blvd.)
Phone 866-4571

This is another of the Sheraton chain, the popular, younger brother of the Sheraton Mt. Royal. The Laurentian, which opened in 1948, has the highest occupancy rate of all the downtown hotels, an average of over 80%—as a pause in its bustling lobby will confirm. While pausing, note the colourful length-of-the-lobby mural, *Migration,* which was painted by a gifted young French-Canadian artist.

One of the main features of the Laurentian is its central location on the west side of Dominion Square, one block from the central Bus Terminus, one block from the Canadian Pacific Railway Station, one block from Place Ville Marie, and a stone's throw from the shopping district. It is the only hotel that has two competitive sightseeing buses departing from its door. For the guests another bonanza, not usually found in a moderately priced hotel, is that each of the recently redecorated 1,000 rooms has air conditioning, television, and private bath. The courteous, efficient service of the staff brings guests back time and time again. The hotel will even arrange to get you a baby sitter at a very reasonable fee. Children up to 14 years of age are free if they share their parents' room.

The Laurel Dining Lounge with its delightful French-Canadian atmosphere serves full-course meals at $2.00 and up. The Au Ballon lounge on the mezzanine floor features pop music played on a Hammond organ, while the Kiltie Lounge is enjoyed by lovers of the bagpipes, kilt, and tartan.

Queen's Hotel . . . Moderate
700 Windsor Street at St. James St.
Phone 866-2531

This large Victorian building was one of Montréal's first hotels. It was constructed in 1893 in anticipation that some of the visitors of the Chicago's World Fair would come to Montréal. In 1929, sixty more rooms were added, giving today's total of 310. To keep up with Montréal's rapidly advancing hotel scene and in preparation for Expo '67, The Queen's has acquired a new general manager, a new chef, and a redecorated lobby.

Although it is not a stylish hotel, it provides friendly service and solid comfort. Only 10 of the 310 rooms have air-conditioning, but all have private baths, television, and radio. Not equipped with "the newest", "the most luxurious", or "the best", it has a well-established reputation for being a "home away from home".

The main dining room has just been moved into the more intimate Venetian Room. Here you dine amidst Italian Renaissance splendour while listening to the hotel's string trio. The Sunday night buffet has long been a favorite with Montrealers. There are also a coffee shop and two lounges. The hotel is well located one block from the Windsor Train Station and the Métro. Parking is free after business hours.

TOURIST HOMES

Visitors on a limited budget should have no trouble filling their lodging needs in Montréal, but not in a budget hotel! This older type of accommodation, unable to survive the current building boom, is doomed to extinction. Even now, few of the budget hotels that are left can pass the test of cleanliness and minimum service. Their place has been taken by a myriad of tourist homes in and around greater Montréal. At the last count there were 120 of these officially registered, ranging from basic bed-and-bureau types to sumptuous suites. From this conglomeration we've chosen eleven that we feel give you the most value for your money. All are highly respected in the tourist trade. All are within, or very close to, Montréal's "golden mile" with its shops, theatres, museums, and squares.

Montréal's tourist homes are a strange breed, a cross between a boarding house and a hotel. Their closest kin is the English "bed and breakfast" place. However, taken as a whole, Montréal's tourist homes do have some common characteristics. Most of them are the large, ornate, private residences of the élite of bygone days, converted to suit their new role. They average 10 rooms each, with each room accommodating two or more guests. Many are family-run establishments which try to express a warm, homey atmosphere by offering comfortable, public sitting rooms, television sets, radios, refrigerator space, and free advice on what you should see during your visit. Ask the manager for whatever you need, for often they keep their extras tucked away. The majority of tourist homes do not serve food or provide cooking facilities. None have liquor licences.

Concerning Rates

The Montréal Association of Select Tourist Homes has established a degree of price standardization among its members, but not all Montréal's tourist homes belong. Generally they are rated as inexpensive when the price is $7.00 to $10.00 for a double. That, of course, is cheaper than almost any respectable hotel. The larger your party of people, the better your accommodations will be, and the cheaper the price. Prices usually fluctuate according to the season, the number in your party, your appearance, etc. Unless the government sets a ceiling, some will shoot sky-high during Expo '67. Inquire about the price before you take a room. If it's too high, tell them so and leave.

A list of the tourist homes in the city can be obtained by visiting the kiosk on Dominion Square or contacting the Association of Select Tourist Homes, 1669 Sherbrooke St. West, tel: WE3-6924. During the six months of Expo '67 you would be wise to write or call well in advance. At any other time you'll get the happiest results by going around to see the tourist homes for yourself.

Sherbrooke St. West Area

BENNETT'S LODGE, 1659 Sherbrooke St. West, Tel. 935-0544. 40 rooms; 19 with private baths, 21 with hot and cold running water. Free parking.

VERSAILLES LODGE, 1669 Sherbrooke St. West, Tel. 935-0224. 24 rooms. All have private baths and televisions. Scandinavian type furniture in rooms. Free parking.

WARRINGTON GUEST LODGE, 1001 Sherbrooke St. West, Tel. 844-0811. 18 rooms, all newly decorated. 6 private bath and shower, the rest with hot and cold running water and semi-private baths. Natural wood interior throughout. Free hot coffee available in the morning.

GLAMIS TOURIST HOUSE, 1624 Sherbrooke St. West, Tel. 935-0116. 9 rooms. 4 with private shower, 5 with hot and cold running water. Free parking.

Sherbrooke St. East Area

MANOIR SHANGRI LA TOURISTES, 157 Sherbrooke St. East, Tel. 844-0331. 9 rooms equipped with television and radio. Free parking.

KENT TOURIST LODGE, 1216 St. Hubert Street, Tel. 842-0961. 8 rooms, equipped with television and radio. 6 with bath and 2 with running water. Near Berri station on the Métro. Free parking.

Central Montréal Area

GOLDEN VALE TOURIST LODGE, 1111 Drummond Street, Tel. 866-6095. 12 rooms, equipped with radios. 9 with private bath and shower, 3 with running hot and cold water.

P. AMBROSE GUEST HOUSE, 3422 Stanley Street, Tel. 849-0526. 14 rooms. 5 two-room-suites with connecting baths, 4 with semi-private baths.

PARE GUEST HOUSE, 3430 Stanley Street, Tel. 842-0841. 9 rooms. 2 with bath, 4 with semi-private bath, and 3 with running water.

PEEL TOURIST HOUSE, 3471 Peel Street, Tel. 849-0133. 11 large rooms. Some with massive, antique wooden beds, 2 with private bath, 9 with hot and cold running water. Some rooms have fireplaces. Parking.

BISHOP GUEST HOUSE, 1242 Bishop Street, Tel. 861-7568. 10 air-conditioned rooms with television and private baths. Parking.

Y.M.C.A. MEN'S RESIDENCE, 1441 Drummond Street, Tel. 849-4171. 250 modern rooms, mostly single occupancy. Available to Christians, non-Christians, and even non-members of the "Y". Swimming pool, gymnasium, restaurant, roof garden, no curfew.

Y.W.C.A. WOMEN'S RESIDENCE, 1355 Dorchester Blvd.West, Tel. 866-9941. 100 single and double bedded rooms, some with private bath. Facilities include swimming pool, gymnasium, restaurant, coffee shop, roof garden, Saturday night dance, and no curfew.

MOTELS

Motels have become as much a part of the North American way of life as suburban living. Both result from the population squeeze in the urban areas, the increased number of cars, and the casual mode of modern living.

People travelling by car, especially those with children, don't want to fight the traffic of a strange city or to stay in the formal atmosphere of a hotel. But they *do* want the comfort of the most modern conveniences. Motels provide the answer. They allow the driver to pull off the road, back up to his own private entrance, unload the bags and the kids, jump into a swimming pool, and then relax in a nearby bar in his shirtsleeves.

Montréal has followed this modern trend, and motels line every incoming highway. The two biggest clusters of motor hotels are located on the western and southwestern approaches to the city. They offer a tremendous number of facilities, from basics such as air conditioning and swimming pools, to private dog kennels and 16th century wine cellars with waiters dressed as monks. Most of the larger motels offer their own bus tour of the city or will make arrangements for you to join one. If you are driving to the downtown district from your motel, we suggest that you leave your car at the Atwater or Guy Street Métro car park and take the Métro to the hub of the city or to Expo. For the hub of the city get off at either Peel or McGill station. This will eliminate the tension and frustration of looking for a parking space downtown.

Western Approaches

(for those entering Montreal on Highway 2 B, otherwise known as Côte de Liesse Road-Autoroute 520.)

Montréal Airport Hilton . . . Expensive

6500 Cote de Liesse Road

Phone 631-2411

Within walking distance of the airport. A futuristic, circular-shaped complex surrounding a beautifully landscaped courtyard the size of a football field, with olympic-sized swimming pool and a children's wading pool. Another of the international Hilton chain, it opened in 1963. Each of the 228 rooms is air conditioned and noise insulated. Overall theme of the décor reflects warm French-Canadian mood. Children occupying same room as parents are not charged. Top luxury motel.

International Motel . . . Deluxe

6425 Cote de Liesse Road

Phone 631-1804

50 modern, tastefully decorated units with every facility for your comfort. Service excellent. Le Fourneau dining room specializes in French cookery. Close to Montréal International Airport.

Grand Motor Hotel . . . Moderate

6126 Cote de Liesse Road
Phone 748-9661

110 air-conditioned units equipped with individual heat controls, hi-fi music, and television. Heated olympic size pool and dining room. Drinks, light entertainment, and dancing in Marine Room and Galleon Bar.

Holiday Inn #1 . . .
Moderate and Expensive

6110 Cote de Liesse Road
Phone 748-7771

One of the chain of Holiday Inns. 210 air-conditioned rooms with gay French Provençale décor that frame a quiet, landscaped courtyard. Year-'round pool with infra-red heated patio for winter suntanning. Light snacks and coffee served on the outside terrace. Interesting assortment of restaurants, banquet rooms, and cocktail lounges, especially the 16th century wine cellar with waiters dressed as monks.

Town and Country Motel . . .
Moderate and Expensive

6061 Cote de Liesse Road
Phone 748-8871

Designed and laid out to look like a Laurentian village. A few minutes drive from the International Airport. The modern suites, and smaller, more rustic rooms, restaurant, and recreation centre are clustered away from the busy highway amidst quiet, landscaped surroundings. 140 attractive, air-conditioned units. Continental dining in Le Tapis Rouge, with a famed hot and cold buffet. Four distinctive lounges. Free parking.

Skyline Hotel . . . Expensive
6050 Cote de Liesse Road
Phone 747-9861

Two minutes from the Trans-Canada Highway and five minutes from the Airport. Quiet, comfortable, air-conditioned guest rooms and suites. Year-'round pool, sun terrace, and cabana club. Leisurely dining in the Salle du Barry, or fast service in the Coffee Gallery. The Pub for light evening entertainment. Children under 12 stay free of charge when sharing a room with their parents. Complimentary airport transportation. Free parking.

Holiday Inn #2 . . . Expensive
6036 Cote de Liesse Road
Phone 748-7822

200 air-conditioned units located halfway between the Airport and downtown Montréal. First of the Holiday Inn chain to be franchised in Canada. Facilities include free transportation to airport, free kennels and rations for pets, beauty salon, barber shop, laundromat, two heated swimming pools, cocktail lounges, and restaurants. Les Caves de L'Abbaye is a romantic wine cellar where waiters and musicians dress as monks — very popular with Montrealers. Le Chateaubriand is noted for its French cuisine.

Ruby Foo's Motor Hotel . . .
Expensive and deluxe
7655 Decarie Blvd.
Phone 731-7701

118 large, ultramodern, air-conditioned units with every comfort and superb service. It has long been a favorite hotel with discriminating visitors. The Rickshaw Alley connects the hotel to the famous Ruby Foo's

Restaurant (see restaurant chapter). Outdoor heated pool and a coffee shop that serves excellent inexpensive meals are on the premises.

Capri Hotel . . . Expensive
6445 Decarie Blvd.
Phone 739-2771

106 air-conditioned units. Situated on "Sunset Strip", Decarie Blvd., it is a short distance from Blue Bonnets Racetrack. It's the closest motel/hotel to downtown Montréal in this section. Le Petit Café offers French and American cuisine. Honky-tonk piano at the Gilded Cage. Baby-sitting facilities, swimming pool.

Southwestern Approaches
(Mercier Bridge)

For those entering Montréal on highway 9C, 3 or 4, cross Mercier Bridge and follow signs to Montréal via Montréal-Toronto Highway (Routes 2 and 17).

Raphael Motel . . . Expensive
7455 Montréal-Toronto Blvd.
Phone 489-4911

A sprawling, stylish, motel complex. Its 90 units feature air-conditioning, television, radio, contemporary furniture, and wall-to-wall carpeting. Heated outdoor pool, cocktail lounge, and French restaurant. Sightseeing tours of Montréal arranged. A ten minute drive from Central Montréal.

Belvedere Motel . . . Expensive
7250 Montréal-Toronto Blvd.
Phone 481-8121

70 air-conditioned, individually controlled units with the latest facilities and smart con-

temporary furnishing. Justly proud of the excellent cuisine of their separate dining rooms. Sightseeing tours arranged. Valet and room service.

Cavalier Hotel/Motel . . . Deluxe
6954 St. James Street West
(Upper Lachine Road)
Phone 488-9561

Restaurant, cocktail lounge, dancing nightly, heated swimming pool. 50 air-conditioned units. Sightseeing tours available. One of the Quality Court chain.

Southern Approaches off the Island

(Approximately 1 mile south of Jacques Cartier Bridge on Highway #9).

Motel Le Champlain . . . Moderate
7733 Taschereau Blvd.
Phone 676-0341

Small but very comfortable motel. 17 modern, air-conditioned units with an attached restaurant.

Motel La Barre (500) . . . Expensive
2019 Taschereau Blvd.
Phone 677-9101

Named after the 500th goal scored by hockey player Maurice "The Rocket" Richard. 50 air-conditioned, opulently decorated units, swimming pool. We recommend this motel's dining room as one of the best in Québec. Organ music and dancing nightly.

Le Versailles Motel . . .
Moderate and Expensive
7200 Sherbrooke St. East
Phone 256-1613

Seven miles east of Dominion Square and the newest motel from this approach. 126 ultramodern, air-conditioned units, swimming pool and wading pool in the inner court, dining room and coffee shop.

Cadillac Motel . . . Expensive
5800 Sherbrooke St. East
Phone 259-4691

60 air-conditioned units with bath and shower, television, dining room, and gift shop.

Motel Fontainebleau . . . Expensive
5500 Sherbrooke St. East
Phone 256-9011

125 units, air-conditioned, dining room, heated pool, cocktail lounge.

Lucerne Motel . . . Expensive
4950 Sherbrooke St. East
Phone 255-2806

125 air-conditioned units, swimming pool, turkish bath, gift shop, daily sightseeing tour, trio and dancing nightly. Special feature is its location adjacent to the municipal golf course and tennis courts. Their French-Canadian restaurant, Le Reveillon, enjoys a good reputation with Montréal's gourmets. This is a Quality Court motel.

7.

GUIDED TOURS

Those visitors who enjoy escorted tours are in for a treat, for Montréal is one of the few cities actively concerned with the welfare of her sightseers. Not only are all tours well organized with excellent facilities, but also the city has passed a special by-law which specifies the duties and sets the fees of the guides.

The qualifications demanded by the city to become a tourist guide are high — once-a-week attendance at a winter course given at the University of Montréal and a passing grade on a written examination on the city's history, economics, politics, geography, and so forth. Once a guide has received his diploma, he must purchase a licence; only then is he qualified to impart his wealth of knowledge to sightseers. By the way, it is illegal for licenced guides to solicit patronage. Visitors can apply for their services either to the guide in person or by contacting any tourist bureau. (See our Listing).

BY BUS

Montréal Transportation Commission . . .

159 Craig St. West

Phone 877-6260

These buses are marked "PROMENADE" and can be boarded at any regular stop that indicates Promenade on its sign. Starting at Dominion Square, they wind their way through the city, stopping to let passengers on and off at any of the twelve principal sights. The buses are equipped with a recorded commentary of the places they pass. If you stay on the bus for the entire trip, the 28-mile ride takes two and a half hours. However, the best thing about this bus tour is that you can get off at any of the sights, stay as long as you like, then get on another Promenade bus — all for one fare, $1.50 for adults and 50¢ for children. The buses run every half hour from 10 a.m. to 5 p.m. and every 15 minutes from 5 p.m. to 10 p.m. M.T.C. Promenade Tour operates only during the summer months. Here is a listing of the principal tourist sights that are on this tour route:

Dominion Square
Place Ville Marie
Redpath Museum at McGill University
Notre Dame Church at Place d'Armes
(see chapter on Old Montréal)
Château de Ramezay
(see chapter on Old Montréal)
Bonsecours Church and Chapel
(see chapter on Old Montréal)
St. Helen's Island
Botanical Gardens
Lafontaine Park
Beaver Lake on the top of Mount Royal
Wax Museum on Queen Mary Road
St. Joseph's Oratory

University of Montréal
Museum of Fine Arts

Murray Hill Sightseeing Service . . .
1380 Barre Street
Phone 937-5311

This large bus-touring operation offers a wide range of tours. Their superbly designed, luxurious buses include *le tram*, a replica of Montréal's earliest trolley car, and the Golden Chariot, an exact copy of a 19th century open-top observation tram.

Murray Hill gives the visitor a choice of five tours of Montréal and surrounding districts. Pickup points are the four central hotels – The Laurentian, The Sheraton Mount Royal, The Queen Elizabeth, and the Holiday Inn on Sherbrooke Street.

TOUR 1, SIGHTSEEING IN MONTREAL: A two-hour lectured excursion through our multi-cultured city with 200 points of interest unfolding before you. Departs daily at 10 p.m. Price is $3.00 per adult.

TOUR 2, MONTREAL AND MOUNT ROYAL PARK: A three-hour trip which includes everything in Tour 1 plus a trailer-train ride through Mount Royal Park to the Municipal Lookout. There you stop for a magnificent view of downtown Montréal and the swift-flowing St. Lawrence River. Operates daily from June 1 to September 15, 10 a.m. and 2 p.m. Price is $3.75.

TOUR 3, ST. LAWRENCE SEAWAY AND CAUGHNAWAGA RESERVATION: A three-hour jaunt that takes you across the Jacques Cartier Bridge for a close-up view of one of the Seaway locks in operation. At the Indian Village of Caughnawaga, the home of 2,000 Iroquois Indians, you'll see the remains of a tiny church and the tomb of Kateri Tekakwitha who died in 1680 for Christian faith at the age of 24. You will also meet Chief Poking Fire, see an Indian dance performed, and be given an opportunity to buy home-made Indian souvenirs. Price is $3.75. Leaves daily at 2 p.m. from June 1 to September 15.

TOUR 4, LAURENTIAN MOUNTAINS: A seven-and-a-half hour journey which includes lunch and afternoon tea. The bus winds its way through the colourful, rugged Laurentian Mountains dotted with quaint French-Canadian villages. At Ste. Agathe-des-Monts a sightseeing launch waits to take you on a cruise on placidly beautiful Lac des Sables. Price is $14.95 for adults and $10.95 for children. Daily from June 15 to September 15, leaving at 10 a.m.

TOUR 5, AN EVENING ON THE TOWN: This tour begins with dinner and a glass of wine at one of Montréal's leading French restaurants. Next comes a lectured tour taking you to the top of Mount Royal for a spectacular view of the glittering mosaic of city lights. The tour continues with a ride through Lafontaine Park to see the illuminated fountain and lagoon. The last stop is a gay nightclub featuring an international extravaganza (a drink of your choice included). All-inclusive tour price is about $12.95. Leaves nightly at 6:30 p.m.

Gray Line Sightseeing Tours . . .

1188 Dorchester Blvd.

Phone 842-2281—866-8461

Gray Line offer much the same tours at the same prices. All are informative and well-organized. Phone either of the above numbers for the details or else pick up a brochure at the central bus terminus listed above. The tours start from either the Dorchester Terminus or Dominion Square. Buses may be chartered for group tours from both companies.

Colonial Coach Lines . . .
1188 Dorchester Blvd.
Phone 866-8461

There are many intriguing points of interest within a 200-mile radius of Montréal. For visitors who wish to broaden their knowledge of the Canadian way of life, both past and present, we highly recommend Colonial Coach Lines' two one-day excursions to Upper Canada Village and to Ottawa.

UPPER CANADA VILLAGE EXCURSION: This is a scintillating tour that operates daily during the summer months. If you wish to drive there unescorted, you will have about a two-hour journey along picturesque and historic Highway 2. The village is located in the 2500-acre Chrysler Farm Battle Park on the shores of the widened St. Lawrence River. The Park is well equipped with a picnic ground, beaches, camp site, restaurant, railway museum, and large marina.

The recently completed Upper Canada Village is the most exceptional reconstructed village we have seen – either on this continent or in Europe. In memory of the men who died in the battle of Chrysler's Farm in 1818 it recreates the pioneer days with startling realism. Once through the entrance gate (adults $2, children free) you step back 120 years into the rugged life of Canada's first settlers. On this tongue of land that licks the St. Lawrence, twenty-five absolutely authentic buildings line the narrow street. Every home, church, tavern, barn, school, bakery is authentically furnished down to the wallpaper. The Ontario-St. Lawrence Development Commission which is responsible for this first-class exhibition scoured the countryside looking for anything from this period of history.

However, don't get the idea that the village is a lifeless museum piece. Rather, it is inhabited by people who dress and work in the same way their ancestors did a century ago. You'll learn first-hand how loaves of bread were made, how sheep's wool was turned into yarn and eventually clothing. And then how the old clothing was turned into blankets and carpets. You'll see a blacksmith shoeing a horse, a schoolhouse straight out of Glengarry School Days, old two-wheeled buggies and a unicycle. There's also a windmill, a lighthouse, and a fort to delight the children. From the lookout you have a superb view of the passing Seaway traffic. The Colonial tour cost is $8.20 (includes entrance fee) with three buses departing each morning from May 14 to October 16.

OTTAWA EXCURSION: This is a trip with special sightseeing treats which only a national capital can offer. Colonial's one-day excursion to Ottawa leaves daily from May 15 to October 15 and currently costs $9.50 per person. If you are visiting Montréal during the last two weeks of May, this side jaunt is a must, for at this time Ottawa's many parks are a brilliant mass of flowering tulips, one of the world's finest displays. Queen Juliana of the Netherlands makes such a show possible as she gives the bulbs yearly in remembrance of the hospitality she received during the war years when she lived in Ottawa.

Taking Highway 17 (either by car or by bus), you travel beside the scenic Ottawa River until it meets the Gatineau and Rideau Rivers. The lush natural setting provided by their union is the site of the City of Ottawa. If you take the Colonial tour, the rest of your day is filled wih interesting sights and activities: the Parliament Buildings, the Governor General's mansion, and the National Museum, to name a few.

BY TAXI

Only taxi drivers holding an official guide licence are permitted to conduct city tours. At the rate of $4 per hour, regardless of the number of people in the cab, a taxi chauffeur will point out the most interesting places in town or the surrounding districts. One of these taxi tours may be arranged at the stand located on the north side of Dominion Square or by calling one of these companies: Diamond VI. 2-3221, Veterans UN. 6-4551, LaSalle UN. 1-2552.

BY PRIVATE CAR

If your prefer to tour the city in your own car or in a rented car, you may obtain the services of a guide by calling the Municipal Tourist Bureau at 872-3561. For $3 per hour these licenced guides will conduct you, either driving or riding, on fascinating tours of the city, the harbour, Old Montréal, or the nightclub circuit. These guides, all members of the University Guide Service Ltd., are also available for excursions beyond Montréal. For details phone the Tourist Bureau listed above.

TOURS FOR CHILDREN

Montréal has many points of interest to which you will want to bring your children. Some of these are the Jardin des Merveilles in Lafontaine Park, St. Helen's Island, the Dow Planetarium, the Wax Museum and the Marguerite-Bourgeoys Chapel (see our description of these places in other chapters). But some attractions extend a special thrill to the kiddies – and Mrs. Olivette Rill knows them all! This young, energetic widow with three children of her own has organized a tour program that will delight every parent. Limousines pick up and return the children to their respective hotels. While on the tour they travel in mini-buses with four bilingual guides. Tuesday and Thursday are full-day tours from 10 a.m. to 5 p.m. The price of $8.95 includes lunch. Wednesday, Madame Rill organizes a "surprise package" tour from 1 p.m. to 5 p.m. Cost is $5.95 with snacks and souvenirs.

These tours for tots are a bonanza to parents who want to shop or just sleep. The kiddyboppers have a ball, seeing new sights, meeting new friends and learning catchy French ditties! For more information contact Gulliver's Trails Canada Limited, 853 Rockland Ave. Tel: 277-6722.

BY CALECHE

Montréal is one of the few cities left in North America that still have horse-drawn carriages sedately clip-clopping along the busy downtown arteries. They are so much a part of the city that cars zoom around them without the least sign of irritation – another example of the perfect meshing of the old and the modern way of life.

These old-fashioned vehicles offer the tourist a leisurely, romantic method of soaking up the sights, sounds, and smells of this vibrant metropolis. Some *calèches* depart from the north side of Dominion Square, winding their way through Montréal and up the flanks of Mount Royal. Others depart from the Chalet on Mount Royal and promenade along the trails of the mountain park, where cars are forbidden.

TWO TIPS: Establish your price before you hire the *calèche*. Don't expect a running commentary of the places you pass, for your coachman is not a licenced guide.

8.

PLACES OF INTEREST

As Canada's biggest, most cosmopolitan city, Montréal has sights to interest everyone. In this chapter we stick to tourist attractions in and around Montreal. Happily, most of the indispensable sights are located within the city's core. We roam from the magnificent St. Joseph's Oratory, high on Mount Royal, to the sights along the bustling waterfront. In doing so we cut across Montreal's three main arteries — elegant Sherbrooke Street, with its boutiques and art galleries; sanguine St. Catherine, with its crowded, neon-lit stores and bars; windswept Dorchester, with its soaring skyscrapers.

You can take three days, three weeks, or three months to discover this area, and every day will bring something new and fascinating. Such is this enticing, bubbly city. Beginning with the visitor's mecca, Dominion Square, we clue you in on the sightseeing musts.

AROUND DOMINION SQUARE

Here lies the heart of Montréal. Shadowed by skyscrapers, this large public square sits astride Dorchester Blvd., bound to the west by Peel/Windsor and the east by Metcalfe.

With its numerous benches, shade trees, and flocks of pigeons, it seems like any public square the world over. But its history is far from ordinary! Over the years Dominion Square has been transformed from a public cemetery, to a tranquil park, to the heart of bustling city and a jumping-off point for tourist activities.

At the end of the 18th century the Catholic Church bought what is now Dominion Square for a cemetery. Its grimmest days were during the cholera epidemic of 1832; within three days 100 bodies lay unburied at St. Antoine Cemetery, as it was then called. No-one could be found to bury the macabre pile. Finally, in response to the cries of the priest, the people dug a deep trench, 100 feet long, laid the dead in layers, and threw dirt over them. Gradually the city recovered, and all that remained evident from those dismal days were the words, *Aujourd'hui pour moi, demain pour vous*, above the mass grave.

By the 19th century the city closed the cemetery. With the old crosses removed, grass and trees planted, and paths set down, St. Antoine Cemetery became a pretty park in one of the best residential districts of the city. But the grim reminders of death are renewed whenever excavations are made around the square. Coffins were found when Dorchester Blvd. and Windsor Street were widened, and even more recently bones were found when the foundations were dug for the Canadian Imperial Bank of Commerce skyscraper in 1959.

From contemplating the past, let's turn to the buildings framing the square. The stately, spreading building to the east is the Sun Life. When it was erected, it was the largest building in the Commonwealth. And even today we consider it one of the most beautiful office buildings in Montréal.

Moving clockwise around the square, you'll see the impressive Basilica of Mary Queen of the World; the dazzling, *avant-garde* Château Champlain on Place du Canada; the imposing, castle-like Windsor Station; the Gothic St. Georges Church, dwarfed by the Laurentian Hotel; the stark steel-and-glass Canadian Imperial Bank of Commerce; and finally, especially for visitors, American Express, Cook's, and the tourist kiosk of the City of Montréal, all located on the north side of the square. Quite a unique framework for an ordinary square!

Before leaving, let's stop for a brief look at the statues scattered around the square itself. On the south side stands Sir John A. Macdonald, placed on a high pedestal and covered with an ornate canopy. As mentioned elsewhere in this book, the curve of the windows of Le Château Champlain was copied from the canopy's curve. (In the summer this section of Dominion Square has an unusual outdoor art display. Further along is an outdoor cafe, La Guinguette, which serves non-alcoholic beverages.)

Poetry is represented by the well-executed statue of Robert Burns on the west side near the Windsor Hotel. The huge Boer War Monument, showing a soldier holding a restless horse, commemorates the first time Canadians participated in an overseas battle, which fact accounts for the statue's size. On the north side of the square, facing Sir John A., is another famous politician, Sir Wilfrid Laurier. Appropriately for these days, the inscription reads, "The governing motive of my life has been to harmonize the different elements which compose our country," a philosophy which incites separatists to occasionally splatter it with paint. The most recent and most controversial sculpture is the work by Henry Moore outside the Canadian Imperial Bank of Commerce. Its title accurately describes it: *Reclining Figure in Three Pieces*. It's been damned by some as a waste of $40,000 and praised by others as "the city's most important artistic acquisition in a hundred years." What do you think?

From Dominion Square you can fan out to whatever interests you. There are lots of places to choose from, as the following pages will show.

CHURCHES

Mark Twain, visiting Montréal at the end of the 19th century, claimed that, "This is the first time I was ever in a city where you wouldn't throw a brick without breaking a church window." Surprisingly enough, the number of churches has continued to increase with the population, until now we rival Rome. In greater Montréal over half the populace is Roman Catholic; the next largest denominations are Anglican, United Church, and Presbyterian, in that order.

St. Joseph's Oratory

City officials estimate that eighty-five per cent of all visitors to Montréal tour this shrine. Pilgrims come from all over the world, hoping to be healed by the miraculous intercession of Brother André, the saintly patron for whom St. Joseph's was built. Towering high on Mount Royal, it's a magnificent tribute to this humble man, an uneducated doorman at Notre Dame College. Imbued with a fervent devotion to Saint Joseph, Brother André was gifted with the power to effect miraculous cures, and he was allowed to build a small wooden chapel on the flank of Mount Royal. Here he ministered to the spiritual and physical sufferings of the pilgrims. Each year more people came, and the small shrine grew into one of the greatest temples in the world. Oven ten million dollars in public offerings have been spent, but it is still not completed. The huge interior, holding over 12,000 people, remains to be decorated.

Space allows us only a few descriptive facts. The vast basilica is topped by a towering dome, 125 feet in diameter, and a cross, 27 feet high. The 5,811-pipe organ inside the basilica took seven months to install. The crypt is dominated by a great white statue of Saint Joseph, while the votive chapel, glowing with the lights of 10,000 candles, houses the crutches and other supports left by the faithful. Behind the Oratory the Stations of the Cross are sheltered in a mountain park. It's especially awesome at night when the way has been illuminated by a myriad of lights. Two million persons visit St. Joseph's annually, and hundreds of pilgrims still climb the ninety-nine stairs on their knees as part of their devotions. The address is 3800 Queen Mary Road; masses are held in French and English. The Museum contains a permanent exhibition of paintings and panels on the life of Saint Joseph. Open daily from 9 a.m. to 5 p.m.

Mary Queen of the World Cathedral

Located on Dorchester Blvd. just east of Dominion Square, this Roman Catholic cathedral dates back to 1870 and is a half-size replica of St. Peter's of Rome. The decoration and even the people seem to be lost in the dim vastness of its interior. One of the chapels is dedicated to the Papal Zouaves, who left Québec over a century ago to fight for the Pope's army against Garibaldi. The beautiful onyx and marble main altar is set under a canopy as it is in Rome. Under the dome is a reproduction of Bernini's *Baldachino*. As mentioned earlier, the statues on top of the façade are the patron saints of the thirteen parishes that donated them. The bishops of Montréal are buried in the crypt. The cathedral is the archiepiscopal see of His Eminence, Cardinal Léger. Masses are held daily in French and English.

Christ Church Cathedral

Located on St. Catherine Street between Eaton's and Morgan's, this church is a fine example of Gothic church architecture, with magnificent stained glass windows and one of the few stone steeples in Canada. The interior has a warm atmosphere, in spite of its large size. Note the intricate carvings in the stone façade. For information concerning services, phone AV 8-6421.

Two other interesting, history-steeped churches, Notre Dame and Bonsecours Chapel, are discussed in great detail in our chapter on Old Montréal. Before finishing, we must mention our favorite downtown church, St. Patrick, on the corner of Dorchester and St. Alexander. It is a wonderful example of 14th century Gothic architecture, with an interior decoration similar to that of St. Mark's in Venice. By the way, this Roman Catholic church has an English-speaking parish.

The most unique church we know is Le Bon Dieu en Taxi (God in a Taxi) at 3019 Sherbrooke E. There Roman Catholic cabbies attend a drive-in mass on Sundays.

These are only a few of the many outstanding churches throughout Montréal. For the closest synagogue or church of your denomination, inquire at the front desk of your hotel.

PARKS AND GARDENS

Montréal has acres of parks (more than any other North American city except Washington), with a great many special attractions that are well worth exploring.

Mount Royal Park

This park has been mentioned frequently throughout this guide. The only wooded mountain in the centre of a North American city, Mount Royal has become a magical retreat from the smoke and noise below. It features a 494-acre natural forest, a popular recreational and cultural centre, and a fabulous view of the city. Designed by Olmstead (who also designed New York's Central Park), this one-time volcanic peak has been a sanctuary for the people of Montréal.

The Chalet and Municipal Lookout provides one of the most spectacular views of central Montréal. Regardless of the time of day or the extreme temperature, there are always people there, for in clear weather you can see 50 miles to the Adirondack foothills. The snack bar in the Chalet is a regular meeting place for teenagers. From here you can take a tour over the mountain summit by *calèche* or by miniature train.

The Pavilion and Beaver Lake, near Cote des Neiges Road, are easily reached by car. In winter the terrace is transformed into a skating rink. The large artificial pond called Beaver Lake is popular for evening stereophonic concerts during the summer. The Pavilion serves light refreshments.

The Mount Royal Art Centre stages excellent art exhibitions in a century-old stone farmhouse near which stands an outdoor gathering of modernistic sculptures. For a breathtaking drive over the mountain (by car or bus), take the Camillien Houde Parkway from Cote des Neiges Road to Park Avenue.

Maisonneuve Park

This is Montréal's largest park, located in the east end of the city at Sherbrooke and Pie IX. From its inception, it developed according to a definite plan. Today it consists of three parts — the golf course, the Maurice Richard Arena, where summer concerts are held, and the spectacular Botanical Gardens. Sprawling over a 200-acre site, the Gardens are the world's third largest, after those of Berlin and London. Visitors can tour the grounds aboard small trains. The divided greenhouse has a central conservatory for special exhibits, while the other sections contain year-'round collections. You can walk through a humid tropical jungle, a colourful display of house flowers, and a sandy desert. The Botanical Garden also has a medieval monastery garden, with herbs, pools, and children's vegetable plots. Each summer 300 youngsters who don't leave the city are picked to cultivate their own plots.

Lafontaine Park

This 100 green acres in densely populated east Montréal (Sherbrooke E. between Papineau Avenue and Amherst Street) is a fabulous place for kids. The Garden of Wonders is a child's paradise, with 40 exhibits featuring 300 small animals in a storybook setting. Open between May 15 and October

15, the park also has two meandering artificial lagoons. For $1.00 an hour you can rent a rowboat or for 10¢ tour a lagoon on a miniature steamer. It's worth a special trip at night to the other lagoon to see a dazzling fountain illuminated with 54 lights with 9 different effects. Nearby is a unique open-air theatre under the stars; the stage is built on a small island, separated from the audience by ten feet of water. During the summer it is used for a number of concerts and folk dances.

Belmont Park

A typical amusement park in the north end of town near Cartierville Bridge, Belmont Park covers fifteen acres on the banks of Des Prairies River. There are all the fun rides that kids love, as well as special rides for tiny tots. If you are not sure of your way, we advise you to take the CNR commuter train from Central Station.

SKYSCRAPER COMPLEXES

The current building renaissance of central Montréal makes this city one of the most modern and aggressive on the continent. Skyscrapers sprout at the rate of a new floor a week. The giant crane, wrecker's ball, and pneumatic drill are symbols of the transformation. The core of the city is incorporating all the latest town planning ideas. In the near future it will be a "3-D" area—Métro below, cars and buses on the streets, and pedestrian passageways above—glassed in against the weather.

Place Ville Marie

The heart of Montréal sprang alive five years ago with the construction of Place Ville Marie or "P.V.M." Its shimmering, cruciform shape has become the unofficial emblem of New Montréal. Named after its first and major tenants, the Royal Bank of Canada, this 40-storey building is the biggest office building in the Commonwealth. Below, at the 7-acre plaza, lies a city in miniature, with offices, shops (see *Shopping in Montréal*), restaurants, and theatres. An underground walkway links P.V.M. to Central Station and the Queen E. Hotel. The entire complex contains more rental space than the Empire State Building, has more telephones than a city of 15,000 people, and uses more electricity than a city of 20,000. Nearly 20,000 people work here, and 100,000 visit it daily. How's that for impressive figures? Here's one more; it was developed at a cost of $105 million, most of the funds coming from the United States and the United Kingdom. All in all, it's a fitting symbol of the New Montréal!

Place Victoria

Situated between St. James and Vitré Streets, this modern skyscraper complex links Old Montréal with the new, via Beaver Hall Hill. The soaring, stark tower is the world's tallest reinforced concrete building. Sir Basil Spence, the famed architect who designed England's Coventry Cathedral and the British Pavilion at Expo, described it as "a world pacesetter". Place Victoria houses the Montréal and Canadian Stock Exchanges, as well as a double-level shopping promenade (see our shopping chapter), restaurants, a bar, and a hand-blown sculpture composed of 3,000 pieces of colourful Murano glass.

The Stock Exchange, with modern automated equipment, is one of the finest in the world. For the first time in the history of the exchange, girls are allowed on the trading floor. Their job is to feed information into the computer, which instantly flips over the appropriate disc to bring the information up to date. At the same time, the data are transmitted to Montréal brokerage offices by means of a closed circuit T.V. monitor. Although the brokers are surrounded by ultramodern furniture and sophisticated electronic equipment, there's still most of the traditional hustling and yelling. Traders still throw their bid paper on the floor, but now the floor is covered with a plush red carpet. For this reason, special pads were designed that do not require carbon paper, so there's no chance of spoiling the carpet.

Place du Canada

This gleaming white complex at the bottom of Dominion Square is dominated by a steel-and-concrete skyscraper nicknamed by Montrealers, "The Cheese Grater" — the magnificent Château Champlain, which we discussed in our accommodations chapter. At the plaza level, activity focuses around a 27-storey office building, a quaint French-Canadian "village" shopping concourse, a heated open-air restaurant, and a skating pond.

Place Bonaventure

This gigantic merchandise mart, international trading centre, and convention hall will introduce a new era in Canadian commerce. With the burning of the Chicago Merchandise Mart, P.B. has become the world's largest commercial building. The complex has 3,100,000 square feet of floor space — almost twice that of New York's Empire State Building. However, don't look for a sky-high building, for P.B. sprawls more than it soars, averaging 14 floors over six hillside acres. It's such a spectacular engineering feat that facts, figures, and adjectives cannot do it justice. It has a prime downtown location — adjacent to C.N.R.'s Central Station, 30 minutes by car from Dorval Airport, a short cab fare from the waterfront, and is a stop on the Métro line. The two-level underground shopping promenade and the luxury hotel have been discussed elsewhere in the book. Both are supporting facilities for the Merchandise Mart in the heart of the mammoth complex. Place Bonaventure is more than a building; it's a happening that will be felt from coast to coast. Don't miss seeing it!

ART GALLERIES AND MUSEUMS

Art in all its varied forms enjoys a terrific popularity in Montréal. The performing arts we discussed under *Night Life*. Now we turn to paintings, decorative objects, and sculptures found in museums. While the Montréal Museum of Fine Arts and the Museum of Contemporary Arts are "musts", don't overlook the private galleries, which often advertise outstanding exhibitions. To see what's currently showing, check *Current Events* magazine, which can be found at the front desk of most hotels.

Montréal Museum of Fine Arts

This distinguished centenarian with its pillared entrance is Canada's oldest art institution. In keeping with its policy of being representative rather than specialist, the museum's permanent collection includes a stimulating variation of old and new masters of Europe, oriental art, Canadian paintings and sculpture, and decorative arts dating back 3,000 years.

Admission is free except for special exhibitions. The address is 1379 Sherbrooke W.

in *le quartier des boutiques.* Across the street you'll find a string of small art galleries between Mountain and Guy that are fun to poke about in.

Montréal Museum of Contemporary Art

Operated by the Québec Department of Cultural Affairs, this museum is housed in a former private mansion built to resemble France's Petit Trianon. The grounds are studded with the works of contemporary sculptors, and the museum's two storeys house travelling collections plus samples of the best from today's local artists. It stands at 4040 Sherbrooke E. at Pie IX Blvd. Admission is free. Open daily except Monday, from noon to 6 p.m., 7 to 9 p.m. Phone 254-7524.

Redpath Museum

If you're interested in geological exhibits and Canadian Indian relics, be sure to see the rich collection at this museum. Its location at McGill University gives you the opportunity to see the lush green campus at the same time.

THE WAX MUSEUMS

Montréal boasts two good, but totally different, wax museums. One is more commercial, with lighter entertainment, while the other is a dignified, history-steeped display—a museum in the true sense of the word.

Musée Historique Canadien Ltd.

Located at 3715 Queen Mary Road, across the street from St. Joseph's Oratory, it's well worth the ten-minute drive from central Montréal. This immaculate, air-conditioned building features 200 startlingly realistic wax figures in scenes of historic

Canada, the Christian martyrs in early Rome, and leading contemporary personalities. A knowledgeable student guide will conduct you through, explaining each scene. It's one of the most fascinating first-class museums of this type we've ever seen, well deserving its label, "the most beautiful wax museum in Canada." Open daily from 9 a.m. to 9:30 p.m. Adults $1.25, children 50¢.

Ville Marie Wax Museum

This museum is centrally located at St. Catherine and Drummond. You can't miss seeing their reproduction of Sleeping Beauty in the large lobby window. Inside are offered 28 scenes with 85 life-size figures supplied by Madame Tussaud's Wax Museum of London. There's entertainment for the whole family in portrayals of many contemporary people — presidents, scientists, movie stars — and of course, a chamber of horrors and fairytale *tableaux*. Open daily from 9 a.m. to 10:30 p.m. No guided tours.

DOW PLANETARIUM

Located within walking distance of Dominion Square, this $1,250,000 building was a gift to the city from the Dow Brewery. The nightly spectacles here are achieved by actual photographs of a star-studded sky projected on an arched aluminum dome, 65 feet in diameter. The movement of the heavenly bodies around the artificial sky comes from an ultramodern $140,000 Zeiss projector, which integrates 152 individual slide projectors to create such effects as rainbows, clouds, thunderstorms, and the Northern Lights. It's fascinating to see a 24-hour change of day simulated on the screen in a few minutes. There are 400 comfortable chairs in which to sit and watch the fabulous wonders of the universe revealed. It's a rewarding and memorable show for adults and children. Several programs are given daily in both French and English. Admisson 75¢ for adults, 25¢ for children.

ALONG THE WATERFRONT

Since the earliest pioneers settled on the Island of Montréal, the harbour has been interwoven in the history of the city. It has been the single most important factor in the development of Montréal as a cosmopolitan centre.

Montréal's twelve-mile harbour spreads east from the foot of McGill Street to the end of the Island. Not only does it lie at almost equal sailing distance from European ports as do principal United States ports; but it is also a trans-shipment point between the Atlantic Ocean and the Great Lakes.

Montréal is the world's largest inland seaport. Although it is located 1,000 miles from the sea, ocean-going vessels are able to reach the harbour without passing through a single man-made lock. Usually the port is open from April to December, but in recent years icebreakers have succeeded in keeping it open longer. By the way, the city presents a gold cane to the captain of the first ship to dock each year.

The entire waterfront area is a city in microcosm, with its own police force, railway system, and towing facilities. The harbour's biggest export commodity is wheat, and nothing has been spared to provide the most modern grain facilities.

The St. Lawrence Seaway

The Seaway has its beginnings at the southern approach to the Victoria Bridge.

Here you'll find parking facilities and an observation platform from which you can watch the workings of the St. Lambert Lock — the smooth, awesome operation involved in lifting ships up 50 feet in a huge basin of water to start them on their long journey into the heart of North America. The Seaway, by making inland cities accessible to huge vessels, eliminates the expense of transshipment of general cargo and also provides much needed hydro-electric power.

Further west, where the St. Lawrence becomes the frontier between Canada and the United States, it became necessary for the two countries to work together. This was an immense international endeavour, for these two neighbouring countries co-operated on every level of development. The entire project took four years to complete at the combined cost of more than one billion dollars. It consists of seven big locks plus a series of minor canals that transformed 189 miles of swift-flowing river into navigable deep water. It was a gala day on June 29, 1959, when Queen Elizabeth and President Eisenhower officially opened this ambitious construction project — one of the world's major achievements.

St. Lawrence Cruises

A leisurely, refreshing way to see the sights along the harbour is aboard *La Madelon II*. This converted ferry boat sails up the St. Lawrence, giving you a spectacular view of the skyline of Montréal, the entrance to the Seaway, the 1967 Expo site, and the port of Montréal. The cruise starts from Victoria Pier every afternoon and evening. Prices vary from $3 to $4 for adults and half-price for children under 12. The lounge and dance floor are popular and cool places on hot summer evenings. For further information, call 288-5933.

On your way to *La Madelon*, you'll pass one of the most interesting landmarks of the harbour — the 155-foot Memorial Tower on Victoria Pier. The cornerstone was laid by the Prince of Wales in 1919 as a tribute to the sailors during World War I.

9.

LISTINGS

TRANSPORTATION TO, FROM, AND AROUND MONTREAL

Montréal is the transportation centre of the nation; in some respects, of the world! As the transport facilities of the continent evolved through successive stages of movement by water, by road, by rail, and by air, Montréal has maintained a leading role.

BY WATER

This city owes its existence to a strategic position at the head of deep-water navigation between the Atlantic Ocean and the Great Lakes. Today it's one of the world's busiest harbours, with the largest inland fleet of ships and 96 shipping companies using it as a terminus. The following passenger steamship lines list Montréal as a port of call:

Canadian Pacific Steamships, Cunard Steam-Ship Co. Ltd., Europe-Canadian Line, Gdynia America Line, Holland-America Line, Oranje Line.

BY RAIL

The explorers and *voyageurs* who paddled across the country established Montréal's reputation as the gateway to the Canadian hinterland. The railway continued this reputation. As the hub of the Canadian National and the Canadian Pacific, the largest transcontinental railways in the world and through liaison with U.S. railroads, Montréal has ready access to every large North American city.

Ticket Offices and General Information

CANADIAN NATIONAL: Central Station. Open daily, 6 a.m. to midnight, tel. 877-5400. City office: 276 St. James St. W., tel. 877-4901. General information, 24-hour service, tel. 877-6550.

CANADIAN PACIFIC: Windsor Station. Open daily, 6 a.m. to midnight, tel. 861-6811. City office: 215 St. James St. W., tel. 861-6811. General information, 7 a.m. to midnight, tel. 866-5581; midnight to 7 a.m., tel. 861-6811.

RESERVATIONS: There are reservations for sleeping and parlour cars, and also for coaches on certain lines. Reservations: Canadian National, 7 a.m. to 11 p.m., tel. 877-5650; 11 p.m. to 7 a.m. tel. 877-6550. Canadian Pacific, 7 a.m. to midnight, tel. 866-1601. Timetables are available at stations, hotels, and travel agencies.

The Fastest Train in the World

As a major supplier of equipment for transportation by rail, it's not surprising that Montréal should build the world's fastest train. For the newest, quickest, and most thrilling way of surface travelling, climb aboard the Canadian National's turbotrain. This sleek silver bullet whisks you from the Union Station in Toronto to Montréal's Central Station (a distance of 365 miles) in a little over three hours.

This is the third turbotrain in existence. The first, built in 1951, operates between Milan and Rome in Italy at a speed of 90 m.p.h. The second, built thirteen years later, travels between Osaka and Tokyo in Japan at 131 m.p.h.

The last, just completed this year, travels at the fantastic rate of 161 m.p.h. between Canada's two largest cities. Its comfortable interior resembles a plush airplane, with air-conditioning and thick carpets. An innovation in the suspension system minimizes the amount of swaying and allows the train to take the curves 30% faster than usual. It's as exciting as an amusement ride!

BY AIR

Montréal is the aviation capital of the world. It is the headquarters of the International Air Transport Association (IATA) and the International Civil Aviation Organization (ICAO). These are worldwide organizations that lay down the policies governing the principles and techniques of international air transport at governmental level.

Through the glittering, glass Dorval Airport, three million passengers pass annually as they move to and from its transatlantic flights alone. Located fourteen miles west of Montréal, the airport employs 6,500 people in a sprawling complex of buildings. It's like a small, self-sufficient city with numerous shops, bars, restaurants, nurseries, beauty salons, etc. The $26,000,000 aircraft servicing base is the largest and most modern in the world. Each of the airlines listed below lands at Dorval Airport. Together they link Montréal to every corner of the globe. Aeronaves De Mexico, S.A., Air Canada, Air France, Alitalia Airlines, British Overseas Airways (B.O.A.C.), Canadian Pacific Airlines, Eastern Air Lines Inc., Irish International Airlines, KLM Royal Dutch Airlines, Lufthansa German Airlines, Nordair Ltd., Northeast Airlines Inc., Quebecair Inc., Sabena Belgian World Airlines, Scandinavian Airlines System Inc., Swissair, Transair Ltd.

MONTREAL AIRPORT: Located at Dorval, 13 miles from the centre of Montréal, 24-hour service year 'round, tel. 636-3191.

INTERNATIONAL CIVIL AVIATION ORGANIZATION: 1080 University St. tel. 866-2551. Open Mon. to Fri., 9 a.m. to 5:30 p.m.

INTERNATIONAL AIR TRANSPORT ASSOCIATION: 1060 University St., Room 800, tel. 866-1011. Open Mon. to Fri., 9 a.m. to 5:30 p.m.

As the nerve centre of the Canadian Railway System, the aviation capital of the world, and the largest freshwater port in existence, Montréal makes it very easy for visitors to arrive and depart from her island home.

ROADS IN QUEBEC

Prior to 1958 the highways of the Province of Québec were notorious for being poorly marked, narrow, and peppered with pot-holes. Since then the provincial government has invested over a billion dollars in a vast autoroute network going over, under, around, and through Montréal. Although the number of roads linking Montréal Island to the rest of the province has doubled in the last five years, so has the number of motor vehicles. Unfortunately, traffic congestion must be accepted as a character defect of any large, modern city. In her inimitable way Montréal provides a colourful solution to the problem. The basic rule of the game is "follow your impulses". This goes for both pedestrians and drivers. In downtown Montréal the pedestrian ignores crosswalks, lights, and even policemen, darting across the street whenever there's a break in the traffic. The driver pays no attention to the nimble figures sprinting past his windshield, except during rush hour when a converging mob forces him to a stop at every corner. One point to remember — the taxi driver is the undisputed king of the road, so don't tangle with him! We urge all visitors uninitiated to the traffic game to rely on the public transportation system for getting about the city.

Heed a warning. Last year Québec accounted for 1,234 of Canada's 3,734 highway fatalities. Since the capricious driving habits of Québeçois are mostly to blame, we hope you practise great caution while driving in the province.

Gasoline

U.S. motorists are reminded that the Imperial gallon measure sold in Canada is one-fifth larger than the United States gallon. So in Canada, fewer gallons are needed to fill fuel tanks.

How to Get to Montréal via New York State

Since 90% of the visitors driving to Montréal from the United States come through New York State, we have outlined the quickest route. Take the New York Turnpike and the Northway Interstate #87 to the Canadian border at Rouses Point. Here you switch to Highway #9, which is an hour's drive from Montréal.

From #9 you have access to three bridges, depending on where you are going on the

Roads into Montréal.

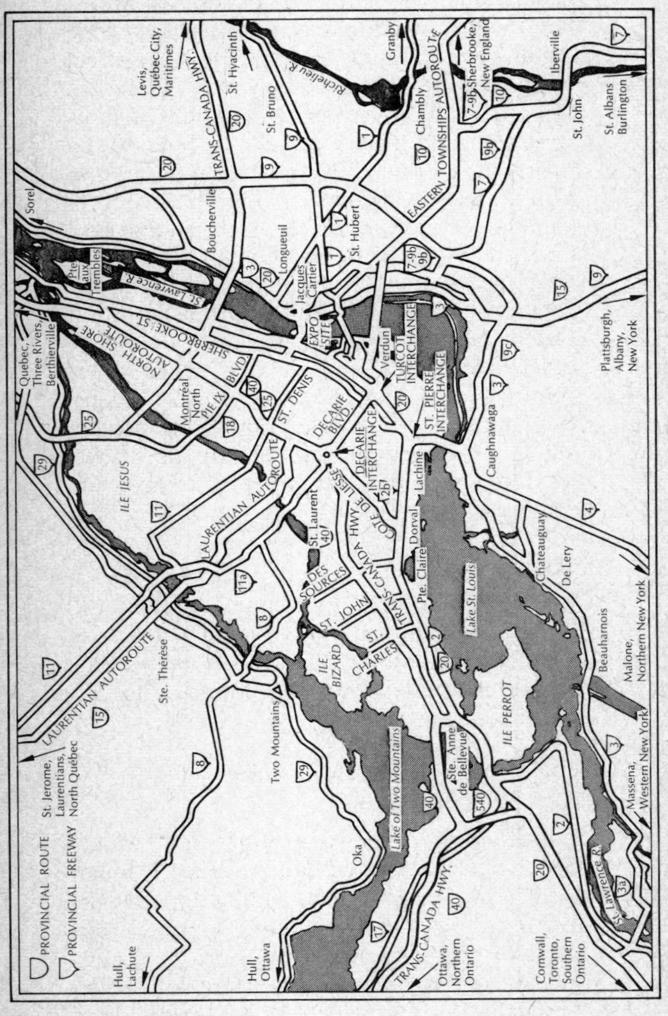

Island of Montréal. For the motels in the southwest sector of the city swing left on to Highway #9 C and cross the Mercier Bridge. For central Montréal swing right onto #9 B and cross the Champlain Bridge (toll 25¢). Then take Atwater Street, turning east on Dorchester Blvd. Further east the Victoria Bridge joins the Bonaventure Expressway, which leads both to Central Montréal and to Victoria Auto Park at the main entrance of the Expo '67 site. For the east end of greater Montréal, take the Jacques Cartier Bridge over the Expo site and head west along Dorchester Blvd. The turnoff to another Expo parking lot, the Jacques Cartier Auto-park, is located just before the bridge.

GETTING AROUND IN MONTREAL

The System of Streets

For the newcomer it might be helpful to know that streets in Montréal are for the most part laid at right angles. The east-west streets run more or less parallel to the St. Lawrence River, while those going south-north are at right angles to the river line.

Montréal's street-numbering system is simple. Numbers start from the river line for streets going north, and St. Lawrence Blvd. divides the east and west numbers on streets running in this direction. Furthermore, parallel streets bear the same numbers between intersections. For example, if you want to go to 1450 St. Denis Street and you are at 1450 Peel St. between St. Catherine and Sherbrooke Street, you will know immediately that the place you are looking for on St. Denis St. it also located between St. Catherine and Sherbrooke Streets. You can always tell how far you are to any given address from the St. Lawrence Blvd. intersection or the river line by the street numbers. The larger the numbers, the farther you are from either one of these two lines of demarcation.

Public Transit

Public transportation on the island of Montréal is provided by 2,000 buses and a 15½-mile Métro. The Montréal Transportation Company operates the biggest transit system in Canada. At this writing, adult fares on all buses, trolleys, and the Métro are 30¢ cash or 4 tickets for $1.00. The price is the same no matter how far you travel. Children under five are carried without charge. They pay half-fare between the ages of 5 and 13. The St. Denis St. lines operate 24 hours per day. Street signs identify the business-district lines that do not operate after 7 p.m.

If you want to get to a specific location but do not know which bus or buses to take, telephone M.T.C. at 877-6260. The operator will provide you with detailed instructions as to what bus to catch and where to catch it.

You board at the front entrance of a bus and drop your fare into a coin machine, or else ask the bus driver for the correct change. Since it's a one-man-operated vehicle, he also gives out the transfers which enable passengers to change buses without paying another fare. Above the front windows of the bus an indicator shows the number and the name of the street that the bus travels on for most of its route.

Taxis

There are more than 4,000 taxis in Montréal. It is always easy to find one, as they are located on stands at the corners of the main streets throughout the city, near the

Montréal Métro.

railway stations, hotels, theatres, restaurants, and stores.

The initial charge including the first sixth of a mile or fraction thereof is currently 35¢. For each additional sixth of a mile or fraction thereof, the charge is 5¢. Waiting time is paid for at the rate of 5¢ per minute or $3.00 per hour. After previous arrangement with the passenger, the driver may suspend the use of the taximeter for trips beyond the limits of the City of Montréal. In such cases, the tariff for automobiles for hire will apply; for each quarter of an hour or part of a quarter of an hour, the trip costs $2.00.

Driving Around Town

Maximum speed allowed for automobiles is thirty miles per hour and must be reduced to twenty miles at intersections. No right or left turns are permitted on red lights. In some cases, green arrows under the red lights allow drivers to proceed ahead or to make right or left turns. Left turns are generally prohibited along main two-way streets. Moreover, the number of one-way streets is growing everywhere in the urban and suburban areas, so watch carefully for green arrows and other traffic signals.

Street Parking

Street parking regulations are clearly outlined on white signs throughout the city. As a general rule, parking is strictly prohibited on main streets during rush hours; signs with red letters forbid parking, either at any time or at specific hours, while those with green letters indicate limited parking time. Visitors will always find places to park their cars, as there are numerous off-street parking garages and lots throughout the city.

Montréal police are lenient with foreign visitors in case of minor traffic rule violations. Visitors are expected, however, to conform with driving and parking regulations just as are the residents. In the event of an accident, even a minor one, stop and furnish any person involved or the police with information concerning identity, driver's licence, car registration, and insurance. If the accident is serious, call the police immediately and inform them of persons injured if there are any. Hospitals and ambulances are called by police.

AUTOROUTE MARKERS

Trans-Canada highway

Provincial route

Provincial autoroute

Tourist facilities

Gas

Restaurant

Camping

Provincial rest area

Mechanics

Picnic

Trailer

QUEBEC ROAD SIGNS

No parking

Obligatory stop

Do not enter

No U turn

No passing

No automobiles

No rubbish

No bicycles

No pedestrian

School crosswalk

Pedestrian crosswalk

Playground crosswalk

Slippery when wet

Falling Rock

Steep hill

School (advance sign)

Traffic circle

First aid post

End of route marker

CUL-DE-SAC

Blind alley

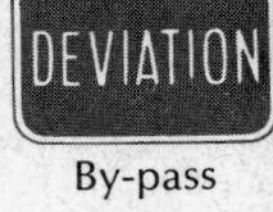

By-pass

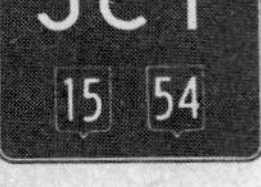

Junction

Hospital

Parking

UNIVERSITIES

These rapidly expanding institutions reflect Montréal's many-faceted personality — the French-language, yellow brick Université de Montréal perched atop Mount Royal; the English-speaking, ivy-covered McGill sprawled in a verdant park at the foot of the Mountain; the multicultured Sir George Williams, "the college with the sidewalk campus" in the heart of the downtown district.

Université de Montréal

High on the steep northern side of Mount Royal, this university complex is hidden from the downtown view except for its 250-foot tower. The location is a lucky one, not because of the spectacular view but because it's the only Montréal university with space for expansion. And how it expands! A total of 13,000 students are enrolled in day, evening, and summer courses, making it the largest French university outside France. With students from more than 60 foreign countries it is as cosmopolitan as Montréal itself.

Founded in 1876 as a branch of Québec City's Université Laval, the U of M became autonomous in 1919, with faculties of theology, law, medicine, dentistry, and pharmacy. Some years later the faculties of arts and sciences were added. A few years ago the Institute of Microbiology won world fame when it produced the Salk polio vaccine. Keeping astride the atomic era, the Université de Montréal is building the largest campus nuclear physics laboratory in Canada, with an atomic reactor second in size to that of Chalk River.

McGill University

Montréal's oldest university rests on the

southern slopes of Mount Royal where the mountain meets the city. The main entrance, framed by the imposing Roddick Gates, opens onto Sherbrooke Street directly west of University Street. Walking up the broad elm-lined avenue of the campus, one finds it difficult to believe that the site of this great university was once the uncultivated country estate of its founder, James McGill (see chapter on *le Vieux Montréal)*. The campus has long since burst its original allotment, spreading west whenever suitable land or buildings could be bought. Now the student enrollment is over 12,000, with about 20% from foreign countries.

McGill answers the challenge of the modern world with such contemporary institutes as the highly respected Institute of Air Space and the Montreal Neurological Institute. Medicine, the oldest faculty, gained world recognition with such great teachers and scientists as Dr. Wilder Penfield and Sir William Osler. The university has won an international reputation from its students and distinguished teachers who have emigrated to all parts of the world.

Sir George Williams University

This steel and glass college without a campus recently added a sleek, escalator-equipped, 12-storey, $26 million building. Over 12,000 students from all walks of life and from ages of 17 to 72 crowd its lecture halls. This figure does not include its night school, its business college, or its school of art and retailing. Sir George's fantastic growth cannot be fully appreciated until you consider that its first B.A. was awarded only in 1936, and that it became a university only in 1959.

Named after Sir George Williams, who

founded the first Y.M.C.A. in London, England, the university developed from a program of evening education and has as its aim the development of individuals. With such an altruistic background it follows that it was a pioneer in the field of student guidance. Sir George can also be justly proud of its fine collection of 200 paintings and sculptures, visible proof of its interest in the artistic and cultural development of its students.

USEFUL FACTS, TIPS, AND ADDRESSES

BANKS: There are several hundred bank branches in Montréal. All are open from 10 a.m. to 3 p.m. Monday to Friday. In addition the three downtown branches of the Montreal City and District Savings Bank are open between 7 and 8 p.m. on these days. They are at 777, 1220, and 1472 St. Catherine St. W.

TIPPING: Tips or service charges are never included in bills. As a general rule an average tip of 12-15% of the bill is expected by taxi drivers and restaurant and nightclub waiters and waitresses. A tip of 25¢ is expected by barbers, hairdressers, cloak-room attendants, bellboys, and porters. Tip hotel doormen if they call a taxi or perform a personal service. Theatre ushers are rarely tipped.

TELEGRAMS AND CABLES: Montréal has two main telegraph systems – Canadian National Telegraphs and Canadian Pacific Telegraphs; both also operate quick messenger services. CANADIAN NATIONAL TELEGRAPHS, City main office, 600 Windsor St., tel. 877-5430. To send a telegram or cable, tel. 866-8411. Messenger service, tel. 877-4203. CANADIAN PACIFIC TELEGRAPHS, city main office, Windsor Station, tel. 866-4531. To send a telegram or cable, tel. 861-4211. Messenger service, tel. 861-1524.

Sports

Montréal is one of the most active sports centres in Canada. No matter at what time of the year you happen to visit the city, there is always a rich and varied program of sporting entertainment awaiting. Hockey in winter, soccer and horse racing in summer, football in the fall are among the many attractions for crowds of enthusiastic spectators. There are also skiing, curling, tennis, golf, yachting, swimming, and other equally enjoyable sports.

The "Sports" section of the quarterly *Calendar of Events* published by the Municipal Tourist Bureau will give you more details than space allows us here.

Weather and Clothing

Depending on the seasons, visitors find in Montréal climates that please nearly all tastes. Summer is warm and sunny, with temperature hovering around 70 degrees Fahrenheit. The spring season is rather mild, while fall is generally cool, and clear skies alternate with snow. During spring, summer, and fall, visitors to Montréal may clothe themselves much as they would if they were visiting any major city in the North Temperate Zone. Heavy clothing and overshoes are needed in winter.

NOTE: Eastern Daylight Saving Time is in use in Montréal from the last Sunday in April to the last Sunday in October.

Holidays

In addition to Sundays, there are fifteen public statutory holidays during the calendar year in Montréal. Their observance, however, is not uniform. Those fully observed are New Year's Day, Good Friday, Sovereign's Birthday (first Monday preceding May 25),

Dominion Day (July 1), Labour Day (first Monday in September), Thanksgiving Day (second Monday in October), and Christmas Day. Those observed in part are the Epiphany (January 6), Ash Wednesday, Eastern Monday, Ascension Day, St. John the Baptist's Day (June 24), All Saints' Day (November 1) Remembrance Day (November 11), and Immaculate Conception Day (December 8).

A LISTING OF PERSONAL SERVICES

Baby-Sitting

Check with your hotel or motel to see if a baby-sitting service is provided, or call: Baby Sitters Service Bureau, 1215 Greene Ave., Westmount, 932-2191; Baby Sitting Service, 2165 Crescent, 849-4503.

Dry Cleaning

Town & Country Cleaners Ltd., Pick up and delivery Call 334-6340.

Branches: Windsor Station, 861-7501
Place Ville Marie, 861-6530
Place Victoria, 861-5049

Formal Wear

Classy Formal Wear Inc. 1227 Phillips Square, 861-3625

McLaughlin & Harrison Reg'd., 2005 Drummond St. 288-3544

Handbag and Luggage Repair

Handbag Repair Co. 1439 Mansfield, 842-3846

Invisible Mending

French Art Weaving Reg'd. 900 Burnside Ave. 288-0610

Magazines for Tourists

There are two free tourist magazines available in most hotels and tourist outlets:

Current Events, a weekly magazine listing local events being held each week in Montréal. It provides an up to date listing of films, theatre, exhibitions and night clubs in Montréal.

The Arrow, a summer guide to Montréal and the Province of Québec. It serves as a directory of useful information for visitors.

Montréal Daily Newspapers

English – *Gazette,* morning paper
Montreal Star, first edition appears at noon.

French – *Le Devoir,* morning paper
La Presse, evening paper

American and Foreign Newspapers

Leading daily papers from cities around the world can be purchased at Metropolitan News Agency, 1248 Peel St. at St. Catherine, 866-9227.

Medical Service and Hospitals

Most of the hotels and motels either have a physician on call, or can arrange for a local physician to come to your room.

Montréal General Hospital, 1650 Cedar Avenue, 937-6011

Royal Victoria Hospital, 687 Pine Avenue, 842-1251

Montréal Children's Hospital, 2300 Tupper Street, 937-8511

Travellers' Aid Society, with booths at both train stations and the airport. Phone 866-2677.

Shoe Repair

Happy Shoe Repair Reg'd. (Pick up Service) 1268 Guy Street, 932-2439.

London Mastercraft Shoe Repair Ltd., 630 St. Catherine St. W., 866-0981.

Travel Agency

McGregor Travel Co., 3 Place Ville Marie, 866-1161.

Telephone

For direct-dialing long distance calls dial "1", the area code, and the number. For person to person calls dial "0" for operator. Information dial "411".

Translators and Interpreters

Berlitz Translations, offices at Place Ville Marie & Place Victoria, 288-3111.

Veterinarians

Animal Hospital of Montreal, 349 Victoria Ave., Westmount (Director, Dr. Paul Villeneuve), 489-8217.

Jasmin and Jasmin, 740 Guy St. (Dr. J. G. Jasmin), 932-3149.

10.

THE INTERNATIONAL WORLD EXHIBITION

Expo '67 is the popular name for the Universal and International Exhibition and will highlight Canada's Centennial celebrations. Voluminous statistics, descriptive superlatives, huge expenditures of work hours and cold hard cash all help to support the statement of the Director of Operations, "It's going to be the greatest exhibition that ever was." Television, newspaper, and radio reporters casually toss about incredible facts.

Would you believe $20,000,000 for entertainment?

Would you believe 55,000 miles of telephone wires and 6,000 telephones?

Would you believe $2,500,000 for an amusement ride that whisks you through a simulated space flight, a volcano bubbling lava and steam, and finally, a bug-eyed metal monster that swallows your cabin in one gulp?

Would you believe that the specially schooled dolphins for Alcan's Aquarium are completely bilingual; that is, they respond to commands in English and French – much to the embarrassment of monolingual Montrealers?

Would you believe a mysterious, cube-shaped labyrinth with a special chest-high railing to prevent those who become disoriented from attempting suicide?

Would you believe a 2½-ounce friendly, informative teleguide that sits on your car, but shrieks if you attempt to carry it out of an exit?

A fantastic fair, *n'est-ce pas?*

WHEN IS A WORLD'S FAIR MORE THAN A WORLD'S FAIR??

When it's a Universal and International Exhibition of the first category, authorized and governed by the rules of the B. I. E.; in short, Expo '67. This is the first time a first category exhibition has been held in North America. According to the B. I. E., Expo '67 must cover the fullest range of activity known to contemporary man. It must stress education and entertainment rather than the commercial approach of a booth-type trade fair, such as New York's, which wasn't officially recognized by the B. I. E. The Seattle Fair was a second category Exhibition which covered one phase of human activity – in Seattle's case, Science.

All the countries that accept invitations to take part in a Universal and International Exhibition must build national pavilions. Since this involves so much time, effort, and money, the B. I. E. laid down ground rules that a universal exhibition could be staged only once in the same country every fifteen years, and that its duration must be limited to six months.

The world's response to Expo '67 has been phenomenal. Seventy nations will be participating, the largest number in the history of exhibitions and twice the number of the last first category exhibition, held in Brussels nine years ago.

Man and His World . . .
thereby hangs the tale!

To stimulate the ingenuity and intelligence of the participants, it is customary for World Exhibitions to incorporate a theme. Previously it was used mainly as an identifying slogan, but for Expo it is the mainspring, its *raison d'être*. Why this departure from the traditional approach? The public, generally, is well aware of the progress in all fields of science and accept nonchalantly the tremendous technological developments of this century. However, what fascinates everyone is *how* these discoveries help to shape the world of tomorrow.

With this in mind Expo '67 searched for a theme. They found it in the writings of Antoine de Saint-Exupéry, the French author, poet, and aviator. The title of one of his works, *Terre des Hommes,* became the main theme of the Exhibition. It tells the story of man and his environment, pointing out how man's environment affects him, how he changes and improves his environment to fulfill his aspirations, and how, in turn, he is influenced by his new achievements. It is a challenging theme, one that is attracting other countries to come and exhibit in Canada. So as to present a logical program *Terre des Hommes,* or, in English, Man and His World, has been developed under the following thematic topics:

Man the Explorer
- Man and Life
- Man, his Planet and Space
- Man and the Oceans
- Man and the Polar Regions

Man the Producer
- Man and Resources
- Man and Progress
- Man in Control

Man the Creator
- Fine Arts
- Fine Photography
- Contemporary Sculpture
- Fine Industrial Design

Man in the Community

Man and His Health

Expo is devoting more than twenty acres to theme pavilions, a fantastic project! In addition all participants, whether national or industrial, must relate their individual presentations to some area of the theme concept. In this way the entire exhibition can be seen as a mosaic of interdependent pieces illustrating the premise of Saint-Exupéry: To be a man is to feel that through one's own contribution one helps to build the world."

The Instant Island

Suddenly rising from the water in front of us there looms a large landform covered with irregular and grotesque shapes. It is not an ordinary island placed there by nature, but a super-island built largely by the hand of man to make his environment suit his need. It is not an ordinary fair site, but rather a super-site, the most spectacular happening of Expo '67. It is hard to believe that three years ago the whole of this island consisted of the 135-acre park, St. Hélène, named by the explorer Champlain after his teenage bride, Hélène. For many years a popular retreat on hot summer days, it has remained untouched. Instead, more land has been added upstream and downstream, another island, Ile Notre Dame, has been built adjoining it; MacKay Pier has been extended and renamed Cite du Havre. In less than a year St. Hélène Island has expanded to a 1,000-acre island complex, the largest fair site in the history of world exhibitions.

This island site offers a super view of the mountain-skyscraper-harbour skyline on one side and the busy St. Lawrence Seaway on the other. Dotted with lakes, lagoons, canals, and footbridges, the man-made Notre Dame exudes a leisurely, Venice-like atmosphere. In contrast, the daringly original architecture thrusting its way skyward creates the appearance of a futuristic fantasyland.

HOW MUCH WILL IT COST?

Another characteristic of a B. I. E. World Fair is that there must be no admission fee to any national pavilion. The admission price to the exhibition as a whole entitles you to see the exhibits of all the countries and private participants without further cost. Only food, beverages, and some entertainment will have to be paid for, and Expo has strictly enforced specifications concerning quality and prices.

Here's the price structure in Canadian currency:

An adult passport for the entire season sells for $35, and a child's passport is $17.50.

An adult seven-day passport costs $12, a child's $6.

A one-day adult passport is $2.50, a child's $1.25.

Whether you buy a passport for a day, a week, or a season, it includes your admission to the site and to most exhibits as well as free rides on the Expo Express.

On-site Transportation . . . ride, don't walk!

Although no automobiles are allowed on the site, no one will have to walk more than 400 yards to find transportation. Linking all parts of the ground, Expo's mass transit system, the Expo Express, has 8 trains of 6 cars each – a total capacity of 1,200 people. A train leaves the main gate every

135 seconds and travels 23 miles per hour over 3½ miles of track. Each fully automated train has air-conditioned cars with panoramic windows. Just to reassure the passengers, there are uniformed college students sitting in the control cabins, but all they do is push buttons to close the doors. Ah, the advantages of higher learning!

At Expo's Express stations you can transfer to one of the three "minirail" loops that snake through St. Hélène's Island, Ile Notre Dame, and La Ronde. For 25¢ to 50¢, depending on the length of ride, you can relax in a canopied car and wind over, around and even through pavilions in each sector. This minirail system was used previously in the Swiss National Exhibition in Lausanne.

For a relaxing scenic ride along the maze of Ile Notre Dame canals, hop on one of the Venetian styled *vaporettos* (complete half-hour trip for 50¢). Or, if you wish, there are many smaller exotic vessels from far-flung parts of the world – gondolas, sampans, Mexican flower boats, etc., each carrying four to eight passengers. Serenaded by music and piloted by gondoliers, these small boats provide a particularly romantic night excursion.

The newest concept in transportation is the Hovercraft. It skims at 60 m.p.h. around St. Hélène's Island in a thrilling 15-minute trip (cost $2.50 per person, $1.25 per child). This ultramodern machine, which rides on a cushion of air and holds 38 passengers, is not only able to glide over the water but can also travel over land and hurdle any obstacle up to three feet in height. When we consider the elaborate system of on-site transportation, we are inclined to agree with the Expo official who said, "This will be a softie's fair!"

WHERE TO SLEEP? ASK LOGEXPO

Accommodations are always a prime concern during any world exhibition. To combat this problem Expo set up a central housing bureau called Logexpo. Its duty is to reserve beds for visitors, using every available vacancy – hotels, motels, university residences, private homes, apartment houses, and trailer camps. This includes lodgings not only on the island of Montréal, but also in the surrounding region, and even at resorts in the Laurentian Mountains.

The cost of hotels and motels ranges between $8 and $25 for a single room and $12 and $40 for a double. Apartments offering hotel services are charging from $20 to $30 a suite. Beds in institutional dormitories range from $2 to $5. Rooms in private homes are expected to range from $5 to $14. All rates have been frozen at levels approved by the Québec authorities. The government also set up a bureau to deal with complaints, so that anyone who feels that he's being unfairly treated, either in price or service, can make a complaint and expect almost immediate action. However, please remember that, with over 5,000,000 visitors requiring paid accommodations, it's not always possible to get exactly the kind of lodging you desire. The biggest difficulty is satisfying the visitor who asks for first choice at one of the major downtown hotels, most of which have been solidly booked for the past year.

During the Exhibition's peak in July and August Logexpo expects to book beds for 115,000 to 162,000 visitors per day. The needs and preferences of these people will vary, ranging from luxury suites to tenting sites. But Logexpo is ready for them. With the use of a computer system, it can keep a minute-by-minute record of every room registered with it.

If you have not already done so, we recommend that you make your reservations as soon as possible, either through your local travel agency or write direct to:

Logexpo, Expo 67
Administration and News Building
Cité du Havre
Montréal, Québec.

Having received over 200 letters daily for the past year, Logexpo has become one of the most popular addresses in Montréal. During the six-month period of the fair, information as to lodgings is obtainable from booths at Dorval Airport, at the railway stations, and on the main highways.

FOOD TO PLEASE EVERY PALATE

Twenty-three thousand seats await the hungry at Expo, in everything from snack-bars serving hot dogs to gourmands to around-the-world restaurants serving mouth-watering delicacies to gourmets. There's even a kiddies' restaurant with child-size portions, utensils, and fixtures.

Half of the 60-odd restaurants belong to national pavilions, so food adventurers can choose dishes from 38 different countries – ranging in price from 85¢ Quiche Lorraine to $5 stewed nightingale. Not only do the menus incorporate the best national dishes, but also the décor, the entertainment, and the staff provide an authentic impression of what the country is like.

Besides national restaurants Expo controls 39 restaurants and 67 snack-bars, most of which are operated by private concessionaires. Very close control is kept over size, location, hours, food portions, and prices. Each restaurant must post its menu and prices outside. Generally, the eating establishments are divided into five categories according to the average price:

Snack-bar	$ .65
Inexpensive	$1.00
Moderate	$1.75
Medium	$2.50
High	$3.75
De luxe	$5.00

E-X-P-O SPELLS HOSPITALITY AND SERVICE

Two hundred and forty gorgeous girls acting as Expo hostesses supply information and orientation to visitors. You'll find them in 12 attractive information booths scattered through the site. A telecommunications system gives them the up-to-the-minute news of events. The successful candidates (2,000 girls applied) started in January to take courses in first aid, protocol, history, and of course Expo '67. All the girls are bilingual, and some speak as many as seven languages.

If you want to know something and can't find one of the pretty hostesses, just ask anyone wearing an Expo uniform – even if he's watering flower boxes. Each one of the 3,000 staff members has been briefed on being helpful. Each day their freshly laundered uniforms have printed cards stuffed in the pockets describing the program of the day.

Expovox is the central information bureau which is supposed to come up with the answer to any question dealing with Expo. The key is an automatic call distributor with 40 telephone-answering units. It's a seven-day operation from 9 a.m. to 10 p.m. Expovox will also work on lodgings during the peak months.

TOURING "THE WORLD IN A THOUSAND ACRES"

The most frustrating thing about a visit

to this stupendous exhibition is attempting to cram everything into a few days, or even into a week. There are simply so many things to see and do that one can only try to make the best use of the time available. To understand the underlying spirit and purpose of the fair, one should start with the grand generalizations of the theme pavilions and gradually work down to the amusement rides at La Ronde.

What follows is a sketchy guide and description of the various parts of the Exhibition. We stress that it's meant to be used solely as an orientation. The major printed source of information is the Expo Guide Book, an official 300-page informatory on this greatest fair ever.

Our outline of "what's where" on the site revolves around the five stations of the Expo Express. We figured this as the best plan for an orientation since the Express is free and also provides a gull's eye view of the entire exhibition.

1. Rendezvous '67, at the Main Entrance on Harbour City

"Man the Creator" is the main theme of this part of the site. The ART GALLERY, a permanent building, is exhibiting 200 of the world's greatest masterpieces that have been borrowed from museums and private collectors all around the globe. Over half the paintings represent the last six centuries in Western Art. The $2 million gallery housing these priceless collections is temperature-controlled, air-conditioned, fire-resistant, and watched over by a bevy of security guards and electrical equipment. The Exhibit, of course, has the same general theme as Expo '67, "Man and His World".

Just behind the Art Gallery the 2,000 seat EXPO THEATRE has planned six months of film festivals, light entertainment, and special attractions.

2. Habitat '67, in the middle of Harbour City

NOTE: The Express stops only on its way *from* Rendezvous '67.

As soon as you step off the train your attention will focus on Habitat '67. Other world exhibitions have contributed great architectural accomplishments, such as the Eiffel Tower of Paris and Crystal Palace of London, but none of them were functional. Habitat is the first functional symbol of a World's Fair. Viewed as the world's most *avant-garde* experiment in urban living. it's currently lived in by Expo personnel.

Described as an Arab village, a settlement of Pueblo Indians, and a child's building blocks, Habitat solves the problem of housing in a densely populated district. Actually, as we understand it, the complex is composed of great concrete blocks, completely prefabricated on the spot (this includes the plumbing) and then lifted into position by a crane. Cables are threaded through the boxes so they are actually suspended. In this way no unit overlaps another, and the roof of the one below serves as a garden for the one above. Oh yes, there's also a tree in the middle of each garden for the use of the dog. The whole fantastic project rises 13 levels, with the lowest used for services. The cost of these 2-storey houses is estimated at $100,000 each.

Adjacent to Habitat is the MAN IN THE COMMUNITY pavilion. Since the 1970's will emphasize man's breakthrough in the social sciences rather than the material sciences, this pavilion takes on an added importance. By means of sculptures, films, sound and light, plus a unique kind of teaching machine, the exhibit examines the effect of technology over certain aspects of today's human conditions.

If you've always wondered what LSD is like, don't miss the cube-shaped LABYRINTH. This $4.5 million experiment in controlled environment sums up Expo's Man and His World theme. Mirrors, lighting, mazes, music, and multi-screened films combine to take you on a thirty-five minute unforgettable "trip". The effect is so weird that a chest-high railing has been constructed to stop you from becoming disoriented.

3. Place des Nations, on Ile Ste. Hélène

PLACE DES NATIONS is an outdoor arena that can hold 10,000 spectators and is a focal point of the "Special Day Celebrations", that is, national days set aside for the participating nations at Expo. For a tour of the international and theme pavilions of this area you can either walk or take a minirail.

On the far side of Swan Lake you have your first view of the unique, futuristic structures of four international pavilions, those of Austria, Switzerland, Belgium, and the Netherlands. Walking east past the Scandinavian Pavilion you'll come to the MAN AND LIFE pavilion and MAN AND THE OCEANS.

In the southeast corner of this section of Expo you can't miss the UNITED STATES PAVILION. From there, a short stroll across the Cosmos Walk, over Lemoyne Channel, brings you to Notre Dame Island. This holds the largest concentration of pavilions at Expo. Most of the international pavilions, some of the theme pavilions, and all the Canadian pavilions are located in this area.

The SOVIET PAVILION is directly across Lemoyne Channel from the United States pavilion (use the Cosmos Walk) on one of the biggest sites of Expo. Directly east of the U.S.S.R. pavilion is an area of 7 acres devoted to MAN THE PROVIDER theme. Called a "Sun Acre" it is composed of open-air agricultural exhibitions and loosely connected subject pavilions. All the walls of the various structures are reinforced with earth so that the verdant sweep of planted surface is unbroken.

Heading upstream, you would be wise to hop a minirail, as it is rather a long walk. Taking the route east along the Lemoyne Channel you pass the pavilions of Tunisia, Africa, Venezuela, Czechoslovakia, Israel, Greece, Great Britain, France, and Canada.

4. Express Station, The Pavilion Area of Ile Notre Dame

Take the minirail to the Expo Express station on Ile Notre Dame for a relaxing scenic ride along the St. Lawrence Seaway to the fifth stop at LA RONDE.

La Ronde is the amusement park of Expo '67. Using the Tivoli Gardens of Copenhagen and Disneyland in California for their inspiration, the planners of La Ronde tried to emulate both the sophisticated, relaxed air Tivoli and the "pure fun" feeling of Disneyland. As Canada's only "in depth" amusement park it is to remain as a permanent attraction after Expo '67 is over. This 135 acres of fun includes marina, a lake park, a 40-acre amusement area, a youth pavilion and Children's World. With the exception of the last two it stays open until 2:30 a.m. daily.

La Ronde offers everything from the carousel (antique Belgian run by steam) to strip-teasers (very modern) and an African Safari (complete with ostrich).

FORT EDMONTON represents a typical Western Village with all TV cowboy trimmings, except Lorne Green. Admission is free. At the GARDEN OF STARS things are humming from morning to late night. This triangular-shaped building serves as a children's entertainment area in the daytime, as a teenage dance hall in the early evening, and as a nightclub, housing popular entertainers, during the rest of the evening. Le Village is a French-Canadian corner with cafés, bistros, chansonniers, strippers and restaurants. The RIDE CENTRE includes 26 varieties. The focal point is the GYROTRON. This $2.5 million spectacular ride takes you into the base of a pyramid and seats you in a cabin that whirls you upward 21 storeys in a space flight past planets, stars, shooting meteorites, and floating astronauts. You shoot out of the mouth of the pyramid, hover 100 feet above the ground, and then plunge into a volcano bubbling lava and steam. The ride lasts seven minutes and costs $1.00 per adult and 75¢ per child.

DOLPHIN LAKE is a half-mile-long lake on which are held water shows and *voyageur* canoe races. Every night is climaxed by a lavish water ski and fireworks display staged in front of a spectacular fountain spurting jets of coloured water. The Alcan AQUARIUM has another fantastic show. This time it's dolphins that perform acrobatic feats for 900 spectators. But there are more than just dolphins. It's a complex of several buildings containing 23 aquariums and an air-conditioned penguin pool as well.

This is just a brief run-through of some of the entertainment at the La Ronde. We didn't mention the INTERNATIONAL CARREFOUR, a complex of bars, boutiques, restaurants operated by the foreign countries participating in Expo. The best part of all this is that there are so many free things to do and see that you can have scads of fun without having to purchase a single ticket.

UNSURPASSED IN THE HISTORY OF ENTERTAINMENT

Never has there been such a mammoth program of performing arts! Expo's World Festival is presenting more than 200 attractions with 100,000 participants and 5 million available tickets. It's the greatest repast of entertainment ever presented in one city in a six-month period. The festival begins on the night of April 29 with a gala concert and ends October 29 with two top drama companies, the Stratford Shakespearean Festival and the National Company of Britain, plus the National Ballet of Canada. Between these opening and closing events is squeezed something for everyone, either off-site paid entertainment or on-site free entertainment. To house this fabulous *pot-pourri* of culture, fun, and frolic, Expo has rented Place des Arts in downtown Montréal. This consists of a complex of three theatres —the existing 3,000-seat Salle Wilfrid Pelletier (one of the most acoustically perfect halls in North America) and two other houses, the 1,000-seat Theatre Maisonneuve and the 800-seat Theatre Port Royal. Other sites of performances, the Expo Theatre (2,000 seats) and the Automotive Stadium (25,000 seats), are located just outside the Exhibition's main entrance gate. With the exception of the Garden of Stars, all entertainment is booked in centres outside the Expo grounds, so that visitor's don't have to pay the entrance fee on top of the price of the entertainment.

But don't get the idea it's all for culture! Three million of the five million tickets on the market are for light entertainment – Marlene Dietrich, Pearl Bailey, Bob Hope, Danny Kaye, Petula Clark, Johnny Mathis, and the Supremes, to name a few star performers. The breathtaking spectaculars are expecting sell-out crowds in the Stadium. For example, the celebrated 700-man Gendarmerie Française, which at one time served as Napoleon's Imperial Guard; a summertime show staged by Radio City Music Hall; a 1700-man Canadian military searchlight tattoo; for horse-lovers, the World Horse Spectacular and the Great Western Rodeo. The biggest razzle-dazzle of them all is Man the Daredevil, a collection of death-defying acts by who else but Ringling Brothers and Barnum and Bailey Circus.

From spectaculars, a double shift into world première films. Movie buffs, remember the dates, August 4 to 18! That's the time of the International Film Festival. Comprising more than thirty feature films, it will be attended by renowned producers, directors, stars, and critics. An additional film attraction is the screening of ten films selected from the entries to an international 50-second film competition based on Expo's theme "Man and His World". The winner receives $10,000.

Sport fans must make it a point to attend the outstanding program set up in the Automotive Stadium. Features include an all-Indian lacrosse tournament, an international soccer tournament, and a two-day Europe versus America track-and-field meet (following the Pan American Games in Winnipeg).

Since the Canadian Government regards the sports aspect as such an important part of the Centennial, it has allotted grants of $500,000 to world championships and international competitions. Many of these events are held outside Montréal, but within a day's journey one can watch championships in world fencing, badminton, and lacrosse at Toronto and junior tennis championships, shooting, and track events at Ottawa. The Expo Canadian Open, to be held June 29 to July 2 in Montréal, is expected to draw some of the greatest golfers in the world. No wonder, with a whopping $200,000 in prize money!

Well, that's it, a very cursory outline of some of the things you'll see between April 28 and October 27, when Expo '67 blazes against the Montréal skyline as the biggest, brightest candle on Canada's Centennial birthday cake.

INDEX

Italics indicate names of restaurants and nightclubs.

NOTES

NOTES

NOTES

NOTES

NOTES

NOTES

NOTES

The Iowa Hill Divide
Volume 2

Towns and People of the Iowa Hill Divide

ALSO BY ROBIN YONASH

The Iowa Hill Divide Volume 1:
Schools of the Iowa Hill Divide

History of the Weimar Joint Sanatorium and
the Weimar Cemetery

The Iowa Hill Divide
Volume 2

Towns and People of the Iowa Hill Divide

ROBIN YONASH

Printing History

Mar. 20, 2016	Original publication
Sep. 13, 2016	Various typos corrected Pg. 37: Names added to photo of Independence Hill 1923
Jan. 23, 2017	Pg. 70: Bio of Milford O. "Mo" Parker added

ISBN-10: 1523933925
ISBN-13: 978-1523933921

Library of Congress Control Number: 2016902634
CreateSpace Independent Publishing Platform, North Charleston, SC

DEDICATION

This book is dedicated to the pioneers, both those who have gone before, and those who are soon to take us to the stars.

PHOTO CREDITS

Daniels Collection:	76, 91, 95, 96
Donaldson Collection	39
Henderson Collection:	Cover, 50, 81, 97, 102, 110
John B Hobson:	8
Macy Collection:	7, 9, 12, 21, 22, 42, 61, 61, 62, 62, 62, 62, 99, 106
McClure Collection:	4
Merz/Dorer Collection:	55
Parker Collection:	68
Placer County Museums:	i, 34, 35, 37
Placer County Historical Society:	41
Schwab Collection:	16, 18, 72
Unknown:	112
Wheeler Collection:	114
Wikipedia:	1
Yonash Collection:	15, 19, 21

On the cover: Patrons of Mike Papa's Saloon

Note that some photos are old, not of very good quality, or the scans available were not well done, so the ability to do restoration was limited. These were included anyway because their historic contribution outweighs any imperfections.

(This version, published in September 2016, includes corrections for various typos.)

CONTENTS

Contents, cont.

ILLUSTRATIONS

Illustrations, continued

Preface

People and the settlements they live in make up the human history of a place. This book is about the towns of the Iowa Hill Divide in Placer County, California and the people who lived in them from the Gold Rush era to the present day.

This book has been extensively researched. Wherever possible, primary sources, such as actual records or recollections of people directly involved, have been relied on. When those were not available, reputable secondary sources were used, such as histories or newspaper articles and other publications based on primary sources from the time. In the few cases where opinions or rumors are quoted, they are so identified and where possible are accompanied by reliable source information to either support or refute them.

In addition to a history, this is also somewhat of a memoir. Items that are *surrounded by a border and italicized* indicate my personal recollections.

I hope you enjoy this history of the hardy people who have lived on the Iowa Hill Divide.

Robin Yonash
2016

A note on names: Foresthill used to be spelled Forest Hill and Yankee Jims had an apostrophe. The modern spellings are used in this book. Succor Flat was variously spelled "Sucker Flat"; the former name was used here. Gleeson was also spelled Gleason. Married women's maiden names, where known, are *italicized.*

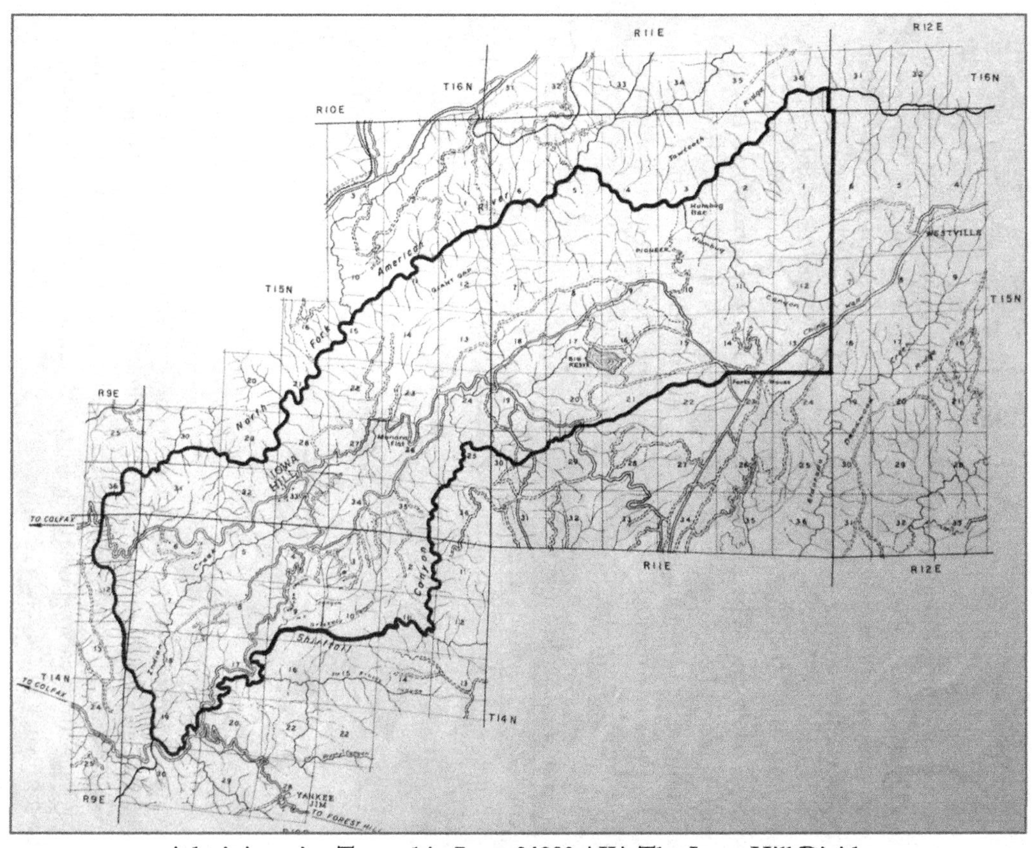

Administrative Township 7 as of 1880 AKA The Iowa Hill Divide

The Iowa Hill Divide—an Overview

Around the time California became the 31st state on September 9, 1850, gold was discovered on the Iowa Hill Divide, the area located between the North Fork of the American River and Shirttail Creek in Placer County, California. The first settlement on the Divide was Elizabethtown, supposedly named for one of the miner's wives.

The Iowa Hill Divide was initially part of Yuba County and transferred to Placer County on April 25, 1851 when that county was formed from parts of Yuba and Sutter. The name "Placer" came from the Spanish word for sand or gravel deposits containing gold. "Placer mining" was the process of washing away the gravel, leaving the heavier gold, and usually refers to surface mining.

Map of California Highlighting Placer County

The Iowa Hill Divide, historically designated as Administrative Township 7,[1] hosted several towns. Only Iowa Hill still exists—all of the other settlements have disappeared.

Iowa Hill has suffered several disastrous fires. The final impactful fire was small—just one building—the "old store," built around 1853. When it burned on July 19, 1968 it took the last operational connection to the gold rush era with it.

But in spite of it all, Iowa Hill survives.

---

[1] Not to be confused with the Township, Range, and Section terms for property, administrative townships were used historically for the Census, elections, etc.

TOWNS
OF THE IOWA HILL DIVIDE

Remains of the Jameson Mine 2015
showing the devastation of hydraulic mining

Iowa Hill/Iowa City

This chapter focuses on how Iowa Hill (also known as Iowa City until 1901) came to be and on the "old" Iowa Hill Store which survived from the gold rush era to the modern day.[2]

Because so many sources disagree or are missing, this chapter is heavily annotated so that the reader can see the reasons for the statements made below. To facilitate following the chronology, **dates are bolded** *so they are easily identified.*

Background—Mine Ownership in Early California

The task of tracing the roots of Iowa Hill is complicated because records from that time are spotty or non-existent due to the legal and political turmoil in the area at the time.[3]

When gold was discovered at Sutter's Mill in Coloma in **January 1848**, the area was still part of Mexico. The United States acquired the California territory when the Mexican-American War ended with the signing of the Treaty of Guadalupe Hidalgo on **February 2, 1848**.

Title to public lands was vested in the United States, to be administered by the General Land Office (GLO)[4] In general, mineral rights and surface

[2] The full history of Iowa Hill will be covered in detail in Volume 3 of this series, *Gold and Fire: A History of the Iowa Hill Divide*, planned for publication in late 2016.

[3] This section is a simplified overview; also its focus is the Iowa Hill Divide. For more detail see the sources used for this section: *Historical Sketch of the Mining Law in California*, John F. Davis, 1902; *Divergent Mineral Rights Regimes*, John Dobra, 2014; and *Seventy-Five Years of Law in California*, Jeremiah F. Sullivan, 1925. All are available online.

[4] The GLO was an independent agency of the United States government responsible for the surveying, platting and sale of public domain lands in the United States. Created in 1812, it was placed under the Department of the Interior when that department was formed in 1849.

rights were owned and transferred separately. Further, a distinction was made between mineral lands and agricultural lands.[5] However, the GLO had no system to administer this in early California. In particular, until 1866 there was no official way to transfer public lands to private ownership.

Prior to California's admission as a state, Congress did not set up any official territorial form of government. The gold miners and other early settlers in California were basically trespassers, with no laws to guide, restrain, or protect them.

Something had to be done, so miners themselves defined rules and customs of ownership for placer (surface) and lode (underground) mines, *governed by local mining districts*.[6] Since an adequate supply of water was crucial to mining, water rights were also included in these rules and customs. From 1848 to 1866 these rules and customs were the common law regulating mines and water on public mineral lands in California.

Even when Congress finally enacted the first legislation regarding mining lands in **1866**, the law stipulated that claims were to be recorded by the local mining districts. Claims were recorded at the County Recorder's Office only if there was no associated mining district.

Unfortunately, many of these mining records are now lost or incomplete. In particular, the records for the Iowa Hill Mining District no longer exist and in any case were not maintained after 1865.[7] All we know is that The Iowa Hill Mining District included "all the quartz, drift and placer mines north to the North Fork of the American River and along Shirttail Canon and Indian Creek in the region about what is known as the Iowa Hill Divide, including Succor Flat, Wisconsin Hill, Independence Hill, Strawberry Flat and Monona Flat camps."[8]

With the passage of the lode mining law by Congress on **July 26, 1866** it became possible for a miner to obtain a "patent" and legally own the mineral rights for a mine. Surface mines were covered by the Placer Law of **July 9, 1870**. The 1866 law was amended on **May 10, 1872** to more appropriately define the extent of lode mines. These laws essentially remain in effect today, defining mine ownership on public lands nearly 150 years later.

However, even when it became possible to patent and own a mine, many mines continued to be worked without patents.

---

[5] Only mineral lands could be patented for mining; agricultural lands could be homesteaded after passage of legislation in 1862, but the Federal Government usually reserved the mineral rights on homestead patents.

[6] At one time California had more than 500 mining districts.

[7] *Historical Sketch of the Mining Law in California*, John F. Davis, 1902

[8] *Report XV of the State Mineralogist*, 1915-1916

The Founding of Iowa Hill 1850-1854

Iowa Hill 1850-1853

Many modern accounts state that gold was first discovered here in 1853, but it actually occurred earlier than that.

In the fall of **1850**[9] the Kennedy brothers discovered placer (surface) gold and quickly organized a town. The brothers were said to be from Iowa,[10] so the new settlement was called Iowa Hill. However, the richness of the claim was not fully realized until 1854.

As early as **1852**[11] the name of that initial mine had changed to Jameson or Jamison (both spellings are used, but Jameson is more common). It was owned by Thomas Jameson[12,13] of the Jameson Company.[14]

Tom Jameson, Owner of the Jameson Mine

---

[9] *History of the Gold Discoveries of the Northern Mines of California's Mother Lode Gold Belt as Told by the Newspapers and Miners 1848-1875*, compiled and written by Lewis J. Swindle, 2000; pages 65 and 163. However, regardless of the title of the book, he does not provide sources for these statements. (This footnote applies to the entire paragraph)

[10] The names of the Kennedy brothers are lost to history; nor could the Iowa connection be verified. The portion of the 1850 Sutter County Census which covered "Auburn and vicinity", the 1850 Yuba County Census, and the Placer County portion of the special 1852 State Census did not list any Kennedys from Iowa (and no brothers from Iowa) but they may simply not have been tabulated.

[11] *California and Oregon Travel Diary of Artist, Illustrator And Future Yosemite National Park Advocate James Mason Hutchings*, 1854-55

[12] Caption on the photo from the Macy Collection.

[13] In his article "Early Day Iowa Hill" published in the *Colfax Record* on August 25, 1951, Waldo Macy says that the father of J. W. Jameson of Dutch Flat made the strike in 1851. This conflicts not only with the caption on the photo from the Macy Collection but also with the biography of James W. Jameson, published in *A Volume of Memoirs and Genealogy of Representative Citizens of Northern California*, 1901 which states "In 1854 he [the father of James W.] became a resident of Iowa Hill, where he followed the barber's trade. He at one time was a mine-owner, but lost money in his mining operations." The Jameson was a high-paying mine so Jameson could not have lost money on it, plus it started before 1854.

[14] The Thomas Jamison [sic] who is listed in Census living in Auburn in 1860 and 1870, and in the 1861 Placer County Directory, appears to be a different person as he was a cabinet maker/undertaker who went on to become the County Coroner (no medical expertise needed). To go from a major mine owner to a cabinet maker seems a stretch. Also, he spelled his name with an "i" and the name of the mine

Probably the Kennedy brothers sold out because when the easy pickings were gone investment capital was needed to pursue underground ("drift") mining (in 1852 hydraulic mining[15] had not yet been developed as a methodology). This capital was provided by the Jameson Company.

The Jameson later switched to the hydraulic process.[16] According to BLM records, the land where the Jameson Mine was located was never patented. When William Weisler bought the property in 1867[17] he paid $15,000 for the Jameson and several other claims compared with one-tenth interest of the Jameson alone going for $13,000 in 1854, as discussed below. Owning multiple adjacent claims provided enough land for hydraulic mining to be used. When this type of mining was banned in 1884, the Jameson would no longer have been profitable and it was probably abandoned.

The 1890 geological map by John B. Hobson, excerpted below, shows the Wisler [sic] claim. Because no property boundaries were given for the claims on the deed, only the approximate location of the Jameson is known.

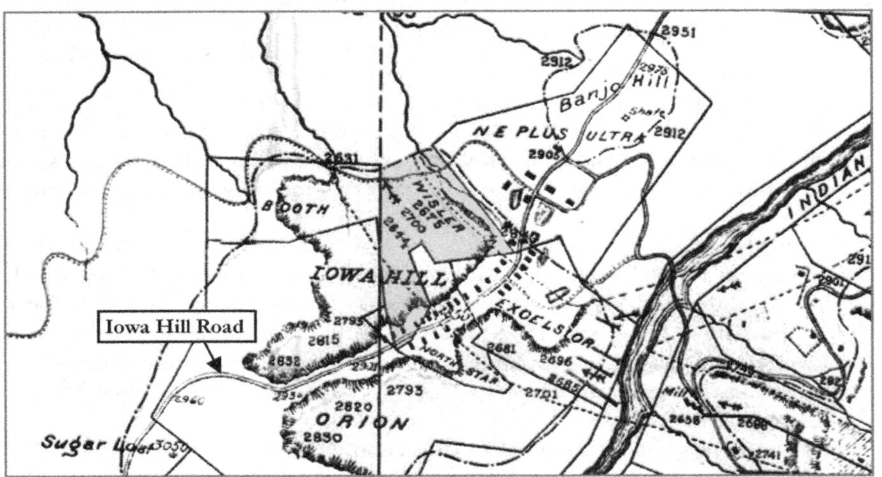

Approximate Location of the Jameson Mine

On **October 23, 1852** the Placer Herald listed Turner's Store in Iowa Hill as one of the two locations in Administrative Township 7 for voting in

---

and its owner is usually spelled with an "e".

[15] Hydraulic mining uses high-pressure jets of water to dislodge rock material or move sediment.

[16] This sequence is evident in that the tops of the old tunnels no longer exist because they have been washed away by subsequent hydraulic mining, as can be seen on the land.

[17] Placer County Recorder's Office deeds Book O, Page 161

the upcoming election. E. P. Turner was a voting inspector. The same issue of the paper included an ad by Charles Rice stating that he had opened a ferry and a general merchandise store at Mineral Bar.

In the **1853** Placer County Assessor Rolls T. C. Jameson stated that he owned a mine with a value of $1,300.[18] This low value is consistent with the statement in Swindle's book[9] that the "richness of the claim was not fully realized until 1854".[9] The same Assessor Rolls document that an H. Parker had a store and goods worth $1,300.

Iowa Hill 1854

The town began growing exponentially in the **spring of 1854**. In late May the population was between 600[19] and 1,000.[20] The town was laid out at this time,[21] consisting of three streets running southwest to northeast, with eleven alleys crossing them as shown on the map below. Main Street (now Iowa Hill Road) went through the center of town. Whim Street was on the north and Milk Street, which led to the Coleman Dairy, was on the south.[22] Eventually Milk and Whim Streets lost most of their existence to hydraulic mining.

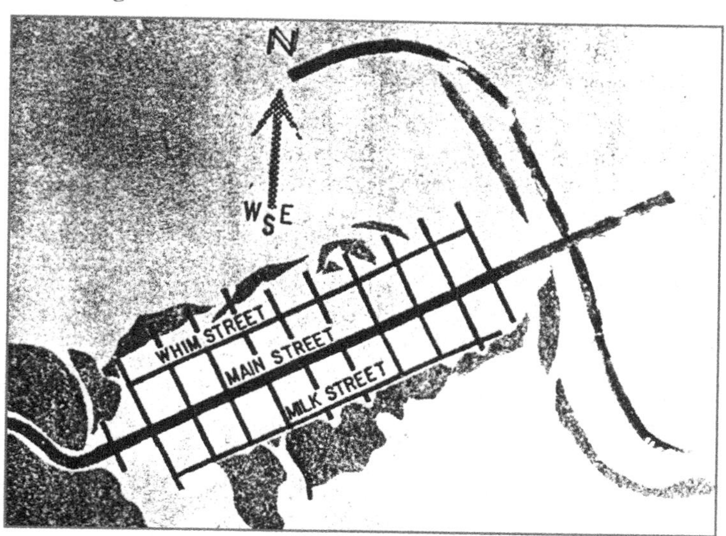

Street Map of Iowa Hill 1854

[18] The 1853 map of California by John B. Trask called the settlement "Iova".
[19] *Placer Herald* newspaper, late May 1854
[20] *Alta California* newspaper, May 1, 1854
[21] *Iowa Hill Weekly Patriot*, January 1, 1859
[22] *The Birth and Decline of Iowa Hill 1849-1899*, Michael Labant Szafranski, Masters Thesis, Sacramento State College, 1962

A nine-mile long canal was built to bring water in from the American River[23] for mining. The Post Office was established on **June 16, 1854** in Colgan's Store.[24] By July over 300 mining tunnels had been started.[25] The Placer County Assessor's Rolls for that year have 63 entries for Iowa Hill and it's probable that many people and businesses weren't included as enforcement was difficult.

The Jameson Mine became a major producer. On **May 21, 1854** the *Daily Alta* reported that a "one-tenth interest in the celebrated Jamison [sic] Company was sold last week for $13,000!" and on **July 1, 1854** the same newspaper said that "The Jamison Company took out of their claims last week $15,000, the result of the labor of ten men for one week—an average of $250 per day to the hand!"[26]

The **August 26, 1854** *Placer Herald* had the following ad:

CREAMER'S HOTEL.
MAIN STREET, IOWA HILL.

This house has been fitted up in a neat and comfortable manner for the accommodation of the public. The rooms are airy and comfortable, and furnished with entirely new bedding. The table will be supplied with the best the market affords.

J. H. CREAMER, Proprietor

Around **September 1854** the first school opened, taught by J. A. Burns.[27] For more details on the Iowa Hill School, see the book *The Iowa Hill Divide Volume 1: Schools of the Iowa Hill Divide.*

Around **October 1854** a Masonic Lodge started and a Sons of Temperance post was established with 94 members.[28]

By **January 1855** Iowa Hill had over 200 houses and 3,000 inhabitants with buildings renting for $25 to $360 per month.[29] While 3,000 people in just 200 houses seems a bit high (possibly this was a typo[30]), Iowa Hill was clearly flourishing.

---

23 *Daily Evening Star* newspaper, May 26, 1854

24 US Government records. The Post Office was called Iowa City until 1901.

25 *Gallipolis Journal* newspaper, July 27, 1854

26 However, the miners, who were employees, were only paid $3 to $5 per day—the huge profits went to the shareholders.

27 On December 2, 1854 the Placer Herald reported that school had been taught in Iowa Hill for three months

28 The Iowa Hill Lodge opened "a few evenings since". *Placer Herald,* November 18, 1854

29 *Daily Statesman* newspaper, January 19, 1855)

30 Since it is impossible to know whether the figure of 3,000 is correct, a value of 1,500 (the average of the 1,000 figure for May 1854 and the 3,000 for January 1855) is used in the population discussions later in the book.

Timeline for Early Iowa Hill

Year	Date	Event
1848	January	Gold discovered at Sutter's Mill in Coloma
1848	Feb. 2	Treaty of Guadalupe Hidalgo
1850	Sep. 9	California became a state; the Iowa Hill Divide was in Yuba County
1850 ~		Kennedy brothers found gold and a settlement named Iowa Hill sprang up
1851	Apr. 25	Placer County established from parts of Yuba & Sutter
1852 ~		The Jameson Company bought the Kennedy Claim
1852 nlt	Oct. 23	Turner's Store in Iowa Hill opened
1852 nlt	Oct. 23	Charles Rice opened a ferry and a general merchandise store at Mineral Bar
1853		Trask map of California showed a community named "Iova"
1854	May	Population between 600 and 1,000
1854	June 16	Iowa City Post Office opened
1854	September	First school opened
1854		Streets were laid out
1854		63 entries for Iowa Hill in the County Assessor's Rolls
1854		Jameson Mine is a major producer
1854 nlt	October	Masonic Lodge plus Sons of Temperance post started
1855	January	Over 200 houses and (possibly) 3,000 inhabitants

nlt = not later than
~ = approximately

The Old Iowa Hill Store 1962

The Iowa Hill Store

NOTE: Because so many sources disagree or are missing, this chapter is heavily annotated so that the reader can see the reasons for the statements made below.

Primary sources for the Iowa Hill Store history in the form of deeds and other recorded documents were diligently researched at the Placer County Clerk's Office and the County Archives. Where these were found, the document numbers are given in the footnotes as either the Deeds Book and Page or the Bills of Sale Book and Page. Post Office and Postmaster information comes from US Government records.

Where primary sources could not be located, some data came from memories of the author, from the anthropomorphized account titled The Old Brick Building *which follows below, or from local lore as annotated.*

To facilitate following the chronology, **dates are bolded** *so they are easily seen.*

History of the Iowa Hill Store

The old Iowa Hill Store, as it was known in its later days, was erected by Joseph Colgan in the early years of Iowa Hill and it survived all of the major fires in the town, plus many smaller ones, only to succumb itself in 1968, 115 years after being built. At its end, the property included the eponymous store, a post office, a bar, and living quarters plus a shed across the street.[31]

The exact date of construction of the store, AKA the "old brick building", is unknown, but was most likely in **1853 or early 1854**.[32] Colgan's store is first mentioned in the Placer County Assessor's Rolls in **1855** with a valuation of $4,000. He paid $24 in State tax and $32 in County tax that year.

Possibly the initial edifice was of canvas and wood, given the construction methods of the time, but it's likely that the brick building was in place before the post office was approved in 1854. In addition to the post office and store, miners could have their gold weighed and purchased, a service which continued for the life of the store.[33]

The building had foot-thick adobe brick walls with iron shutters on the doors and windows in the main structure[31] which was twenty-one feet wide, sixty-two feet long, and eighteen feet high.[34] Later on, living quarters constructed of wood were added to the back with walls were insulated with newspapers.[31]

---

[31] Memories of the author

[32] In the October 1852 special California Census, the occupation of Joseph Colgan, the original owner, was given as "miner" rather than "merchant", but by June 16, 1854 he had been named the first Postmaster of Iowa City [sic].

[33] Per photos below

[34] From the anthropomorphized account titled *The Old Brick Building*, written by Charles Schwab, which follows below

When Joseph Colgan died on April 9, 1861 the store property was split and sold to James Collier on **September 26, 1861**,[35] which included the building, and George Hawkins on **August 5, 1861**, "on which formerly stood the store of Joseph Colgan."[36] Collier paid $2,250 but the price for Hawkins was not stated in the deed.

Both new owners ended up with property with a frontage of 20 to 22 feet along the south side of Main Street (now known as Iowa Hill Road). In 1905 the two properties were merged again as discussed below.

Main St. (now Iowa Hill Rd.)

King's Butcher Shop	**Property sold to George Hawkins**	**Colgan's Store sold to James Collier**	George Haycock --- P. H. Sibley	(later Papa's Stable)
	Joseph Colgan's former Property			

Map of Colgan's Property after Split in 1861 (not to scale)

James F. Brown bought the store **~1862.**[34] Iowa Hill "old timer" Mike Gleeson recalled a Samuel E. Parker owning the store at some point. However, the *Pacific Coast Business Directory for 1876-78*, compiled in 1875, shows Parker and Brown owning separate general merchandise businesses.

In October 1897 another fire hit Iowa Hill, and on **November 6, 1897** James F. Brown sold the store for $100 to Seymour Waterhouse,[37] who was one of the Directors of the Ursa Major Supply Company, formed in November 1897 by Seymour Waterhouse, E. Waterhouse, and Enoch E. Scott as a general mercantile, commercial, freight, and manufacturing business.[38] Ursa Major also got into mining, owning the Big Dipper and the Morning Star Mines, among others. The property description of the store includes many references to "bounded by the lot recently occupied by…" and is very sad to read. But the store survived, now renamed Ursa Major Supply Company.[39]

---

[35] Deeds Book G, Page 409

[36] Possibly a portion of the store, presumably not built of brick, had burned in the February 2, 1857 fire. Hawkins built his own store on this property, made of the same adobe brick, but only thirteen feet high and thirty feet deep (per Schwab).

[37] Deeds Book 67, Page 558

[38] Bio of Enoch E. Scott in *A Volume of Memoirs and Genealogy of Representative Citizens of Northern California*, 1901

[39] Various deeds found in the Placer County Recorder's Office

Mailbox Area of the Old Store ~1958

(Note one of the steel shutters for the doors/windows on the left.)

Carl Adamson and the Gold Scales in the Old Store ~1958

Privies, or outhouses, were the toilets of the day, and in fact the facilities at the store for public use never advanced beyond this. Once a four-year-old cousin of mine was visiting from the city. She was in the privy for some time, and when she finally came back she was wailing, "It won't flush!"

The men's privy was in the back of the shed across the street from the store, but the men preferred to use the nearby cliff, leftover from hydraulic mining, instead. On a New Year's Eve one of the men missed his footing and fell off the cliff where he held on tightly to some blackberry brambles while the other men figured out how to pull him back up. At midnight my step-mother noticed that there were no men in the bar to welcome in the New Year, so she went out in the road and hollered, "You men, drop what you're doing and get in here!"

A month later, on **December 7, 1897**, Waterhouse sold the property to the Ursa Major Supply Company for $10 in gold coin.[40]

The business was purchased on **July 26, 1904** by the Iowa Hill Supply Company (a partnership of M. B. Cross, F. H. Schulze, E. E. Armstrong, and W. H. Russell, each of them owning a one-quarter share).[41] They changed the name of the store to the Iowa Hill Supply Company.[42]

Iowa Hill Supply Company ~1904

(Note the bell sign in the photo above, indicating a telephone. By 1898 Ursa Major had installed a phone line to Iowa Hill, with seven subscribers. The McGeachin Mining Company may have put in a line even earlier.)

[40] Deeds Book 67, Page 599

[41] Book 82, Page 565

[42] Name inferred from information in the deeds when they sold their interests.

M. B. Cross sold a ⅛ interest in the store to V. E. Spencer on **December 17, 1904** for $10.[43,44] Spencer then sold this share to R. L. Neal on **June 17, 1905** for $10.[45] That **same day** Neal bought the ¼ interest owned by W. H. Russell for $10.[46] Neal had already acquired E. E. Armstrong's ¼ interest for $10 on **May 24, 1905**.[47]

On **July 15, 1905**, according to a handwritten note by G. W. Cross, the Iowa Hill Supply Company purchased the store next door, owned by Cross, thus unifying the two pieces of Colgan's original property which had been split in 1861. The buildings were subsequently joined and Cross's former structure eventually became the bar.[34,31]

On Cross's note, the owners of the Iowa Hill Supply Company were listed as being R. L. Neal, Postmaster; R. H. Schulze, Superintendent of Mines; and T. L. [Ted] Schwab, mine owner. This implies that Schwab bought Cross's remaining ⅛ interest, resulting in Neal having ⅝ share, Schulze ¼ share, and Schwab ⅛ share, but no deeds were found.

Ted Schwab bought the rest of the store in **1906**.[34] On **February 2, 1915**, he transferred the title to the Iowa Hill Supply Company to his wife, Anna AKA Myra for $100,[48] but Ted continued to operate the business, and served as Postmaster until August 1, 1922.

Ted tried to sell the store in January 1922. An ad in the *Colfax Record* for **January 6, 1922** read: "Iowa Hill Supply Co. offers its general merchandise business for sale. Large stock of groceries, brick building 20x60 feet, large warehouse, two horses, harness, wagons, telephone line between Iowa Hill and Colfax and Post Office which pays 145 percent on cancellations. Everything included for $2500 cash. T. L. Schwab, Iowa Hill." The attempt to sell the store was unsuccessful, and so Ted closed the business in **1923** and then retired.[34]

In the **early 1930s** Ted's son Stuart re-opened the store,[34] possibly because business had improved due to the "little gold rush" of the Depression years. He changed the name to Schwab's Store.[34]

---

[43] Deeds Book 90, Page 108
[44] Bills of Sale Book 1, Page 238
[45] Bills of Sale Book 1, Page 250
[46] Bills of Sale Book 1, Page 251
[47] Bills of Sale Book 1, Page 247
[48] Bills of Sale Book 3, Page 205

Schwab's Store 1937

Note the gas pump, also seen in the photo of Adamson's Store opposite. It was gravity-feed, so it didn't need any electrical power. The gas was hand pumped until the glass tank at the top of the unit was full, then the gas was dispensed with the hose. The gallon markers on the tank ran in reverse, so as gas level went down they indicated how much had been used. The amount to be paid was then calculated manually.

The property next changed ownership on **December 17, 1940** when Mable E. De Mond (later Blaise, and then Booth) bought it from Anna (Myra) Schwab for $10.[49] Mable acquired the garage across the street from the store, the "three room house built on the back of brick store building", and various other fixtures for $1.00 on **December 31, 1940**.[50] She altered the name to De Mond's Store. Stuart Schwab originally leased the bar to Jack Blaise and then sold it to him in **1949**.[34]

The bar only served beer and wine. I remember when I was kid (and I assume prior to that), from time to time during an evening gathering some of the men would go outside and pass around a bottle of the "hard stuff" to add to their cans of soda. I used to stand in the circle with my own soda can hoping to get an addition, but no one ever indulged me. I figured it was because I wasn't tall enough and I couldn't wait to grow.

Mabel sold the business to Carl Adamson on **September 9, 1949**, but she retained title to the land.[51] This transaction was completed on **October 1, 1949** with the execution of a mortgage financed by Mabel in the amount of $3,296.75 ($33,011.27 in 2015 dollars) at 6% per annum due October 1,

[49] Deeds Book 406, Page 93
[50] Bills of Sale Book 3, Page 434
[51] Deeds Book 555, Page 466

1954.[52] Mable transferred the on-sale beer and wine license (#A 878 D) to Carl on **September 9, 1949** at no charge.[53] Carl changed the name of the business to Adamson's Store. He married Evelyn "Eva" *Rossi* in Reno on June 23, 1950 and together they ran the business. Carl was also the Postmaster.

Adamson's Store ~1955

While it was small, the store carried a full complement of groceries, including flour and sugar in large bags made of printed cotton, as they had been packaged historically. My grandmother made many of my shirts out of the material from the bags.

I rode a horse to school every day, five miles each way. If we knew in advance that a bad storm was coming, I would stay with Carl and Eva until it blew by.

The next proprietors, Gordon "Jake" and Emma Jacobsen, had moved from Modesto to Iowa Hill to be closer to Gordon's sister, Esther *Jacobsen* Yonash, who lived with her husband Frank on nearby Kings Hill.[31]

Gordon and Emma became the new owners on **September 30, 1959**.[54]

---

[52] Deeds Book 559, Page 160

[53] Deeds Book 555, Page 467

[54] Deeds Book 808, Page 176 (This deed is for the "intent to sell"; the document recording the mortgage was not be found, so the price of the sale is unknown.)

The liquor license was also transferred at no charge also on **September 30, 1959**.[55] The business was henceforth referred to as the (old) Iowa Hill Store. A photo of the store at this time is shown at the beginning of this section.

After the death of her husband in June 1963, Emma Jacobsen sold the store to Emmet and Ann Hill in exchange for a mortgage.[56] She gave them the liquor license for $400.[57] Title transferred to the Hills on **November 15, 1963**. Again, these deeds are for the "intent to sell"; the deed for the mortgage was not located, so the amount of the sale is unknown.

On **May 1, 1968** the Hills sold the Iowa Hill Store to Floyd and Delores "Billie" Sibley.[58] While a deed for the sale of the liquor license was not found, presumably it was also transferred.

The store finally succumbed to fire on **July 19, 1968**. The blaze, which started at 11:30 p.m., was attributed to a propane explosion in the kitchen of the living quarters.[59] It took with it the last remaining business in Iowa Hill from the pioneer days. Now the only links to the gold rush roots of Iowa Hill are a rusting remnant of the Wells Fargo vault and some gravestones in the cemetery.

On **September 3, 1968**, Mable Booth, AKA Blaise AKA De Mond, sold the land where the store had been to Charles Schwab for $10.00.[60] The property is still in the ownership of the Schwab family as of 2016. According to a Schwab family member the old steel shutters are buried there.

For a while the old shed across the street[61] was used to house the Iowa Hill Telephone Company, but that building is also gone now.

However, the store lives on in a way. When a new store was built across the street in **1969**, some of the bricks were also used as rubble for fill around it. Then in **1986**, in order to preserve a connection to the past, some of the bricks were used to build the base of the sign for the new school as shown in the photo below.[62]

---

[55] Deeds Book 807, Page 90

[56] Deeds Book 988, Page 216

[57] Deeds Book 985, Page 588

[58] Deeds Book 1195, Page 653 (This deed is for the "intent to sell"; the mortgage deed was not found so the amount of the sale is not known.)

[59] Iowa Hill column in the *Colfax Record* on August 31, 1972

[60] Deeds Book 1212, Page 456

[61] The date when the parcel across the street became part of the Iowa Hill store property is unclear, but it was certainly prior to the 1940 purchase by Mable De Mond since it is mentioned in that deed.

[62] *The Iowa Hill Divide Volume 1: Schools of the Iowa Hill Divide*, Yonash, 2nd Edition, 2016

Shed across Street from the Iowa Hill Store ~1958

Old Iowa Hill Store after Fire 1968

Solar-Powered Schoolhouse Built in 1987 (sign erected in 1986)

Timeline of the Old Iowa Hill Store

In the list below, *italics* indicate information that was not able to be verified in the Placer County land records. A ~ means approximately.

Year	Date	Owner(s)/Event	Store Name (if known)
1853 ~		Joseph Colgan	Colgan's Store
1861	Sep. 26	James Collier	
1862 ~		James F. Brown	
1897	Nov. 6	Seymour Waterhouse	Ursa Major Supply Company
1897	Dec. 7	Ursa Major Supply Co.	Ursa Major Supply Company
1904		M. B. Cross F. H. Schulze E. E. Armstrong W. H. Russell	Iowa Hill Supply Company
1905		R. L. Neal F. H. Schulze *Theodore Schwab, Sr.*	Iowa Hill Supply Company
1906		*Theodore Schwab, Sr.*	Iowa Hill Supply Company
1915	Feb 2	Anna (Myra) Schwab	Iowa Hill Supply Company
1923		business closed when Theodore Schwab retired	
early 1930s		(name changed)	Schwab's Store
1940	Dec. 17	Mabel De Mond* AKA Mabel Blaise AKA Mabel Booth	De Mond's Store
1949	Oct. 1	Carl Adamson	Adamson's Store
1959	Sep. 30	Gordon & Emma Jacobsen	Iowa Hill Store
1963	Nov. 15	Emmet & Ann Hill	Iowa Hill Store
1968	Jun. 1	Floyd and Billie Sibley	Iowa Hill Store
1968	Jul. 19	Store destroyed by fire	
1968	Sep. 3	Charles Schwab bought the land	
1986		Bricks from store used to build sign for new school	

* Mabel De Mond/Blaise/Booth retained title to the land; only the store building (with bar), the contents, and ancillary structures were sold.

The Old Brick Building

NOTE: What follows is a anthropomorphized account of the history of the Iowa Hill Store, as if the old brick building was narrating the tale itself. It was written by Charles Schwab in 1975 and originally published in Iowa Hill: the Town that Refused to Die *by Mary Parker. Used here by permission.*

The story contains some factual errors. Punctuation and spelling have been preserved from the original. The only change to the text, beyond a few footnotes, is that years of the form 'nn have been expanded to include the prefix "18" or "19" as appropriate. (Certain readers may find some of the text offensive. Read at your own risk!)

The author, Charles Schwab (1920–1982), was also known as "Buzz." The Schwab family history is intertwined with that of the store. Please see the family tree for the Schwab Family in the chapter on Founding Families for details on the relationships.

Young whippersnappers don't even know how old I am; they go and talk and try to tell someone who I belonged to. Well, as best as I can remember—I should be about a hundred and twenty-two this year. Yeah, and I have belonged to a lot of people. Colgan built me, and he built me good. I was about twenty-one feet wide and sixty-two feet long and eighteen feet high. I had a good cellar too. Of course he had to use what was at hand, so most of me was made right close by. In fact, I can look down there now and see some part that weren't quite good enough for me. Yep, I remember that damn Kennedy Claim started it all. Christ, they laid out a town and sold lots twenty feet wide for $150.00 cash—can you imagine!

Pretty quick they had almost a hundred and forty buildings on Main Street. The damn fools didn't know there was going to be a fire at 3:00 o'clock in the morning on February 2, 1857. I watched it all. I saw McCall & Co. Brewery go along with Harkin's and Deliano Store. Creamer's Hotel sure went fast too. It looks to me that it must have started in the back of Smith's Bakery. I can still see old P. J. Edwards running around. I guess I would have too it I were the Town banker and a hundred buildings were on fire. Sure hated to see the St. Louis House going, but was glad to see that the newspaper, "The News," was saved.

Then, I remember in March of 1859 in back of me and across the street there was what the ladies of town called a house of ill repute. Well, it was sure burning. Two of the girls came running out all burning. I can't exactly remember but I kind of think it was Jacob Neff and China Tom who grabbed one of them, threw her right in the water trough in the middle of the street, had burned hell out of her but it saved her life. You know Neff came here on a jackass, went blacksmithing and then got tied up with John C. & Ed Coleman. The bought up a lot of claims. They ran a tunnel that went up and hit the Jameson and that being the old Kennedy Claim, before you could say twenty-three skidoo they hit it rich. Took out about $600,000 in the first six months and I've heard whispering outside my walls how much was highgraded. About the only one that could really tell you just about what they did get would have been J. W. Chinn, him being the Wells Fargo, Nevada Express Agent. But as I remember he was pretty close mouthed for being a Virginian. Before I forget, you know that Neff. Well, he left here and damned if he didn't become Lieutenant Governor of California. His partners didn't do as well. They wound up out in Grass Valley and bought into either the Empire or Baltimore Maryland Mine. Old Charles Macy claimed they made a smart move and I guess time will tell.

Then there was that night in 1862. Damned if a fire didn't break out in the Star Bakery. It burned nearly every business in town. Pretty soon people are going to get tired of building up again. The Weekly Patriot, that's the one that took the place of the News as town paper, well, they got burned out along with everyone else. I sure hated to see the theater go. People just couldn't get enough water from Cap Hill's reservoir or any place else. Oh, that's about the time Brown bought me. He tried to buy George Hawkins out next door. Now you must remember him. They called him Walking George because they couldn't pronounce his name. His great-grandson, Ellard Schwab, is out in back of Hawkins' place. Right now he must remember. You know that an awful lot of people that stop here, gawk and take pictures. Well, I heard some dum dum thought that I was one store. Well, 'taint so. It looks like it now, but 'taint so. You see this here George Hawkins had a store in Sacramento, down at 7th & K. Well, he heard about all the gold at Wisconsin Hill and Elizabeth Town [sic]. He just loaded up a couple of jackasses and went drumming. Well, he wound up here, looked around and said, "I'm going to build a store." Well, he built right up against me. He only went thirteen feet high and thirty feet deep, but he made it twenty feet wide and made it out of the same thing I was made of. I always thought we came from the same place, but maybe not, because Hawkin's store is a little different from me. His daughter Josephine, well, she up and married Charlie Schwab. They were living over on Wisconsin Hill when he got blown up trying to catch those Mexicans robbing his sluice boxes in Refuge Canyon. It seems he set some dynamite and triggered it with a wire. Well, one look was all it took. So at thirty five he crossed the divide. If you want to visit, you can see him still on Banjo Hill.[63] Oh, there I go drifting off.

Excuse me, just saw Bud Cannon. You know his father and whole family—F. E., Rance, Sr., Rufe and all the rest. Can see from here that he has a masonic ring on. Wish I could tell him about the party in Carter's Saloon right after Libanus Chapter No. 17 Royal Arch Masons was

---

[63] This is a reference to the cemetery, which is located east of town on Banjo Hill.

chartered. That was on May 8, of 1857. That same year in October the Ionic Lodge organized under charter of the Grand Lodge of California. Then there was the Rosy Crown Lodge of the Independent Order of Good Templars. But, that wasn't until the 1860s.

Say, talk about Ghosts, Fred Coleman, Deed's, John Parker, China Tom, Mike Gleeson, John Papa, (Butcher Bill) Robinson, Elliot West, Garret Booth, Billy Christian, Jim Austin and John Bonham—well, they were sitting out on my front porch last night. Must be the full moon. Nigger George was there strumming that damn banjo of his. Always wondered why they named a canyon after him. I always thought he was crazy living down there. I always thought they should name something after John Stemple because he made the best doughnuts I ever seen. I heard somewhere he went to San Francisco to open a little bakery. I hope he makes it. All the one's around here get burned.

Well, I'm getting tired. Could talk for a long time but there is so much to remember and I'm so old that I'm just going to tell you what I started out to do in the first place. You wanted to know who I belonged to. Well, first off, I guess to every one that ever came in me, to the people who laughed here, cried and died here, I was the first of my kind and the last. Well, as I said I belonged to Colgan, then to Brown. Brown almost lost me in 1892. You remember, that's where John Hobson and Mike Gleeson wanted to patent the whole town. They did too, but Brown had an agreement, too. Seems like he was a mucky muck in business with Dave McGetchin. It seems he had a law suit in Superior Court in Sacramento and one in Auburn too. "So John," he says "here's what I'll do. You give me the right to the store, and the land too, along with my old store, Carder's Saloon, Smith's Stable, and I'll drop the suit. If you ever do,[64] the town will wash away. You'll pay me a fair price for buildings and land if you don't wash. I'll keep it forever." Now, John, what could he do? He wanted the land, that was true. So he said "alright" and set his hand to a document due in witness of L. L. Chamberlain. Now this paper was lost for many years, but turned up in time to someones good cheer. Well, then Brown sold to old Waterhouse, you know, Seymore. Well, now Seymore, he sold me to the Ursa Major Supply Co. In fact, he became president of Ursa Major, them owning the Big Dipper and Morning Star. Yep, he sold me on December 7, 1897. That's when I become known as Ursa Major Supply Co. Then in 1904, I was sold again, this time to M. B. Cross, F. H. Schulze, E. E. Armstrong, and W. H. Russel. Each one of them owned one fourth of me. Well, they renamed me Iowa Hill Supply Co. Then in 1906, Theodore Schwab, you remember Peanut, well, he made some money

[64] There may be some text missing here. Brown is referring to the potential of Hobson hydraulicing the portion of the town covered by his mining claim.

working Refuge,[65] so he bought me. He became Postmaster in 1907 and lived just across the street where that old Vault of Wells Fargo is. In fact, that Vault was in the house until one day Ted, one of Peanut's boys, started a fire in the stove to cook. It seems he had to because his mother was out of town having a baby. Well, Ted started a fire alright. He burned everything in town. That was in September, 1920, or else his brother is two years younger than he should be. Well, Schwab moved up to the house they still have and keep [kept?] the store going even with business bad. Then in '23, he closed me down tight, so he could retire as was his right. I stayed closed until the early 1930s when Stuart, one of the Schwab boys, opened me. He called me the Iowa Hill Store. Then he started to fix up Hawkin's or Cross's old store which was next door. Well, he put on a roof and a floor to keep Jack Dempsey[66] just out the door.

Well, in 1940, Myra Schwab, Stuart's Mother, sold me to Mabel E. DeMond. Stuart leased the bar to Jack Blaise. He[67] was Mabel's husband and in 1949 sold the bar to them. Well, Mabel kept me until 1968 and right after the fire that finally got me, one of the Schwab boys bought me back. If I could have only told him then where to look for that recorded paper from Hobson to Brown, because when he bought me, he owned everything and didn't know it. Hobson never owned me or the ground I was on. Now, for that ghost who wants everything true, all I can say, you must be too new. This is it for now. Maybe I'll awake when I next hear of a fake.

Sincerely,
Old Brick Building
Christ what I've been through

---

[65] Since Refuge Canyon is near Wisconsin Hill, he is probably referring to the mine owned there by the Schwab family.

[66] Jack Dempsey, a donkey, was the duly elected mayor of Iowa Hill. See his bio in the Vignettes of Iowa Hill Residents chapter.

[67] "He" refers to Jack Blaise.

Legends Examined

Several legends and inaccuracies exist about Iowa Hill. Collaboration was actively sought during research for this book, and the results are discussed below. These legends are:

- Iowa Hill was founded in 1854
- Iowa Hill once had 10,000 residents
- Iowa Hill was once the third/fifth/sixth-largest city in California
- Iowa Hill was once considered for the State Capitol
- The economy crashed when hydraulic mining was banned
- The last Iowa Hill fire was in 1922
- Iowa Hill's first telephone service was in 2010

Iowa Hill was founded in 1853 or 1854

Here it depends on how you define "founded." As discussed above, people were living in a place called Iowa Hill possibly as early as 1850 and certainly by 1852. However, in 1854 the town was formally laid out with streets and lots. It was also 1854 when the Post Office was established. Thus it seems reasonable to say that 1854 was the year that the town was really founded.

Iowa Hill once had 10,000 residents

The belief that Iowa Hill once boasted 10,000 residents appears to have come from a tongue-in-cheek document written by Iowa Hill resident Pierson Tuttle in 1969 which said that Iowa Hill had 9,347 residents in 1870. This document was quoted as fact in at least one publication and then that source was quoted in other places without being fact-checked. Over time, the weight of the number of quotes made the information appear accurate.

An article in the November 13, 1893 *Oakland Tribune* newspaper about Iowa Hill said it had 10,000 population in 1856 and further stated that "San Francisco alone could boast of more voters." These statements appear to have been hyperbole.

The special statewide census done in 1852, due to so many new counties having been created, showed a population of less than 11,000 for *all of Placer County* (unfortunately this census did not record where people lived so we don't know what the count was for Iowa Hill, but it was probably small as the town had just been established).

As discussed in the chapter on Population below, in 1855 the estimated population was about 4,300 for the entire Divide.

In 1860, the *entire Iowa Hill Divide* showed 1,586 residents in the Census. Placer County as a whole had 13,270.

The 1870 Census tabulated 754 people for the entire Iowa Hill Divide.

In fact, the population of all of Placer County was 9,582 in 1870.

So unless the population surged from 1,500 in early 1855 to 10,000 and back down to less than 1,500 by 1860, the town of Iowa Hill probably never approached 10,000 residents.

Iowa Hill was once the third/fifth/sixth-largest city in California

This idea could have come from a couple of places. The bio of Charles F. Macy in the 1901 book *A Volume of Memoirs and Genealogy of Representative Citizens of Northern California* which says "Ten years previously [e.g. 1856 as this statement was referring to 1866—indeed, he may have been misled by the *Oakland Tribune* article mentioned in the previous section] this place had been the fifth in population in the state." Another is the article "Iowa Hill: Once California's Third Largest City," published in the April 15, 1951 edition of the *Sacramento Union* for which no source information was provided. And, as mentioned above, an article in the November 13, 1893 *Oakland Tribune* newspaper about Iowa Hill stated that in 1856 "San Francisco alone could boast of more voters."

Again, precision is difficult, because the highest population of Iowa Hill occurred between US Census periods. However, the entire Iowa Hill Divide, let alone Iowa Hill by itself, was unlikely ever the third or even the sixth largest city in California.

Iowa Hill was just being settled in 1852, and as mentioned in the chapter on the founding of Iowa Hill, the estimated population in early 1855 was ~1,500. This was most likely close to the peak population because the glory days of the individual gold miner had passed by 1854 and many miners had moved on.

By the time of the 1860 Census, when the population of the entire Iowa Hill Divide was 1,586 and Placer County reported 13,270, the top six cities in California were: San Francisco with 56,800, Sacramento with 13,800, Marysville with 4,700, Lewiston with 4,500, Los Angeles with 4,400, and Nevada City with 3,700. Since the 1860 Census did not break out the population of Iowa Hill alone, it can't be ranked, but that of the entire Divide was less than sixth-ranking Los Angeles.

This legend does not appear to bear up.

Iowa Hill was once considered for the State Capitol

This is a rather momentous thing to happen. If it had, wouldn't it have been reported in at least one of the publications about Placer County history: *Directory of the County of Placer for the Year 1861*, *History of Placer County (1882)*, or *History of Placer and Nevada Counties (~1924)*? Yet none of these publications makes a mention of this topic, although the failed attempt to split the county in 1855 *is* covered. It would have been reported in various newspapers as well, but not a peep was found.

Perhaps this rumor arose as an embellishment of "Iowa Hill once had 10,000 residents" conflated with "Iowa Hill was once the sixth-largest city in California" and then combined with the fact that Iowa Hill *was* considered for County Seat under the 1855 proposal to split the county.

The economy crashed when hydraulic mining was banned

When hydraulic mining was banned in 1884, many of the mines on the Divide were already underground drift or quartz mines.[68] The actual crash occurred 15-25 years later, between 1899 and 1910, when both the population and mining output dropped by 75% over a decade.

In 1882, mining engineer John B. Hobson stated (italics added): "The great body of the Divide, from the Watts Mine, near Iowa Hill, to Secret House, a distance by the blue gravel channel of about sixteen miles, is almost untouched. This blue gravel channel, about 600 feet in width, with white quartz and other auriferous deposits of much greater width and depth, is known to be rich in gold, but *can only be reached by long bed-rock tunnels, or sinking deep shafts.*"

While annual gold production numbers specific to the Iowa Hill Divide are not available, gold production for Placer County exceeded the 1884 value for the next 16 years, except for 1887 and 1888, and even those years were close to the 1884 value.

Thus the ban of hydraulic mining did not result in an immediate economic crash.

The last major Iowa Hill fire was in 1922

A typo in *The History of Placer and Nevada Counties* erroneously gives the year as 1922, but California Department of Forestry records, as well as newspaper articles,[69] state that it was 1920, specifically September 29th.

---

68 And not all of the hydraulic mines ceased work, in spite of the law. In newspaper articles as late as 1891 some Iowa Hill Divide mines were being cited for illegal operation.

69 The September 30, 1920 issues of the *San Bernardino County Sun* and *Oakland Tribune.*

Iowa Hill's first telephone service was in 2010

Iowa Hill was first connected to a formal, official, public utility for telephone service in 2010, but there were telephones in the area long before that. By 1898 Ursa Major had installed a phone line to Iowa Hill, with seven subscribers. The McGeachin Mining Company may have put in a line even earlier, according to local lore.

In the early 1900s the Department of Forestry and Fire Protection (now known as Cal Fire) put in a ranger line which was credited with preventing the 1920 fire from being worse than it was because resources were able to be called for by phone. This line, which ran between Iowa Hill and Colfax, was sold to residents of the town in 1950 and upgraded to support dial lines a few years later. However, the number of connections was limited and maintenance had to be done by the users.

The history of Iowa Hill's phone service will be discussed in detail in Volume 3 of this series, *Gold and Fire: A History of the Iowa Hill Divide*, planned for publication in late 2016.

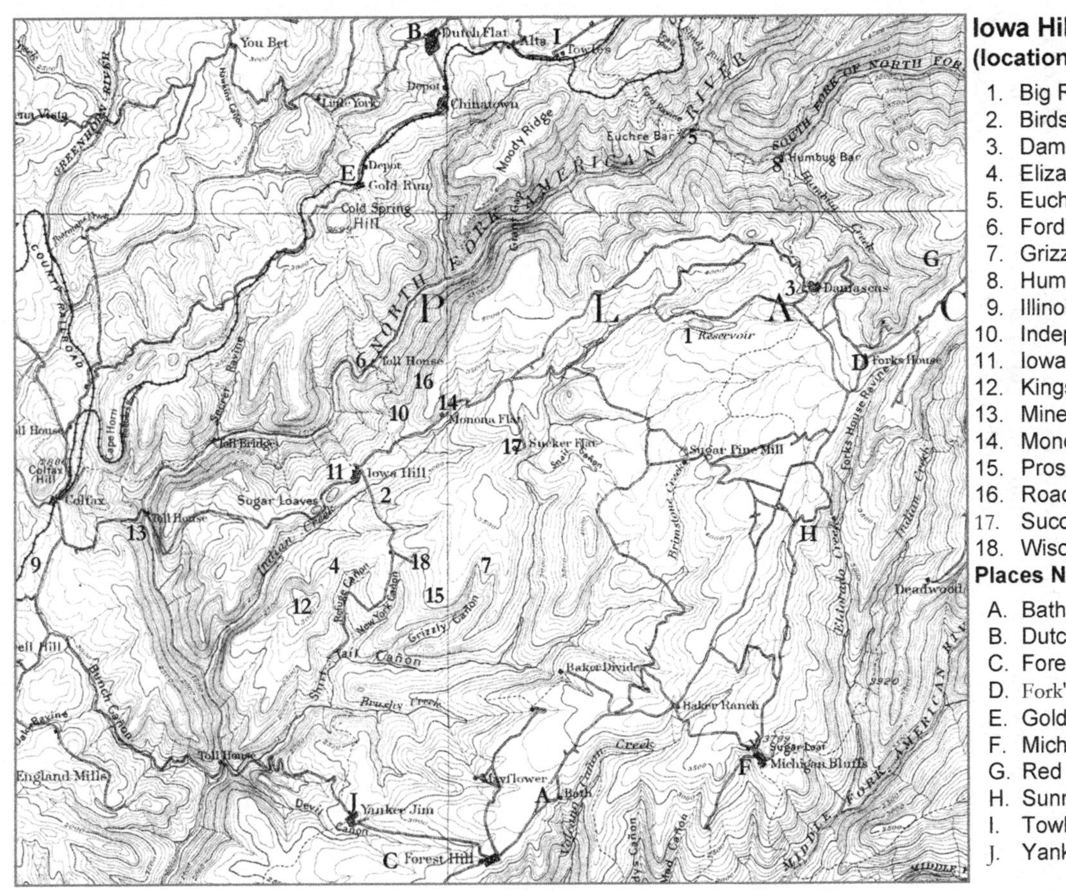

Iowa Hill Divide in Gold Rush Days
(locations are approximate)

1. Big Reservoir
2. Birds Flat
3. Damascus
4. Elizabethtown
5. Euchre Bar
6. Ford's Flat
7. Grizzly Flat
8. Humbug
9. Illinoistown (precursor to Colfax)
10. Independence Hill
11. Iowa Hill
12. Kings Hill
13. Mineral Bar
14. Monona Flat
15. Prospect Hill
16. Roach Hill
17. Succor Flat
18. Wisconsin Hill

Places Nearby

A. Bath
B. Dutch Flat
C. Foresthill
D. Fork's House
E. Gold Run
F. Michigan Bluff
G. Red Point
H. Sunny South
I. Towle
J. Yankee Jims

Other Towns on the Iowa Hill Divide

Settlements are listed alphabetically. Please refer to the map for approximate locations. All of these places have now disappeared with little or no trace left behind.

Bird's Flat

Bird's Flat was located east of Iowa Hill across Indian Creek. Supposedly it was named for a Mr. Bird, who had a store there. An 1855 newspaper article reported it had about 50 houses and a 250 foot high pine tree, five feet in diameter at the base, which had been trimmed of branches and had halyards attached so as to "hoist the stars and stripes to its dizzy heights." The 1880 Census showed a population of 48. In 1882, 10 mines were operating in the vicinity of the town. Today all that remains is the grave of little Amelia Leonard, daughter of John and Nancy Leonard, who died on November 16, 1857 at age two.

Centerville

For a while a settlement called Centerville existed northeast of Iowa Hill on the way to the Blue Wing Mine. (This location is not to be confused with the place of the same name near Michigan Bluff on the Foresthill Divide. In 1896 that Centerville changed its name to Bullion.)

John VanDiver (~1812-1882), a partner in the VanVactor and VanDiver mining claim at Independence Hill and a prominent business man, had a home in Centerville.

Clarksville

Clarksville was near Wisconsin Hill.

Damascus

The town, located about 10 miles east of Iowa Hill, was originally called Strong's Diggings after Dr. D. W. Strong, who discovered gold there ~1852. The name was changed in 1856 when the post office was established. Damascus was the only other town on the Divide, besides Iowa Hill, to have a post office. It operated until January 1908 except for a one-year move to nearby Forks House from May 1860-July 1861 and a closure from 1867 to 1888.

Harold T. Power was the first white child born in Damascus, on February 7, 1857. Among other accomplishments, he was elected to the State Assembly representing District 13 in 1896. See his bio in the Notable Residents chapter for more details on his life.

The settlement grew to include several businesses, a hotel, and a school, but it was primarily a mining operation, having about 45 miners in 1858. The Mountain Gate drift mine[70] and the Damascus claim were the major gold producers in the area. In 1882 the Mountain Gate was yielding an average of $3.00 per yard of gravel. Owned as a cooperative, its 21 shares were selling for $35,000 to $40,000 each.

Damascus Hotel

Some discussions link the Hidden Treasure Mine to Damascus. Although that mine shares the same gold producing channel as Damascus, it is on the Foresthill Divide. Other discussions place Damascus itself on

[70] The Mountain Gate Mine was the result of the 1863 merger of the Golden Gate, first established in 1854, and the Mountain Tunnel Co. It eventually connected to the Hidden Treasure Mine at Sunny South on the Foresthill Divide.

the Foresthill Divide, but it was in Township 7 with the town of Iowa Hill.

Fruit was also grown in Damascus. One newspaper article mentions Bartlett pears weighing one pound six ounces. Collins and Marshall opened a store here in 1855. In 1867 the *Pacific Coast Business Directory* listed a grocery & provisions store, a hotel, a butcher, two physicians, and an attorney as well as a Justice of the Peace. The 1876 Directory showed a butcher, a general merchandise store, and a combination hotel/general merchandise establishment. After the hotel and store were destroyed by fire in 1880, the two-story hotel was rebuilt and named the Union Hotel. In the 1883-4 Directory, the butcher had also become a deputy sheriff. (These entries are probably incomplete because a business had to pay to be listed.)

In addition to the businesses, Damascus had a baseball team, a brass band, and a chapter of the Royal Arch Masons.

Damascus Brass Band 1885
Standing (from the left): Rufus Cannon, Leo Dorer, Wiley Tiner, Jim Donald, Henry (?) Greenbower, Griff Thomas; Seated: Rance Cannon, W. Thomas, Jake Boswell, Billy Brome, Plumb Elliott, A. B. Campbell

In February 1858, 40 residents of Damascus signed a protest to the Legislature against a "Sunday Law"[71] stating: "The undersigned citizens of

[71] Sunday laws prohibit or limit commercial business or the holding of recreational activities on Sundays.

Placer County believing that any legislation having in view the regulation of the conduct of the citizen upon the first day of the week on Sunday, prescribing a different rule for said day, is in effect to legalize a particular religion, and is in violation of the genius of free government; believing also that the practice of true devotion and sound morality is in no manner aided by such sumptuary laws, we earnestly protest against the passage of such laws, and pray the Legislature will concede the privilege of regulating such matters to a healthy public opinion operating upon the police authorities of the several community of this State."

The Damascus School District, established in 1867, included Humbug. Maximum enrollment was 33 in 1881-1882. In 1900, a portion of the district split off to form the Red Point School District. Just four years later attendance at Damascus had declined to only one student. In 1904 the district closed and joined the Red Point District, thus moving Humbug to that district. For more details on the Damascus School District, see the book *The Iowa Hill Divide Volume 1: Schools of the Iowa Hill Divide.*

The population of Damascus probably never exceeded 150. The 1880 Census, the only one to break out the individual towns of the Divide, gave it a population of 71. In 1890, the *Placer Argus* reported that Damascus "is in a depressed condition" and it continued to decline. As mentioned above, the school closed in 1904 when only one student was in attendance, and the post office shut permanently in 1908. In 1920 Damascus had only seven registered voters and eight in 1922. In the early 1900s what little was left of the town was destroyed by a forest fire.[72] On December 10, 1989 the Foresthill Divide Historical Society installed a monument to mark the town.

Elizabethtown

Elizabethtown, established in 1850, may have been the first settlement on the Divide. Lore has it that the town was named for the wife of one of the miners, the first white woman in the camp. Jacob Neff (see bio in the Notable Residents chapter) is listed in the County Assessor's Rolls for 1851 as having property worth $4,000 here. Elizabethtown grew quickly, having several stores, saloons, and hotels, but just as quickly declined when the gold yields dropped. By 1854 it had been eclipsed by Wisconsin Hill and Iowa Hill and it soon disappeared as residents moved on to more lucrative locations.

---

[72] This is according to *History of Placer and Nevada Counties, ...*, W. B. Lardner and M. J. Brock, 1924; unfortunately, the official records of fires is incomplete so no more details could be found.

Euchre Bar

Euchre Bar was a crossing place on the North Fork of the American River that connected the Damascus/Humbug/Red Point/Forks House area with Towle and Alta/Dutch Flat on the north side of the river. Several bridges were built and then replaced due to storm damage. One is shown below. In 1895 a wagon road was constructed to replace the former trail that had only been suitable to pack trains and foot traffic.

Euchre Bar Bridge (date unknown)

Grizzly Flat

Located about 2 miles southeast of Iowa Hill, Grizzly Flat was home to around 12 drift mines, including the Occidental and Jupiter. Gold was first discovered here about 1856. In 1880, 48 people lived here per the Census.

Humbug Canyon

Humbug Canyon was initially called Tennessee (or possibly Mississippi) Canyon. Two tales exist about how it got the name Humbug. One is that the miners got fed up with their initial lack of success so they called it a humbug. Or perhaps the Chinese named it for the numerous ladybugs.

Initially settled ~1850, at one point Humbug had three stores, a boarding house, two saloons, a school, and several homes. It was very isolated. With no road to Humbug on the Iowa Hill Divide side, supplies and mail came in by pack train from Towle, near present-day Dutch Flat, fording the North Fork of the American River at Euchre Bar. Barrow's Store was a polling place for the September 1854 election. Doctor Collins was the Inspector with James Howeth and Dr. Strong as Judges.

The population in 1880 was 50 people. In 1882, 12 quartz mines were operating in the Humbug area, including the Dorer, which had a 10-stamp mill, and the Pioneer. The Dorer family was a mainstay of the region for many years (see their bio in the Founding Families chapter).

Humbug was part of the Damascus School District from its start in 1867 until it closed and joined the Red Point district in 1904. The school was located in Humbug for several years. For more details, see the book *The Iowa Hill Divide Volume 1: Schools of the Iowa Hill Divide.*

By 1912 Humbug had become renowned as a source of ladybugs, which were used to combat the plant lice that threatened the fruit and vegetable crops of California's Central Valley. That year California used 90,000,000 ladybugs to protect its crops, especially melons. One day of harvest in Humbug yielded 400 pounds of the little critters. At 30,000 ladybugs per pound, this was a daily crop of 12,000,000. They had to be carried out by pack train. In 1910 one of the ladybug harvesters got caught in an unusually heavy snowstorm and was stranded for two days without food or shelter. He reached safety by hanging on to the tail of his mule and trusting the animal's sense of direction.[73]

On November 18, 1915 a delayed explosion of a dynamite charge in the Pioneer Mine resulted in the deaths of Peter Colso and Fred Bardsley. When the Pioneer Mine closed in 1918, most of the inhabitants left. In 1936 the area was threatened by the Westville Fire and the remaining residents fled to the river for safety.

---

[73] "Ladybird, Ladybird, Save the Melon Crop," *San Francisco Call*, June 23, 1912

Independence Hill

Independence Hill was located a bit east of Iowa Hill. In 1855 about 200 people were said to reside here, with 50 houses. Five mines were operating by 1882.

Independence Hill 1923
Left to right: Mamie Sparhawk, Ruby Sparhawk Brown, Theresa Sparhawk Donaldson, Ellen Sloan, Ellen Sparhawk Van Voltenburg, Frank "Shorty" Sloane

Kings Hill

Kings Hill, still found on USGS maps even though no town exists, is located about five miles southwest of Iowa Hill and west of Elizabethtown. On November 10, 1851, H. King and Company signed an agreement concerning draining and fluming through Elizabethtown. This agreement was recorded as Kings Diggings. In 1882 G. Robinson owned the King's Hill Hydraulic mine.

Mineral Bar

Mineral Bar was the location of the ferry and general merchandise store established by Charles Rice ~1852 on the road he built between Iowa City and Illinoistown (precursor to Colfax). Later the ferry was replaced with a bridge. In the present day, this is the location of the Mineral Bar Campground in the Auburn State Recreation Area.

Rice's Store at Mineral Bar was a polling place for the September 1854 election. Johnson was the Inspector with Judges Mundy and Stewart.

Mobile

Laid out in 1854 about 1½ miles from Iowa Hill on the other side of Indian Creek, Mobile had a "good" wagon road to Sacramento via Yankee Jims/Foresthill, and thus it was easier for miners in the vicinity of Wisconsin Hill to obtain their supplies there instead of hauling them from Iowa Hill. This was prior to the road being built from Iowa Hill to Wisconsin Hill in 1856, now known as Big Dipper Road.

Monona Flat

Also called Monona Town, the population of 320 in 1860 had declined to just 47 by 1880. Monona Flat had a school district from 1859 to 1863, when it closed and joined the Iowa Hill District. In 1883 a business directory listed John Smiley as having a general merchandise store here.

Monroe City

Monroe City was near Wisconsin Hill.

Pickering Bar

Pickering Bar was a ford on the North Fork of the American River. It provided access between Gold Run and Iowa Hill.

Prospect Hill

Settled in 1854, Prospect Hill was located near Wisconsin Hill, southeast of Iowa Hill. From 1899-1903 it revived the former Wisconsin Hill School District as the Prospect Hill district, then merged back with the Iowa Hill District. The Lebanon Mine, a drift mine, was a major producer.

Red Point

Red Point was located near Humbug Canyon and Damascus.[74] The population may have peaked at 200. The Red Point quartz drift mine became a major producer in the area after 1882. In 1899, 60 men were employed by the mine. The mine closed in 1906. On April 21, 1990 the Foresthill Divide Historical Society installed a plaque on a safe from the former mine to commemorate the town.

In addition to a saloon and grocery store, Red Point had a school district from 1900 to 1921. Maximum enrollment reached 18 in 1900. After the

[74] Some sources put Red Point on the Foresthill Divide rather than the Iowa Hill Divide. However, it was located in Administrative Township 7, with Iowa Hill.

closure of the Damascus School District in April 1904, the Red Point District included the town of Humbug Canyon. For more details on the Red Point School District, please see the book *The Iowa Hill Divide Volume 1: Schools of the Iowa Hill Divide.*

Red Point Mine Stamp Mill 1904

Roach Hill

Located about a mile east of Iowa Hill Roach Hill had 15 active mines in 1882.

Strawberry Flat

Located about three miles east of Iowa Hill, Strawberry Flat was home to four drift mines in 1882, including the mine owned by the Watts family (see their bio in the Founding Families chapter).

Succor/Sucker Flat

Succor/Sucker Flat was located about 1½ miles east of Iowa Hill, and had a population of 21 in the 1880 Census. In 1882 it had five drift mines either producing or in the process of being drilled, in addition to five quartz mines.

Tanyards

Originally established by Joseph Nahor and purchased by John B. Rutherford in 1860, the tanyards was located in the Indian Canyon about 2½ miles east of Iowa Hill. In 1861 the Tanyards processed two thousand hides a year. Spruce, balsam, and oak bark from the surrounding forest supplied some of the raw materials used in the tanning process.

Wisconsin Hill

Wisconsin Hill was situated about two miles from Iowa Hill. It began in 1852 (the first time it appears on the Assessor's Rolls) when gold was discovered on the hill upon which the town was built. Very quickly the influx of miners, including those from surrounding areas who came to shop or play, supported six saloons, five hotels, several restaurants, a theater, clothing stores, grocery stores, etc. The population was estimated at 700 in 1854. Apple's Store was a polling place for the September 1854 election, with Robert Cummings the Inspector and Duff and Scofield for Judges.

Wisconsin Hill had a school district from 1856 to 1889, with a maximum enrollment of 47 in 1881-1882. For more details on the Wisconsin Hill School District, please see the book *The Iowa Hill Divide Volume 1: Schools of the Iowa Hill Divide.* The town also boasted a militia company, an Odd Fellows Lodge, a Masonic Lodge, and a Sons of Temperance group. The Franklin Guards Militia had a complement of 25 men on November 30, 1857.

Wisconsin Hill ~1856

By 1856 the mine output declined, and the population of Wisconsin Hill waned. The 1860 Census put the population at 160. In 1861 the town had two provision and grocery stores, two butcher shops, two boarding-houses, a hotel (the American Hotel, owned by Stephen Lucas & Martha W. Irish), and several saloons. On June 8, 1861 a fire destroyed a dozen buildings at an estimated loss of $30,000. By 1880 the Census listed only 66 inhabitants.

In 1882 there were five hydraulic mines, six drift mines, and nine combination drift/hydraulic mines in the vicinity of Wisconsin Hill, down from 100 in 1854. The Big Dipper and the Gleason were major producers.

Wolverine

Wolverine was located east of Iowa Hill, near Monona Flat.

PEOPLE
OF THE IOWA HILL DIVIDE

Iowa Hill Precinct Registered Voters as of June 3, 1958

On June 3, 1958 the Iowa Hill Precinct had 41 registered voters: 20 Republican, 17 Democrat, and 4 Unknown.

Aasen, Ivor (R)
Adamson, Carl (R)
Adamson, Mrs. Evelyn M. (R)
Belieu, Zoe (U)
Bidstrup, Mrs. Anna (D)
Bidstrup, Peter S. (D)
Davis, Forest S. (D)
Frolic, Otto F. (D)
Haymes, Charles S. (D)
Henderson, Mrs. Jodine W. (R)
Henderson, Melvin O. (D)
Howard, Fred M. (R)
Howard, Mrs. Gladys G. (D)
Howard, William L. (D)
Jacobsen, Mrs. Emma (U)
Jacobsen, Gordon, M. (U)
Kelly, Jack E. (D)
Leonard, Roy J. (R)
Macy, Mrs. Georgia May (R)
Macy, Herbert C. (R)
McAllister, Lawrence F. (R)
McAllister, Mrs. Mabel (R)
Noering, Bern H. (D)
Pettit, Dolph G. (R)
Pettit, Mrs. Gladys V. (R)
Randall, George W. (D)
Randall, Mrs. Minnie (D)
Rose, I. Elmer (R)
Schultz, Frank H. (R)
Schwab, Ellard C. (U)
Simpson, Mrs. Agnes T. (D)
Sparhawk, Mrs. Jessie F. (R)
Stott, Katie F. (D)
Stott, Sherman H. (D)
Thompson, W. E. (R)
Watts, Alvin J. (R)
Weston, Stanley (R)
Yonash, Mrs. Esther Mary (D)
Yonash, Frank (D)
Yonash, Robert F. (R)
Yonash, Virginia Doerr (R)

Population

Population figures for Iowa Hill per se and the Iowa Hill Divide are difficult to ascertain because (1) the Iowa Hill Divide missed the 1850 US Census and the 1852 special state census did not list where people lived, (2) except for the 1880 Census, the towns on the Iowa Hill Divide were lumped into a township and not tabulated separately, and (3) many people were probably overlooked because access was so difficult.

Estimates of the population prior to the 1860 Census come from various sources, primarily newspapers, and some numbers appear exaggerated. Still, a reasonable, though rough, estimate of the population in 1855 is possible.

Elizabethtown is generally recognized as being the first settlement on the Divide, starting in 1850. Iowa Hill had people living there by 1852 as did Wisconsin Hill. While Elizabethtown grew very quickly, by 1854 it was eclipsed by Iowa Hill and Wisconsin Hill and soon disappeared.

Wisconsin Hill also grew quickly, reaching an estimated population of 700 by 1854, but the mine output started to wane by 1856 and the population declined. In 1855 Iowa Hill stood at around 1,500.

Bird's Flat had an estimated 50 houses and 200 residents in 1855, as did Independence Hill. Damascus is said to have peaked at 150. Humbug Canyon was never large due to the extremely mountainous geography. Monona Flat was probably somewhat substantial since it started a school district in 1859 and had 320 residents in 1860.

Putting all of this together, the population of the Divide in 1855, excluding Iowa Hill, was an estimated 2,800. Adding in Iowa Hill gives an estimated total of about 4,300 for the entire Divide.

Beginning in 1860, the Census of Administrative Township 7, which covered the Divide, illustrates the decline in population, as shown in the following table:

Census Population of Administrative Township 7
(Iowa Hill and Environs)
1860-1920 Census

Census	Population
1860	1,586
1870	754
1880*	952
1890†	993
1900	841
1910	187
1920	106

* Birds Flat 48, Damascus 71, Grizzly Flat 48, Humbug 50, Iowa Hill 456, Monona Flat 47, Succor Flat 21, Sunny South 145, and Wisconsin Hill 66 (since Sunny South is actually a part of the Foresthill Divide, it is not discussed in this book)

† While the details of the 1890 Census were destroyed by fire, the Abstract published by the Bureau of the Census survives, so the overall population of Township 7 is known

Initially, the population consisted of primarily lone miners—either single men, or married men who had traveled to the gold fields without their families—hoping to strike it rich quickly. They soon moved on, either to other potential riches or back home, and the population shifted more to families. The precipitous drop in population between 1900 and 1910 paralleled a decline in mining output that occurred during this timeframe.

After 1920, the towns of the Divide were folded into Administrative Township 13 along with Colfax, Dutch Flat, Alta, Weimar, and Applegate, etc. so no specific Census information is available. However, the list of 41 registered voters in the Iowa Hill Precinct for the Primary Election of June 3, 1958 is shown in the chart at the beginning of this chapter.

In the 1950s we used to joke that if you beat the brush hard for a 5-miles radius of Iowa Hill you could rustle up a couple dozen folks on a Saturday night.

One tongue-in-cheek article put the 1969 population at 7 people and 22 dogs.[75]

The population saw a brief surge during the early 1980s due to the combination of an economic downturn, a rise in gold prices along with new dredging technology, and "free" housing provided by abandoned miner's cabins.

An estimate by the Fire Chief puts the 2016 population at around 300, scattered throughout the area of the Divide.

[75] This data came from a spoof written in 1969 by Pierson Tuttle which some editors apparently did not realize was a joke and published the article as fact.

Morning Star Mine Crew ~1895

The Miners

The miners came from around the world in answer to the clarion call of "gold!" The first were nicknamed the "Argonauts," a reference to Jason and the Argonauts and his search for the Golden Fleece.

Travelers had three main routes to the California gold country from the East Coast. None of them were easy. The overland route of 2,000 miles took three to four months. Sailing "around the Horn" was an 18,000 mile trip requiring five to eight months. The quickest method was to sail to Central America, take mules across the Isthmus of Panama, and then sail on to San Francisco. Initially this took three to five months, but eventually the time was reduced to two months or less. Both sea routes left the traveler in San Francisco and required additional overland travel to get to the gold.

Most of the initial miners were men, either single, or lone married men who left their families behind—planning to return to them once they struck it rich, or to bring them along later.

These first gold seekers were often able to simply pick up nuggets on the surface of the land or in streams, or use basic hand mining techniques. This is called placer (or surface) mining. They could work individually or in small groups.

However, the easy pickings soon ran out and mining turned into an industry requiring capital investment. Most miners became company employees instead of working on their own. Initially mines were tunneled, but once hydraulic mining was invented whole hillsides were washed away until it was outlawed in 1884.

Once companies took over the mining effort, the population became more settled and women and children formed a larger portion of the population. The life of miners will be explored in more detail in Volume 3 of this series, *Gold and Fire: A History of the Iowa Hill Divide*, planned for publication in late 2016.

Founding Families

This chapter highlights some of the families who have been associated with the Iowa Hill Divide for multiple generations—most of them from the gold rush to the present day. **Names in bold in the family trees** are the members who were involved with the Divide. Only those people are discussed in detail here. The names of people who are still living are omitted for privacy reasons, unless permission was given to include them.

Information on the families was compiled from various sources: family trees on ancestry.com, historical documents including the Census, vital records, cemetery transcriptions, memorials on the Find a Grave web site, books, newspaper articles, oral histories, interviews, and personal knowledge.

Dorer Family

The Dorer family lived in the Humbug/Damascus/Red Point area. Much appreciation to Richard Merz, a Dorer descendant, for providing information and photos about the Dorer family.

First Generation

Richard Dorer (1828-1904)

Richard Dorer was born in Pfiefenhansenhof, Furtwangen, Baden, Germany on March 1, 1828. He immigrated to Louisville, Kentucky in 1849 at age 21 and moved to California in 1852. Richard was naturalized on March 11, 1861 in Nevada City, California. Although he lived in Placer County, it was probably easier to travel to Nevada City in Nevada County due to the condition of the roads at the time.

In 1853 he and his younger brother Leopold settled in the Humbug Canyon area as miners. In addition to the usual gold, the Dorer Mine on the property where the Dorer Ranch was located also produced copper, lead, and zinc. Richard, with his son Leopold, patented the mine on May 18, 1899; 40 acres in Township 15N Range 11E, patent #57220.

After a courtship by mail, Richard traveled by horseback to New York City and married Augustine Anna *Develey* (1847-1871) on July 20, 1865. The couple returned to Humbug where they had three children: Louise, Leopold, and Anna Isaline.

Born on March 2, 1847 in Eschalene, Switzerland, Anna *Develey*[76] was the daughter of Henri Keysner and Lisette *Develey*. She immigrated with her family to Long Island, New York at age 4 to live with her sister Isaline. Isaline eventually married Michael Harold Power (see his bio in the Notable Residents chapter) in San Francisco and moved to Damascus where she was the first white woman.

Richard's wife Anna died in childbirth (the baby also died) on March 13, 1871 in Humbug at age 24. Richard passed away on January 29, 1904 at age 73. Both were living in Humbug Canyon at the time of their deaths. They were buried in the Iowa Hill Cemetery.

---

[76] According to one of her great-grandsons, for unknown reasons the family called Anna by her mother's maiden name of Develey. In contrast, her sister Isaline used Keysner-Develey and all other siblings used Keysner.

Leopold Dorer & Wilhelmina *Ebbert*
with Richard Dorer 1897

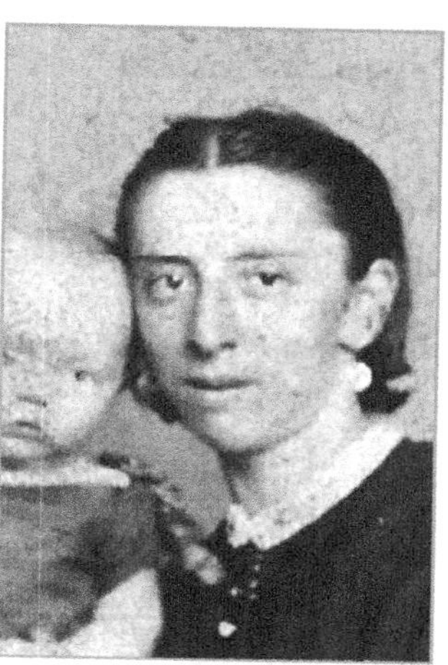

Anna *Develey* Dorer 1860s

Dorer Family 1922
Back: Andrew, Theresa, Lutie, Raymond, Wilhelmina (daughter)
Front : Anna, Richard, Fred, Wilhelmina (mother), Arnold, Blend, Leopold

Second Generation

Louise (1867-1949)

Louise was born in March 1867 in Red Point, which was close to Humbug. In 1892, she married John Mottram (1866-1909) in Sacramento. The couple continued to live in the Humbug area and eventually had five children: Adele, Thomas, Alice Isaline, Louise, and John.

John was the co-owner of the Rawhide Mine on the North Fork of the North Fork [sic] of the American River.

After she was widowed in April 1909, Louise and her family moved across the river to the Dutch Flat/Towle area and later relocated to Sacramento to live with her daughter Adele. Louise passed away on March 10, 1949 in Sacramento.

Leopold "Lee" Richard (1868-1954)

Leopold, also known as Lee, was born in Damascus, near Humbug, on May 17, 1868. He lived most of his life in the Humbug area and was a miner like his father. Lee met his wife Wilhelmina R. *Ebbert* (1879-1952), when she worked at the Damscus Hotel, which was owned by a Mrs. Buckley. They married on September 5, 1897 at her parents' home in Deadwood, Placer County. They had eleven children: Fredolina (who died 5 days after her birth), Wilhelmina, Richard (who died at age 23), Leopold Lute "Lutie," Theresa, Raymond, Andrew, Arnold, Frederick, Anna, and Blend. All of the children were born with the assistance of a local midwife. While they all grew up on the Divide, only Raymond, Andrew, and Theresa remained actively involved there as adults and are discussed below.

Wilhelmina, the daughter of Louis Ebbert and Fredolina *Friedmann*, was born February 18, 1879 in Rose Springs, near Rescue, in El Dorado County. Her father and grandfather came to California by wagon train from Missouri in 1852.

Lee worked as a millwright at the nearby Pioneer Mine (which had a 20-stamp mill), until the mine closed during World War I. After that he was employed as a blacksmith, where he worked six-day weeks for $90 a month.

Lee played the coronet in the Damascus Brass Band in the 1890s. The family has donated his uniform to the Placer County Museums.

On January 18, 1895, the bridge at Euchre Bar collapsed, dropping Leopold, with his pack animal, into the river. Lee survived.

The children, like Lee himself, attended school in the Red Point District and the Damascus District. The school building was located in Humbug for a time. Many years found the schoolteacher boarding with Lee's family. With ten children in need of schooling, plus various cousins, the Dorer clan was able to keep the school open several years all on their own. Around

1922 or 1923 Lee moved his family to Auburn for access to a better education for his family. Dorer Drive in Auburn is named for him.

He remained active as a miner, and in the 1930s he acquired two more mining patents. The Empire Placer Mine was for 20 acres, granted October 12, 1931, #1050615. The other was #1079060 for Empire Placer Mine 2, also for 20 acres, granted on October 11, 1935. These were adjacent to the existing Dorer Mine patent, forming an 80-acre L-shaped parcel in Section 3, Township 15N, Range 11E near the intersection of Humbug Canyon and the North Fork of the American River.

Lee passed away on January 12, 1954 in Auburn and was buried in the Old Auburn Cemetery with his wife, who died on March 13, 1952 in Auburn.

Anna Isaline (1869-1906)

Anna was born in Damascus on August 9, 1869. She married John Patrick (1864-1941) ~1892, and they had eight children: Ellen, Richard, Annie, George, Leo, Robert, Wallace, and Vernon. Anna passed away in Dutch Flat on October 18, 1906. She was only 37.

Third Generation

Of Lee and Wilhelmina's ten surviving children, Raymond, Andrew, and Theresa were active on the Iowa Hill Divide as adults.

Theresa (1905-1994)

Theresa was born on July 16, 1905 in Humbug Canyon and attended school there. She married Joseph Merz, Jr. (1892-1990) on January 7, 1923 in Auburn. Joseph was an Army Private First Class in WWI and served in an artillery truck company in France. They had a son and daughter and lived out their lives in Auburn, except for a a few years at Humbug in the 1930s when the mines were briefly reopened. In 1934, Joseph built a cabin there.

Joseph was a fruit farmer in the Mount Pleasant District of Placer County from 1925-1934. In 1934-1935 he worked as a miner for the American Mining Company, which had leased the old Dorer Mine in Humbug Canyon and re-opened it for a few years. At the time of the 1940 Census he worked as a steam fitter and plumber at the Auburn Lumber Company.

Theresa passed away on June 10, 1994 in Auburn and was buried in the New Auburn Cemetery with her husband.

Raymond (1907-1980)

Ray was born in Humbug Canyon on May 28, 1907. After attending school there, on February 28, 1927 he married Marie *Pettit* (~1908-?) and they had two sons. At the time of the 1930 Census he was employed as a salesman at a hardware store. Later in the 1930s he worked as a forest ranger in various parts of the state. The family returned to Auburn in 1936. In 1940 Ray was the manager of linoleum sales at a roofing and lumber company. In the 1950s he owned the Dorer's Floor Covering Company in Auburn.

During the 1950s, Ray kept his parent's 1890s home on the Dorer Ranch in repair. He also built the first road into Humbug Canyon from the Iowa Hill side. He passed away on July 23, 1980 in Auburn and was buried in the New Auburn Cemetery.

Andrew (1909-1996)

Born on July 31, 1909 in Humbug Canyon, Andy went to school there. At the time of the 1930 Census, he was a salesman for a grocery store in Auburn. On September 6, 1936, he married Loretta *Drish* (1909-1996) in Auburn. They made their home there and had one son. By 1940, they owned the Auburn Grocery at Lincoln Way and Cherry Avenue. Loretta was the bookkeeper. From 1945 until his retirement in the 1970s Andy was a manager of a liquor store in Auburn.

On April 13, 1996, Andy passed away in Auburn and was buried in the New Auburn Cemetery with his wife.

Fourth Generation/Present Day

Today the Dorer Ranch is still owned by the family where Andrew's son spends time on the property.

DORER FAMILY TREE

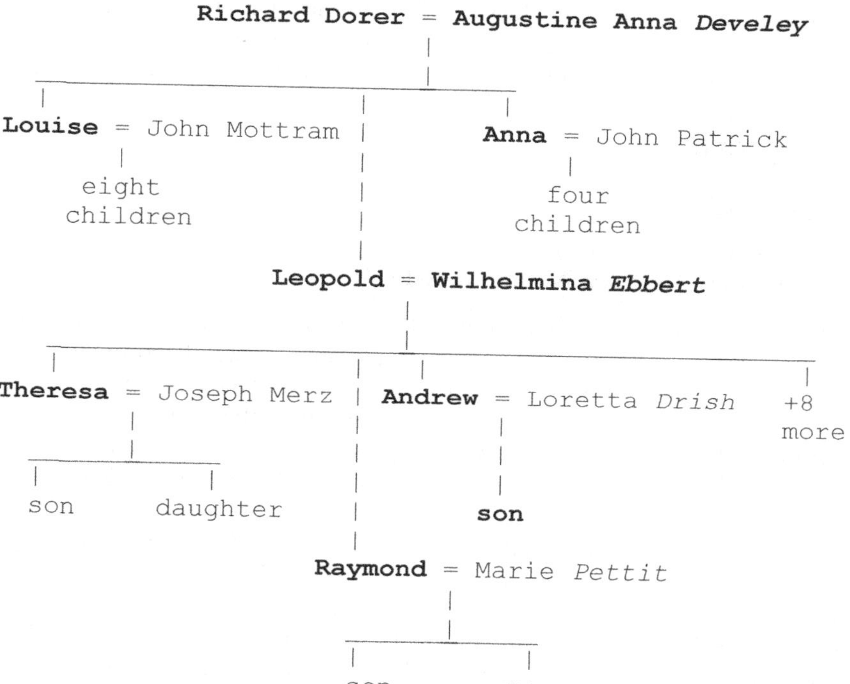

Macy/Nahor Family

Five generations of the Macy family have lived in Iowa Hill, and six generations of Nahors are represented there. Much appreciation to Paula Macy Bruton for her aid with information and photos of the Macy family.

First Settlers

Nahor Family

Joseph Nahor (1807-1871)
Mary Eleanor *Shattuck* Nahor (1812-1904)

Joseph Nahor was born on June 24, 1807 in New Hampshire, and his wife Mary Eleanor *Shattuck*, also of New Hampshire, was born on July 23, 1812. They married on October 6, 1833 in Lowell, Massachusetts, and they had six children. Mary Elizabeth, one of the two children to make it to California, was born on June 25, 1845 in Nashua New Hampshire.

Joseph left for the California Gold Rush from Lowell, Massachusetts in 1849, leaving his wife and children with his brother-in-law, Horace Shattuck. He came to California on the ship Edward Everett, with Alexander's geological surveying party. Their stated purpose was to locate the gold in this state, but nearly all of them died poor. Joseph left the party soon after arriving in the state, and in the winter of 1850-1 he located at Auburn, camping in front of the future site of the American Hotel (home of the Shanghai Restaurant & Bar and the Auburn Alehouse as of 2016).

His family joined him in 1857 and settled near Iowa Hill in a little valley called Strawberry Flat. Only two of the six children, Alfred and Mary Elizabeth, survived to make the trip. Mary Elizabeth was 12 at the time.

Joseph was an Iowa Hill pioneer, a farmer, and original owner of the tanyards. He died at age 64 on August 29, 1871. Mary Eleanor passed away on April 9, 1904 at age 91. They were buried next to each other in the Iowa Hill Cemetery.

Charles F. Macy (1828-1910)

Charles Frederick (C. F.) Macy was born in Nantucket, Massachusetts on Oct. 4, 1828, the son of Alexander Macy and Maria *Pinkham*, and a cousin to the founder of the Macy's department store empire.

After serving his apprenticeship as a tinsmith (now the sheet metal trade) in Nantucket, he sailed around Cape Horn (South America) to California ~1850. For the first few years he focused his efforts in what eventually became Nevada County. There he lived in You Bet, mined, was a tin and sheet metal worker, joined the militia in Little York, and was a member of the Red Dog IOOF, Brooklyn Lodge #46 from 1865 to 1868.

Joseph Nahor and Mary Eleanor *Shattuck*

Charles Frederick (C. F.) Macy and Mary Elizabeth *Nahor*

Top left: Waldo and Everett Macy as Children ~1890

Top right: Waldo Macy

Center: Ida May *Williams* Macy

Bottom: Big Herb Macy ~1942

Charles made two contributions to the development of mining technology. One was called the "undercurrent". When attached to a sluice box or flume, the undercurrent facilitated collection of very fine gold and platinum particles which would otherwise be washed away by the force of the water. These particles can account for 10-20% of the mined value.

His second contribution was to add rifling to the water monitors used in hydraulic mining. This overcame the tendency of the water to come out of the nozzle in a spray rather than a powerful stream, and greatly increased the efficiency of the monitors. The invention was widely used in subsequent mining efforts. Charles, along with Seth Martin, received U.S. Patent No. 40,847 for an "improvement in hose-nozzles" on December 8, 1863. The patent is still referenced in modern-day inventions.

Charles later sued Richard Hoskins, of Dutch Flat, for patent infringement by Hoskins' "Little Giant" hydraulic system. The suit, initially filed in Placer County Superior Court, went all the way to the Supreme Court. On January 23, 1872, that Court decided in favor of Macy. Macy sold his patent rights to his attorneys, Hale and Craig, who reached a compromise with Hoskins which allowed him to use the Macy patent on a royalty basis.

By 1854 he had arrived in Iowa Hill, where initially he worked as a clerk in a general store owned by King & Butler.[77] Using his experience as a tinsmith apprentice, he suggested that his employers build a shop for making stovepipe and other sheet metal fittings. Charles showed Butler the art of making stovepipe and Butler trained him as a pharmacist. Charles then obtained his certificate as a registered pharmacist.

Eventually, Charles and Hoppert (first name unknown) bought out King & Butler. Then Macy sold his interest to Hoppert and built a drugstore with living quarters upstairs and a sheet metal shop behind it. He operated the drugstore for over 30 years. Charles was a also a Justice of the Peace. In addition, he studied mining law and served as a legal advisor for many miners.

After buying the nearby home of Walter Lyons, Butler's brother-in-law, Charles used the living room of the drug store for his office as Justice of the Peace and arranged for an old sea captain named Bowers to look after the drug store. In an October 1965 letter (quoted in a May 12, 1977 article in the *Colfax Record*), his son Everett reminisced: "Charles would put up a prescription and then go back to his office to give legal advice or attend to his duties as secretary of the Iowa Hill Canal Company. When he had the time he'd go out to the shop to make stove pipe fittings or tin household utensils." Both the drugstore and the tin shop survived the 1897 fire.

---

[77] However, Charles continued to be involved part-time with mining in Nevada County until 1868.

During the hydraulicing era, Charles made hydraulic pipe in partnership with John Bisbee of Auburn. In ~1873 Charles was one of the organizers of the Iowa Hill Canal Company. This endeavor was initially very valuable, but became less so after the outlawing of hydraulic mining in 1884. Other investments included a part interest in various mining properties, such as the Orion, the Rule, the Success, and the Juno.

On April 13, 1873, Charles and Mary Elizabeth *Nahor* (1845-1908) were married. The couple had three children: Eleanor, who died of typhoid fever at age 12, Waldo Shattuck, and Charles Everett (known as Everett).

In the 1901 bio of her husband C. F. Macy in *A Volume of Memoirs and Genealogy of Representative Citizens of Northern California*, Mary Elizabeth was described: "She is a lady of marked intelligence and a splendid representative of the brave pioneer women who came to California in an early period in its development and are entitled to great credit for the part they have taken in the settlement of this great commonwealth."

Charles passed away from natural causes on June 28, 1910 at age 82 and was buried in the Iowa Hill Cemetery next to his wife, who died July 22, 1908 at age 63, also of natural causes. They were buried next to their daughter Eleanor.

Second Generation

Waldo and Everett carried on their father's tradition of being an active member of the Iowa Hill community.

Waldo Shattuck Macy (1877-1956)

Waldo Macy was born in Iowa Hill on July 17, 1877 and graduated from elementary school there in 1891.

He was a self-employed mine operator, Justice of the Peace, and druggist in Iowa Hill. He also provided medical services to the community, making his rounds with a horse and buggy. In ~1912, Waldo was put in charge of the PG&E medical department and hospitals in the Colfax area. Later he was temporary superintendent of the Placer County Hospital.

With his father and wife Ida, Waldo ran the C. F. Macy & Son store (replaced by the Red & White store in 1898) in Iowa Hill for many years, and he was the Iowa Hill Postmaster from October 1929 to October 1940. In the 1920s he also served as Deputy Coroner and Undertaker and was the last Justice of the Peace in Iowa Hill. In 1951 he was chosen to be one of the people who unveiled the historic monument marking the founding of Iowa Hill. Waldo married Ida May *Williams* (1883-1952) in November 1914, and they had two sons: Stanley Waldo and Herbert Charles.

He was also involved in mining activities, working to bring the mines back to a profitable basis, including the Morning Star Mine. To support this, he served as a Director of the Western Mining Council.

Waldo passed away on October 17, 1956 at age 79. He was buried next to his wife in the Colfax Cemetery.

Charles Everett Macy (1887-1968)

Everett was born in Iowa Hill on January 18, 1887 and graduated from school there in 1905. He was a Notary Public and co-owner of the family store in Iowa Hill. He also worked in the mines.

On February 9, 1926 he received Patent #1,572,441 for an "Automatically-Operated Electric Iron." The invention improved the safety of an electric iron by causing the current to turn off when the grasp on the handle was released, thus eliminating the danger of fire due to an unattended iron. Ironically, Iowa Hill still doesn't have electricity.

Everett never married. He passed away on April 10, 1968 in San Francisco and was buried in the Colfax Cemetery.

Third Generation

Herbert "Big Herb" Charles Macy, Sr. (1920-2006)

Born July 7, 1920 in Oakland, "Big Herb" Macy graduated from elementary school in Iowa Hill in 1933. He first worked in the Iowa Hill mines and as a clerk in his father's store, then went to Mare Island Naval Base. He married his first wife, Edith Arvilla *Hunt* (1925-1988) of Colfax on July 27, 1941. They had two sons, John, who died in infancy, and Herb, Jr.

In 1942, Big Herb joined the Navy and served in the South Pacific during World War II, receiving an honorable discharge on January 25, 1946. After the war and a divorce, he returned for a time to Iowa Hill, and then he went to work for PG&E, subsequently to R. J. Miles in Colfax, followed by a stint with the Placer County Road Maintenance Department.

On November 20, 1951 he married Georgia Mae *Hilton* in Reno and they had two daughters. Big Herb retired in 1979 and passed away at age 86 on October 22, 2006 in Rocklin, California. He was buried next to his wife Georgia, who died May 1, 2005, in the Colfax Cemetery.

Stanley Macy (1918-1990)

Stanley was born on Oct. 15, 1918 in Oakland, California and graduated from the Iowa Hill School in 1933 with his brother Herb. He served in the Navy during World War II. He married Elaine *Walkoff* on November 25, 1954 in Berkeley, California and they had three children. Stanley died in Auburn, California on January 6, 1990 and was buried in the Colfax Cemetery.

Fourth & Fifth Generations

Herb, Jr. "Herbie" Macy is the fourth generation and last full-time Macy resident of Iowa Hill. Some of the fifth-generation went to school there but have since moved away, although they and the sixth generation are frequent visitors. Herbie followed in his father's footsteps to PG&E and R. J. Miles. He is now retired and is a local historian.

The family generously shared their Iowa Hill photos and knowledge of Iowa Hill and family history for both this book and *The Iowa Hill Divide Volume 1: Schools of the Iowa Hill Divide.*

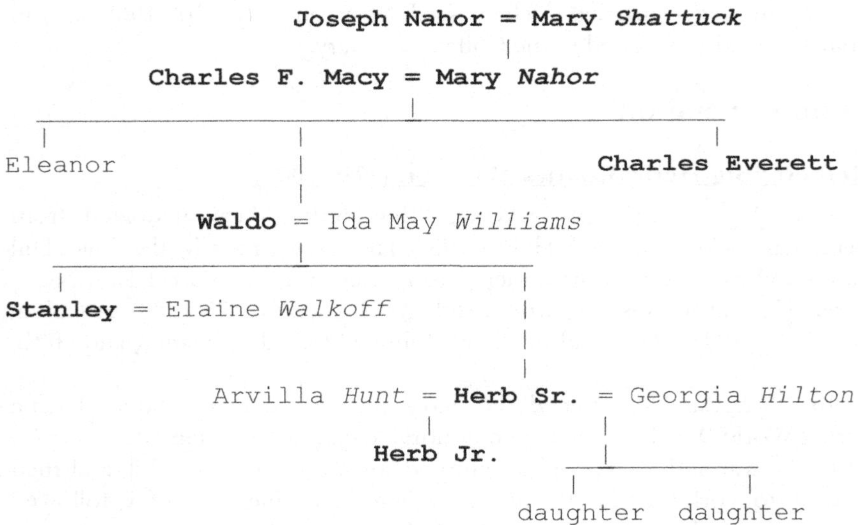

Parker/Cantrell Family

Three generations of the Parker/Cantrell family have called Iowa Hill home. They are considered a founding family not only because of the length of time they have been associated with Iowa Hill, but also because they ushered in the beginning of the modern era when they built the new Iowa Hill store in 1970. Much appreciation to Mary Parker for her assistance with this section as well as with this book and with *The Iowa Hill Divide Volume 1: Schools of the Iowa Hill Divide.*.

First Generation

Martin L. "Pop" Parker (1889-1976)

Pop Parker was born on April. 11, 1889 in Searcy, Arkansas, the son of William Parker and Josephine *Loggins*. He later worked as a farmer. Pop married Laura *Fields* on May 21, 1910 in Logan County, Arkansas, and they had six children: Herman, Bonnie, Amos, Milford, Grover, and Betty. In 1936 he moved to California, initially working as a farmer in Tulare County. In the early 1940s he worked for the Santa Fe Railroad in Contra Costa and San Joaquin Counties. The family next moved to Richmond where Pop operated the Parker Brothers Bakery at 16th Street and Hoffman Boulevard with his brother Milford.

A friend of Bud Cannon, a fellow hunter, Pop began visiting Iowa Hill in the late 1940s and then moved there permanently in 1953. He lived in Iowa Hill for the next 23 years, until shortly before his death on February 11, 1976, just a month before his 87th birthday. Buried in the Iowa Hill cemetery, he was survived by three sons, two daughters, twelve grandchildren and eleven great-grandchildren.

From *Iowa Hill: the Town that Refused to Die* by daughter-in-law Mary Parker: "Pop Parker ... raised and trained hunting dogs and was one of the oldest, active bear hunters in the state. Pop was the author of many outdoor and hunting stories. His articles had been published by several magazines and as a result he was featured on Channel 8 TV in 1970. This was covered by the *Sacramento Bee* and the *San Francisco Examiner*. He wrote many bear stories and about training hunting dogs which appeared in *American Cooner* magazine, the *National Treehound*, and the *Western Hound and News*. In his jeep, he was also known as 'Hot Rod Harry'."

Pop passed away in Richmond, California on February 11, 1976 and was buried in the Iowa Hill Cemetery.

Top: Grover Parker

Left center: Pop Parker

Right center: Hub & Bonnie Cantrell

Bottom: "New" Iowa Hill Store

Second Generation

Grover Parker (1923-2015)

Grover Parker, born March 26, 1923 in Perryville, Arkansas, was the fifth of six children born to Martin "Pop" and Laura *Fields* Parker. As a youth he was scouted by professional baseball, but decided to go a different route in life. He served in the South Pacific with the US Marine Corps during World War II and earned the rank of Lieutenant.

He and his wife Mary were married on December 12, 1952 in Contra Costa County, California. The couple moved to Sacramento in 1953, the same year that Grover's father moved to Iowa Hill. Grover ran his own fence business in Sacramento for over 40 years and was president of the California chapter of the International Fence Industries Association.

After the "old" Iowa Hill store burned in 1968, Grover and Mary built the current store across the street, and Grover's sister Bonnie and her husband Hub Cantrell initially ran it. In 1989, Grover and Mary moved to Iowa Hill and stayed for the next 20 years. Grover helped found and train the Iowa Hill Fire Department and was the Chief in 1999. In 2008, the couple returned to Sacramento but continued to visit "the hill."

During his free time, Grover loved to fish and hunt. He also enjoyed baseball, dancing, and country music. He passed away peacefully on August 1, 2015 at age 92, surrounded by his friends and family. He was buried next to his father in the Old Iowa Hill Cemetery. He is survived by his wife Mary, three children, five grandchildren, and three great-grandchildren.

Bonnie *Parker* Cantrell (1913-2014)

The second of six children of Martin and Laura *Fields* Cantrell, Bonnie was born on March 8, 1913 in Perryville, Arkansas. She moved to California in 1936 and married Herbert "Hub" Cantrell (1903-1972) in 1937.

Bonnie and Hub moved to Iowa Hill in 1970 to be ready to lease the new store being built by her brother and sister-in-law, Grover and Mary Parker. Hub, a carpenter, helped build the store. In 1972, Hub passed away and Bonnie remained with the store until it was sold in 1975. She continued to live in Iowa Hill for many years and was known as the Queen of Iowa Hill, loved by all in the community. Bonnie passed away on August 16, 2014 at age 101 and was buried next to her husband in the Iowa Hill cemetery.

Milford O. "Mo" Parker (1921-1999)

Mo ran the Iowa Hill Store in the late 1970's and early 1980's, often wearing a loaded revolver on his hip. He was born November 4, 1921 in Arkansas, the fourth child of "Pop" Parker and Laura *Fields*, and served in World War II. He was married to Mary Ward, but they divorced in 1974. On November 15, 1975 he married Fay Evans in Nevada County, California. Mo died on April 18, 1999.

Third Generation/Present Day

As of 2016, Mary Parker, wife of Grover, serves on the Iowa Hill Community Cemetery Board of Directors, a post she has held for several years. Grover and Mary's son Keith Parker lives in Iowa Hill on property owned by the Parker family.

PARKER/CANTRELL FAMILY TREE

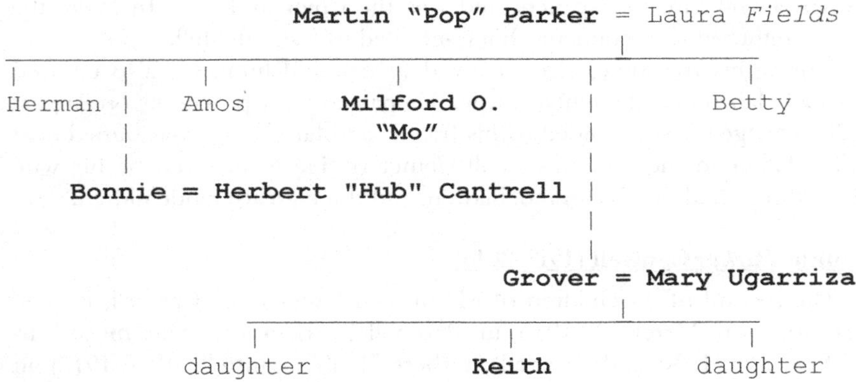

Schwab Family

Four generations of the Schwab family have made Iowa Hill their home. Many thanks to Marilyn Schwab Carter for her assistance with this section.

First Generation

Karl/Charles Frederick "Carl" Schwab (1843-1878)

Karl Friedrich Schwab was born on April 2, 1843 near Stuttgart, Germany, the son of Karl Ludwig Schwab and Christiana Catherina *Idler*, both of Germany. He immigrated to the United States, and by 1862 he had settled as a miner in Wisconsin Hill, where he went by the name Charles or Carl.

During the Civil War, he enlisted at Auburn as Charles Schwab on December 8, 1864 and was mustered into Company D, 7th California Infantry on December 16. Private Schwab was posted to Fort Mason, Arizona Territory, where he was mustered out December 8, 1865.

After the war, he returned to his mining claim at Wisconsin Hill, marrying Josephine E. *Hawkins* (1849-1925) on December 25, 1871. She was the daughter of George Hawkins, a merchant in Iowa Hill. They had three children, all born at Wisconsin Hill: Carl, Theodore L. Sr., and Annie.

On April 7, 1878 Charles was killed in an accidental explosion at his mining claim. He had set up some blasting powder as a deterrent to thieves who were robbing his sluice boxes when, from some unknown cause, the powder exploded, killing him instantly. He was only 35. Charles was buried in the cemetery at Iowa Hill. His obituary in the *Placer Weekly Argus* said: "The funeral was one of the largest ever seen at Iowa Hill. At the grave, even strong men wept like girls, for the deceased was a man well liked by his neighbors. In his death the community loses a good, industrious citizen, and his family a loving husband and father."

After his death, Josephine married George W. Cross (1828-1907). On February 6, 1892 she and her children received patent #54819 for the Schwab Mine of 47 acres in Sections 3 and 10 of Township 14N, Range 10E east of the present-day Gleeson Diggins near former Wisconsin Hill.

Second Generation

Carl (1872-1914)

Born in October 1872 in Wisconsin Hill, Carl resided on the Divide most of his life. On May 3, 1902 he received patent #54956 for 27 acres in Section 9, Township 14N, Range 10E near the former Wisconsin Hill. He died in 1914 and was buried in the Colfax Cemetery next to his mother.

Top: Annie, Theodore, and Carl Schwab as Children ~1882

Bottom: Carl Schwab ~1870

Theodore L., Sr. (1875-1927)

Theodore L., Sr., known as "Peanut" for being short, was born in Iowa Hill on January 21, 1875. He went to school in Iowa Hill and resided there for most of his life. In 1899, he married Anna Myra *Stuart* (1878-1950) and they had four sons: Stuart, Ellard, Theodore L. Jr., and Charles "Buzz." He bought the Iowa Hill Supply Company store in 1906 and was postmaster from then until 1922. He was only 52 when he died on August 25, 1927 and was buried in the Colfax Cemetery.

Annie (1877-1938)

Annie, an Iowa Hill native, was born in 1877. She attended school in Iowa Hill and then taught there for six terms, from 1897-1903. She married Alfred Enslin (1874-1950) around 1904 and moved away from the Divide. They had four children. Annie died in 1938.

Third Generation

Of the four children of Theodore, Sr. and Anna Myra *Stuart*, only Stuart and Ellard continued to be involved with Iowa Hill past young adulthood.

Stuart (1899–1966)

Stuart was born on December 8, 1899. After attending school in Iowa Hill, he married Edith *Hull* (1905-1977) on July 22, 1927. They had one child. In the early 1930s Stuart re-opened the old store in Iowa Hill and renamed it Schwab's Store. He operated the business until 1940, when he sold it to Mabel *DeMond* (who later married Jack Blaise), and moved away. He died on January 29, 1966 in Orangeville, California and was buried in Rocklin next to his wife.

Ellard (1901–1984)

Born August 15, 1901, Ellard attended school in Iowa Hill. He married (date unknown) Eva *Moore* (1905-1991) and they had one daughter. After living in San Francisco for many years and operating the Castro Street Garage, he retired in 1958 and moved back to Iowa Hill. For several years he maintained the old "farmer's" telephone line[78] to Colfax as well as taking care of the fire engine and fire house. He also contracted with the US Postal Service to carry the mail three times a week between Iowa Hill and Colfax for many years. He passed away on March 10, 1984 and was buried in the Colfax Cemetery.

---

[78] Farmer's telephone lines were informal systems installed and maintained by the users without the benefit of a formal utility. In some places, barbed wire fences were used as the transmission medium.

Theodore L. Jr. "Ted" (1905–1973)

Ted was born on January 1, 1905 and used to boast that he was responsible for the September 1920 fire which destroyed most of what remained of downtown Iowa Hill. However the official reason for the blaze was a faulty flue in the Schwab home. Ted attended elementary school in Iowa Hill. In ~1926 he married Edna *Smith* (1903-1997) and moved away. They had one child. Ted passed away on November 9, 1973 in Alameda, California.

Charles "Buzz" (1920–1982)

Born August 15, 1920, Buzz attended school in Iowa Hill, but by 1940 he had moved away. He married Florence *Clark* and they had two children. He died March 16, 1982 in Alameda and was buried in the Colfax Cemetery.

Fourth Generation/Present Day

While growing up, the fourth generation of the Schwab family spent a lot of time in Iowa Hill. After the old store burned in 1968, a family member bought the property. As of 2016 he lives there part-time. The family generously shared their Iowa Hill photos and knowledge of Iowa Hill history for both this book and *The Iowa Hill Divide Volume 1: Schools of the Iowa Hill Divide.*

SCHWAB FAMILY TREE

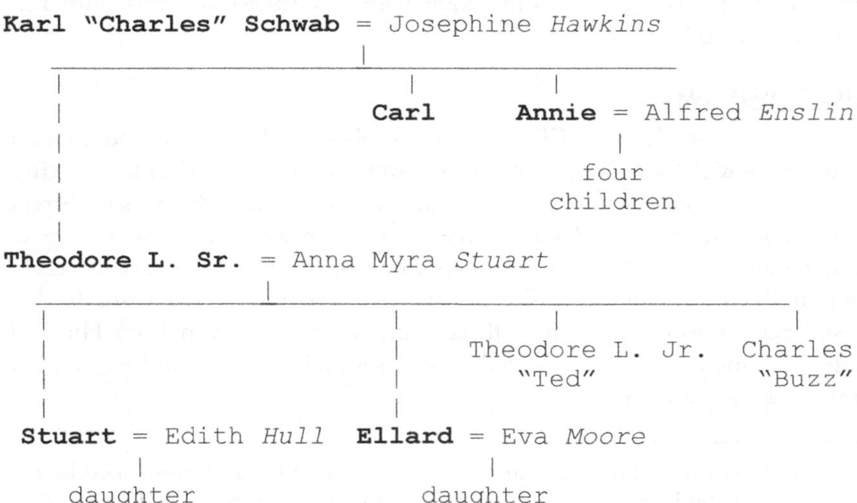

Watts Family

Four generations of the Watts family have lived on the Divide. This was a prolific family, so in the interests of space only those family members who were involved with the Divide are listed here. (A James Watts family lived in the Colfax area in the same timeframe. The families do not appear to be related although it's difficult to be certain.)

First Generation

John Watts (1841-1930)

John was born in Lancashire, England on February 7, 1846. He manufactured soap in Werrington, near Peterborough in Cambridgeshire, England, where on Christmas Day 1865 he married Sara Ann *Alcock* (1846-1924). The couple had ten children: Mary, Frederick, John H., Samuel Gaylord, Arthur, Edith, Albert, Walter, William, and Edwin.

In 1875 he and his family immigrated to the US, and joined his older brother William, who had come to the Divide in 1868. There they purchased the Strawberry Mine, among others, at Monona Flat (near Iowa Hill) for $600. The Strawberry Mine produced gold, silver, and tungsten and employed as many as 14 men.

John later moved to Auburn, where he died on March 1, 1930. He was buried in the Old Auburn Cemetery with his wife.

Second Generation

Samuel Gaylord (1874-1931)

Sam was born in England on January 14, 1874 and immigrated to the US with his family in 1876. He attended school in Iowa Hill and then taught there for four terms, from 1895-1899. Sam married Mildred *Sprague* (1881-1946) in 1899 and moved to Auburn, where he continued to teach for a while. From 1903-1913 he was the Postmaster in East Auburn. By the 1920 Census he was age 45, divorced, and living with his parents and his son Sidney in Auburn. His occupation was insurance agent.

Sam passed away in Sacramento on November 29, 1931 at age 57.

Arthur (1877-1930)

Arthur, born in August 1877 in Placer County, married Ebba Johanna *Leckman* (1880-1910) and had four children: Alvin J., Walter, Beatrice, and William. They mostly lived in the Colfax area, although Arthur also did some mining in Iowa Hill.

Third Generation

Alvin J. "Al" (1904-1975)

Al, son of Arthur Watts and Ebba Johanna *Leckman*, was born July 19, 1904 in Placer County. He was 19 when he married his first wife, name unknown. By the 1930 Census they were living separately and had divorced by 1940. Al was a water well driller in Walnut Creek in 1930, but by 1935 he had moved back to Iowa Hill to the family mines. In addition to being a miner, Al was also a logger.

During World War II, Al was a Private in the U.S. Army, serving from August 25, 1942 to May 5, 1943. He had four children with his second wife Mildred *Ross*: John, Dennis, Jimmy, and a daughter.

He died on July 8, 1975 at age 69 and was buried in the Iowa Hill Cemetery.

Al Watts

Fourth Generation/Present Day

John (1944-2011)

The son of Alvin J. and Mildred *Ross* Watts, John was born April 19, 1944 in Payson, Utah. He grew up and attended school in Iowa Hill. After graduating from the 8th grade there in 1958, he went to high school in Colfax. He joined the Navy at age 17, serving in Viet Nam, and was honorably discharged in 1965.

John worked as a cross-country truck driver for various companies, then began his own trucking business. In his leisure time he loved the outdoors.

John passed away on November 6, 2011 in Pine Bluff, Arkansas, where he resided. He was 67 years old and was survived by his wife of 30 years, three sons, six grandchildren, a brother, and two sisters.

Dennis (1945-2011)

Dennis, another son of Alvin J. and Mildred *Ross* Watts, was born on October 11, 1945 in Placer County. He also grew up in Iowa Hill, attending school there and graduating in 1959. He married Juanita *Berglund* in 1971, but they divorced a few years later. Dennis died on February 12, 2011 in Colfax.

Jimmy (1948-2008)

The third son of Alvin J. and Mildred *Ross* Watts, Jimmy was born on January 10, 1948 in Placer County and graduated from the Iowa Hill School in 1961. He died on February 22, 2008 in Reno, Nevada.

WATTS FAMILY TREE*

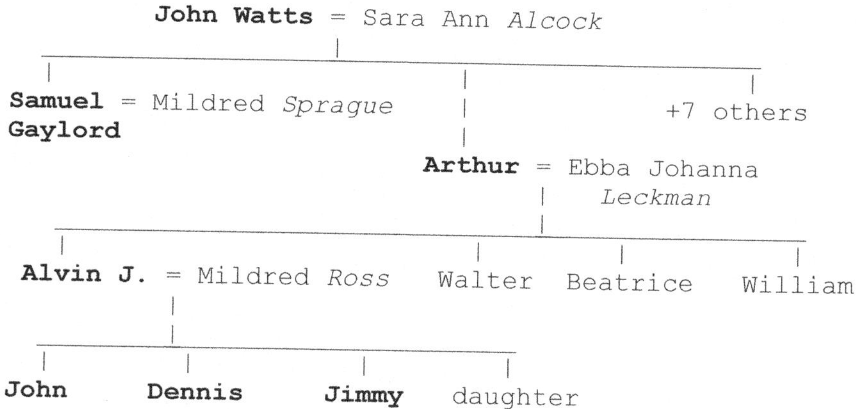

* As noted above, this family tree includes only the Watts family members who were active in Iowa Hill, so it is very abbreviated.

Notable Residents

Many residents of the Iowa Hill Divide deserve mention for their accomplishments. Some of these people are highlighted below. (Dates came from various sources. When a conflict arose, the date of the earliest source was usually used, under the assumption that it was probably the most accurate.)

John G. Bisbee

John Gould Bisbee was born in Lisbon, Maine on March 31, 1837. On November 8, 1858 he married his first wife, Mary Elizabeth *Madden* of Ireland (1838-1877), in Leavenworth, Kansas.

John and Elizabeth left for California the day after their marriage via New York City and the Isthmus of Panama. They arrived in Iowa Hill in January 1859 where John operated the Morning Star mill and for a while was the Superintendent. In the 1870s he built a sawmill for the Iowa Hill Canal Company.

The couple lived in Iowa Hill for 21 years where they had at least seven children. One of them, Effie Viola, died of pneumonia at age 5 and was buried in the Iowa Hill area. Elizabeth was also buried there, having died on April 21, 1878.

In 1879, John was elected as the first Treasurer of Placer County, a post he held for almost three years. He later served two years as County Coroner. After moving to Auburn in 1880, he established a business in blacksmithing plus wagon and carriage manufacturing.

He married twice more: to Minetta *Morgan*, who died just two years later (date unknown), and on December 25, 1896 to Lola *VanAuken*.

John was a member of the IOOF and also a Mason. He died on January 31, 1921 at age 83 in Colfax and was buried in the Old Auburn Cemetery.

Lyman W. Gilmore, Jr.

The eccentric aviation pioneer Lyman Wiswell Gilmore, Jr., was born on June 11, 1876 in Beaver Creek, Washington.[79] He was the sixth of eleven children born to Lyman Wiswell Gilmore (1836-1913) and Sarah Augusta *Gray* Gilmore (1846-1916).

In 1893 or 1894 he moved to his uncle's home in Red Bluff, California where he experimented with a glider pulled by a horse. He later relocated to Placer County.

By 1897 Gilmore was working a placer mining claim at Birds Flat, near Iowa Hill, with his brother Samuel. The 1900 Census shows him living in Iowa Hill.

Around 1905, he and his brother Charlie opened what is thought to be the first commercial air field in the country near Grass Valley, California. The 1910 Census shows him living in Grass Valley, but he remained involved with the Iowa Hill area until the mid-1930s.

He tested his aircraft designs by flying off of the cliff at Cape Horn, near Colfax, and claimed to have demonstrated powered flight in May 1902, some nine months before the Wright brothers. This assertion was never substantiated because all of Lyman's records were lost in a fire.

Gilmore also continued his mining efforts, and received financial backing from the Pittsburgh Syndicate in 1921 for exploration of the famous blue gravel channel (location of the Morning Star and Big Dipper Mines) near Iowa Hill. In 1922 he purchased the nearby General Grant Mine.

In 1923 he pledged funds to help develop the Stevens Trail into an actual road. This project was initially approved by the Placer County Board of Supervisors, but it never came to fruition.

After the record snowstorm of 1932, he was one of the first people to make it through the snow to bring supplies to the town (see adjacent photo). In 1934 he was listed as a Director when the Iowa Hill Gold Mining Company filed articles of incorporation.

Although he was involved with mining in Iowa Hill, his main interests were aviation and invention. Gold mining was a means to provide funding for his true vocation. He invented a rotary snowplow, but his design was stolen before he could patent it. He also conceived several aviation firsts, including an all-metal fuselage with an enclosed cabin and retractable landing gear. Gilmore foresaw the possibility of aircraft in wartime,

[79] Some sources give his birth year as 1874. However, in the July 2, 1877 Washington State Census, he was listed as being 1 year old, which means he was born in 1876.

dropping dynamite from the skies. On May 8, 1906 he received patent #819,752 for a steam engine, primarily aimed at aviation use. (His patent was cited by patent #US3898787, filed on May 9, 1973 and granted on August 12, 1975.) He was an advisor to other aviation pioneers including the Wright brothers, who visited his Grass Valley aerodrome, and Samuel Langley.

Lyman Gilmore (on right) after the 1932 Snow Storm

His first documented powered flight was reported in the *Grass Valley Union* on August 15, 1911. By then he had switched to gasoline-powered engines because the steam-powered ones were too heavy and too dangerous.

In 1929 the Grass Valley Council voted to make Gilmore Field a municipal airport. A fire in 1934[80] destroyed his records and most of his aircraft. Today the Lyman Gilmore Middle School occupies the site of the former airfield.

Gilmore passed away at age 74 on February 18, 1951 in Nevada City following a severe stroke.

On May 9, 2002 the town of Iowa Hill held a Lyman Gilmore celebration to honor his contributions to the community.

---

[80] Most present-day sources give the year as 1935, however, the November 1934 issue of *Popular Aviation* says "When fire swept through the old hangar in Gilmore's Field, Grass Valley, recently…."

Melvin Oliver Henderson

Born in Colfax, California on November 10, 1922, Mel Henderson was the grandson of an early settler in Yankee Jims. He was raised in Iowa Hill and graduated from that school in 1936. He continued to visit Iowa Hill as an adult and lived there for several years.

During World War II, he initially worked as a P-38 mechanic before being sent to Europe in 1943 where he flew seven missions in P-38's and P-51 fighter planes as a Second Lieutenant. After the German surrender, he was a security observer at the courthouse where the Nuremburg trials were held.

Upon returning home in 1945, he received a Bachelor's Degree in Art Sculpture from the College of Arts and Crafts in Oakland. He then took a post at San Francisco State University where he taught painting, design, and sculpture until his retirement. He was also a miner in addition to being a sculptor.

Between 1983 and 2006, he was a Djerassi Resident Artist[81] seven times. While there he created a mill called "Water Wheel" which caused a stone to rise and fall to "stamp out evil." His art reflected his connection to the earth and his concerns about peace and justice. His leisure time included whistling, classical music, watching birds, and eating fresh corn.

In 1996, the City of Colfax appointed him the Director of Art in Public Places. Mel, with his son Theron and John Barrow, restored the sculptures of a bull and bear which are now on permanent display next to the Colfax Area Historical Society Museum in Colfax, California.

He passed away peacefully at his home in Nevada City on October 4, 2014, one month before his 92nd birthday. He was survived by his wife, his sister, two daughters, a son, and a granddaughter. He is fondly remembered by students, friends, and family. The Smithsonian Institution requested his archives when he died.

Captain John T. Hill and Adelia *Reid* Hill

John T. Hill was born in 1812 in Maryland. He came to Iowa Hill in 1852, and on October 11, 1855 he married another Iowa Hill resident, Adelia (AKA Delia or Adelaide) *Reid*, in Illinoistown, Placer County with Rev. Dolton of Grass Valley officiating. Adelia was born in 1831 in

[81] The mission of the Djerassi Resident Artists Program, located in Woodside, California, is to support and enhance the creativity of artists by providing uninterrupted time for work, reflection, and collegial interaction in a setting of great natural beauty, and to preserve the land on which the Program is situated.

Connecticut.

The source of the honorific "Captain" could not be verified; possibly it was through service in a militia company, perhaps it was an affectation.

Hill was a major ditch and reservoir owner, including the Indian Canyon water ditch built in 1852. He supplied water to the mines and settlements in the Iowa Hill Divide area. On the County Assessor's Rolls in 1853, he claimed ditches in Iowa Hill worth $6,000 and in 1854 he claimed property in Iowa Hill worth $13,000 on which he paid $78 in state taxes and $104 to the County.

On January 29, 1855, Hill's Reservoir burst, killing three and injuring one.

Hill died on October 23, 1857 in Iowa Hill at age 45 from an unspecified illness. Adelia was only 26 at the time.

He left an estate worth $14,700, which included "one water ditch 3 miles in length leading from Indian Cañon to the town of Iowa Hill with reservoir and all appurtenances thereto belonging" valued at $6,000 and "one water ditch 11 miles in length leading from Indian Cañon via Birds Flat and Wisconsin Hill to Kings Hill with reservoir and all appurtenances thereto belonging" valued at $3,500.[82] His probate also listed a ditch eight miles long between Humbug Canyon and Damascus and on to the Quartz Mine which cost $14,000 to build, but was no longer in use so was valued at only $100.

Adelia took over the management of the ditches and mining interests after John's untimely death. In 1860 she acquired two more ditches, the Union Ditch and Priest's Ditch. As part of being a ditch owner, she filed multiple lawsuits in attempts to protect her ditches and their water supply. One case, against the Iowa Hill Canal Company, went as far as the U. S. Supreme Court in 1878 but it was declared "plaintiff in error."

Adelia also owned at least five mines: two hydraulic mines on Roach Hill, two drift/hydraulic mines at Wisconsin Hill, and a hydraulic mine at Elizabethtown. She also planted many fruit trees, some of which still produce today.

John T. Hill was a Mason. Curiously, at their Seventh Annual Communication in May 1856 in Sacramento, the Grand Lodge of California accused Hill of being "John Tothill formerly of Holmesville Mississippi but now a resident of Iowa Hill under the assumed name of J.T. Hill who was convicted of larceny and sent to the penitentiary of Mississippi for four

---

[82] This is at odds with the information on ditches on page 224 of the 1882 *History of Placer County, California with Illustrations and Biographical Sketches of Its Prominent Men and Pioneers* by Thompson & West, which lists a 25-mile long "Hill's Ditch" valued at $6,000 in 1856 and $5,000 in 1857. The *Directory of the County of Placer for the Year 1861* states that Hill's Ditch is 10 miles long and valued it at $5,600.

years." Hill said that while he was indeed this person, he was innocent of the charges. The Grand Lodge directed Iowa Hill Lodge 63 to expel Hill. No record was found as to whether or not they followed this directive.

Regardless, when he died the following year the "funeral was attended by a large number of Masonic Fraternity, who buried him with the honors usually bestowed upon those who have advanced sufficiently in the order to be enabled to remove the veil which enshrouds the 'sublime degree'. They have carefully laid him amid the golden hills." (*Placer Herald*, October 31, 1857) He was initially buried in Iowa Hill, probably in the Catholic Cemetery.

On April 6, 1861, his wife reburied him under a $3,000 monument, in the Calvary Cemetery on Lone Mountain in San Francisco. On August 12, 1940 he was reburied once again, this time as part of the mass move of remains from Calvary Cemetery to Holy Cross in Colma prior to the demolition of the Calvary Cemetery.

Adelia, a true pioneer woman, passed away on Feb. 12, 1904 at age 72 and was buried in St. Dominic's Catholic Cemetery in Iowa Hill. Adelia Hill Road, near the Iowa Hill cemeteries, is named for her.

John B. Hobson

John Bogard Hobson was born on March 7, 1844 in County Carlow, Ireland, the son of Thomas Hobson (1822-1883) and Mary *Bogard* Hobson (1811-1871). The family immigrated to New York in 1848 when John was four years old. In May 1859, they moved to San Francisco, where John found work as a gas fitter.

In 1866, he married his first wife, Mary *Healy* (1844-1917), and they had six children. By 1870, the couple had moved to Sacramento, and he continued to work as a gas fitter. John was one of the contractors who built the California State Capitol building, installing the plumbing, gas fittings and fixture, as well as the electric lighting fixtures in the dome of the Capitol.

John became interested in mining and operated several hydraulic mines in the Iowa Hill area, including the Independence Hill Mine and the Excelsior Mine, from 1871 to 1891.

He also studied to become a mining engineer, which entitled him to add "E. M." after his name, and was an "assistant in the field" to the State Mineralogist for several years. In this role he published many articles in the *Report of the State Mineralogist* journal. He also developed various geological maps, including one of the Iowa Hill Mining District done in 1890.

Sometime between 1880 and 1891 he and Mary parted ways and John married for the second time, to Sara Julia *Reid* (1863-1940), the niece of Adelia *Reid* Hill. The couple had three sons, including Richmond Pearson Bogard Hobson (1907-1998), who was buried in St. Dominic's Catholic Cemetery in Iowa Hill.

The 1884 Sawyer ruling, which ended hydraulic mining in California, impacted his mining interests and in 1891 he joined with another Iowa Hill resident, Jacob Neff (see his bio in this section), and others to organize the California State Mining Association. In 1892, John testified in Washington at the Congressional Committee on Mines and Mining. This led to passage of the Caminetti Act of 1893, which allowed hydraulic mining to resume under state regulation as long as the mines prevented their tailings from entering navigable streams or injuring lands owned by others. In California, oversight was provided by the California Debris Commission.

In 1892, at the invitation of the Canadian Pacific Railroad, John decided to immigrate to British Columbia, Canada, where hydraulic mining had no restrictions. Hobson Creek and Hobson Lake there are named in his honor for his contribution to hydraulic mining in Canada. He eventually became a naturalized Canadian citizen.

John was a Mason and a member of the Knights Templar. After his death from heart failure on January 10, 1912 in British Columbia, his body was transported to San Francisco for the funeral, followed by burial in the Woodlawn Cemetery in nearby Colma in San Mateo County.

William L. "Seattle Bill" James

Born in Iowa Hill on March 12, 1892, William Lawrence "Seattle Bill" James was one of four children born to William H. James (1864-1921) and Emma *Schmidt* James (1870-1938). His father was a foreman at the Morning Star Mine and also owned a butcher shop in Iowa Hill.

Called "Willie" as a boy, Bill attended school in Iowa Hill in the late 1890s to early 1900s. He played baseball for the Iowa Hill "Wide Awakes" until his father, a mining engineer, had to move the family to Oroville, California in the early 1900s due to the decline in mining in the Iowa Hill area. Bill graduated high school from Union High in Oroville and continued to play ball.

He pitched a very fast ball. In 1912, at age 20, Bill signed with the Seattle Giants, who won the Northwest League Championship that year. Bill spent many nights practicing his pitching by throwing balls into hotel pillows. In 1913, the Boston Braves purchased his contract.

In 1914, the Braves came from last place to play in the World Series against the "unbeatable" Philadelphia Athletics. James entered the third game in the 11th inning with the score tied. He pitched two innings of no hits, winning the game. The "A's" lost the next four games straight and the Braves won the pennant. However, the season cost Bill a serious arm injury.

During World War I, Bill was an instructor in bomb-throwing for the US Army, appropriately enough. He ended his career playing for Sacramento and eventually managed the Sacramento Solons. After leaving pro ball, he returned to Oroville High to coach baseball.

In 1925, he married Harriet Everial *Newman* (1897-1973), and they had one daughter. Harriet served as the Butte County Clerk for eight years.

In 1949, Bill was named "1914 Athlete of the Year" by Bay Area sports writers for the Helms Athletic Foundation. In 1951, US sports writers named the 1914 defeat of the Philadelphia Athletics by the Boston Braves the number one outstanding news upset of the era.

Bill passed away in Oroville on March 10, 1971, just two days short of his 79th birthday. He was buried in the Memorial Park Cemetery next to his wife.

Charles F. Macy

Please see his bio in the Macy/Nahor Family section of the Founding Families chapter.

Waldo Shattuck Macy

Please see his bio in the Macy/Nahor Family section of the Founding Families chapter.

Anna Catherine *Murphy* Markham

Anna Catherine Murphy was born in Iowa Hill on December 16, 1859, the daughter of a miner. She attended school there, and after receiving her teaching credential, she returned to teach in Iowa Hill for two terms. In 1881 she first met her future husband, poet Edwin Markham, at a teacher's convention in San Jose, California. It was fifteen years before they met again.

After graduating from the San Jose Normal School (for teachers) in 1883, she returned to Iowa Hill where she became principal of the school and taught for a third term. She then taught in Yolo and Colusa Counties before moving to Los Angeles, where she taught from 1887-1892. During the 1890s she independently edited the Second and Fourth readers and collaborated on the grammar and other readers used in California schools. In 1898 she completed a two-year course at the University of California, Berkeley, which entitled her to a high school teaching certificate. Her focus was English literature.

On June 18, 1898, at age 38, Anna became the third wife of acclaimed poet Edwin Markham. The couple had a son, Virgil. Later they moved to New York and lived in Brooklyn and Staten Island. A poet herself, Anna Catherine also guided her husband's career and was his collaborator and editor.

After a lecture in San Francisco in the early 1920s, she ended by reciting her poem, *A Sierra Memory*, referred to by the *Placer Herald* newspaper as "the best ever written of scenes and old times of Placer's mining country of the Iowa Hill and Forest Hill Divides."

Anna Catherine served as Secretary of the California Teachers Association, Corresponding Secretary and Member of the Executive Committee of the Poetry Society of America, and Vice President of the Mary Fisher Home of Tenafly, New Jersey. She was also a member of the New York Browning Society and a founding member of the Pacific Coast Women's Press Association. Her works were printed in several publications, including the *Overland Monthly* and *McClure's*.

Anna Catherine believed that each individual has the power to build their character and advance their station in life. She passed away on April 17, 1938 in Staten Island, New York at age 79.

Jacob Hart Neff

Known affectionately as "Uncle Jake" at the time of his death, Jacob Hart Neff had three very successful missions during his 78-year life: a miner and businessman, a politician, and a Mason.

Born on October 13, 1830 in Strasburg, Pennsylvania, he became a blacksmith after his family moved to Iowa. He was 20 when he headed for the gold fields of California in 1850, initially going to Hangtown (Placerville) and then on to the Iowa Hill Divide in 1851 where he got his start in mining and business. The Placer County Assessor's Rolls for that year show Jacob with property worth $4,000 in Elizabethtown (this may have been a saloon rather than a mine). He later became one of the organizers of the Morning Star Mine. In 1875, he was a partner in the Pioneer Mine near Humbug Canyon.

He also had mining interests with the Rising Sun Mine in Colfax, where he was Superintendent, and the Idaho-Maryland Mine in Grass Valley.

In 1880 Jacob received two mineral land patents. One, #54506, granted on June 30 was for 130 acres straddling the road east of Iowa Hill. He was the sole owner. The other one, #57178 granted on February 6 and shared with four other investors, was for 62 acres in the vicinity of Humbug Canyon.

Jacob provided financial backing in 1863 for an effort with Ben Taylor and others to build a toll road and bridge across the Bear River to facilitate travel between Grass Valley and Illinoistown . He lost his investment when the bridge collapsed in 1880. Another more successful business venture was the 1887 founding of the Placer County Bank with several men in Auburn.

In 1880 he built a home in Colfax at Grass Valley and Kneeland Streets, which still stands today. In 2006 the current owners renovated it back to its former Victorian era glory.

Jacob's Masonic vocation[83] began in 1855 with Wisconsin Hill's Lodge No. 74 where he reached the level of Master Mason. When that Lodge closed, he became a charter member of Ionic Lodge No. 121 in Iowa Hill on October 15, 1857, where he held several offices, including Worshipful Master. He also participated with Libanus Chapter No. 17 in Iowa Hill until 1869 where he advanced to Royal Arch Mason and served in several roles, including High Priest for four years.

In 1869 he left the Iowa Hill Masons and assisted in forming Siloam Chapter No. 37 in Colfax and was High Priest for thirteen years.

Jacob achieved the 32nd Degree of the Scottish Rite in 1882. Along the way he held numerous offices locally and at the state level. On December 12, 1889 he was elected Active Member of the Masonic Veteran Association of the Pacific Coast and a Life Member on October 17, 1896.

His political career commenced in 1861 when he was elected Tax Collector for Township 7 (the Iowa Hill Divide). He was then elected Sheriff of Placer County from 1867-1869 and went on to be a State Senator from 1871-1887. President Grant then appointed him as one of three commissioners to inspect the Oregon & California Railroad. He also served as a Trustee of the State Library. In 1892 he took the post of Prison Director for Placer County, and in 1898 he reached the pinnacle of his political career with his election as Lt. Governor of California.

Jacob's mining and political interests overlapped during his six-year term as President of the California Miner's Association, which he had been

[83] Jacob's accomplishments as a Mason are too extensive to list all of them here, so the primary focus is on what he achieved while living on the Iowa Hill Divide. For details of his impressive Masonic record see pages 19-21 of the book *Fifty Years of Masonry in California, Volume 2* by Edwin Allen Sherman, 1898 (available online).

instrumental in forming in 1891 (John B. Hobson was also involved—see his bio in this section). He is credited with forming the alliance between the miners and the Sacramento Valley farmers which resulted in the Caminetti Act of 1893. This act allowed the resumption, under limited conditions, of hydraulic mining, which had been banned in 1884.

He was also a philanthropist, donating much of his fortune to the needy and in 1908 giving a fountain to the City of Auburn, which still sits in front of the historic Placer County Courthouse.

Jacob never married, and on March 26, 1909 he passed away after a brief illness at his home in San Francisco, where he had moved to in 1900. He was buried in the Woodlawn Memorial Park in Colma, San Mateo County. Over 100 people traveled from Placer County to attend his funeral.

Michael Harold Power

Michael Harold Power, born in County Waterford, Ireland on September 29, 1829, was a lawyer. He was appointed Clerk to the Crown for the District of Waterford until he immigrated to America in 1847. While living in New York he met his future wife.

When his physician advised taking a sea voyage for his health, he set sail from New York to California via the Isthmus of Panama[84] (hardly an easy trip for a man in poor health!). He arrived in September 1852 and made his way to Iowa Hill.

His first accomplishment was to survey a toll road between Iowa Hill and Illinoistown.[85] He then managed ditches for John T. Hill before moving to Damascus in 1854. There he purchased an interest in the Mountain Tunnel Mine, which later joined with the Golden Gate Mine to form the Mountain Gate Mining Company.

On June 1, 1856 he married Isaline *Keysner-Develey*, a native of Switzerland and the sister of Anna *Develey*, wife of Richard Dorer in nearby Humbug Canyon (the Dorer Family bio is in the Founding Families chapter). Isaline was a governess for the H. Crocker family in New York, and came to California in 1855 via the Isthmus of Panama route.

Isaline was the first white woman to live in Damascus. Imagine coming from living with a wealthy family in New York City to a three-room cabin with no indoor plumbing! On February 7, 1857 their son Harold Thomas Power was the first white child born in Damascus. The couple later had two other children: Henry M. and Lizzie P.

---

[84] Or possibly Cape Horn—sources conflict.

[85] It is unknown whether this was the Rice's Mineral Bar and Iowa City Turnpike or Rutherford's Stevens Trail. Probably it was Rice's.

In 1875 or 1876, after nearly 20 years in Damascus, Michael and his family moved to the nearby Foresthill Divide. There he prospected the Hidden Treasure Mine in Sunny South. His wife is credited with naming the mine, where he was Secretary and Superintendent for many years.

In 1867, Harold was elected a Supervisor of Placer County, and in 1869 went on to serve in the State Assembly. In 1873 he was nominated for the State Senate but was defeated.

Isaline was known in her own right as a historian of the area. On her 66th birthday in 1899 she read a paper titled *The Gold Belt of the Sierras* at the annual meeting of the pioneers of the County. The paper was subsequently published in the press throughout the County.

Sadly, their son Henry M. passed away at age 26, but son Harold went on to have an illustrious career, serving as Superintendent of several mines, including the Hidden Treasure and the Morning Star (in Iowa Hill). He was also president of the Placer County Miners' Association and a member of the executive committee of the California Miners' Association with the aim of rehabilitating hydraulic mining after the 1884 ban. Harold was also a director and stockholder in the Placer County Bank, along with Jacob Neff, and served a term in the California State legislature in 1897. In addition, he was a delegate from California to the Republican national convention held in Philadelphia, in June 1900. Harold married Mary V. *Sweeney* of San Francisco on November 23, 1871 and they had seven children, one of whom was named Treasure.

Both Michael and his son Harold were Masons. Michael died on July 17, 1885 in Auburn and was buried in the Old Auburn Cemetery with his wife and two sons.

In 1901, the family moved into what is now known as the Power Mansion in Auburn, but lost it to foreclosure in 1917.[86] Today the building is operated as a bed-and-breakfast and wedding location.

Charles Rice

Charles Rice was a native of Ireland, born there in 1819. By 1844 he had married an Englishwoman named Hester (last name unknown) and they were living in Louisiana where their daughter Mary had just been born. Around 1850 Charles came to the Iowa Hill Divide, and his family followed later by way of the Isthmus of Panama and San Francisco.

Charles made a major contribution to the viability of Iowa Hill when he opened his ferry and general merchandise store at Mineral Bar in 1852. In 1854 he organized the building of the Mineral Bar and Iowa City Turnpike

---

[86] See the *Placer Republican* September 14, 1901 and *Placer Herald* October 27, 1917. Contrary to popular belief, the house was not built by the Power family, but by Ashael Huntley, once a Placer County Sheriff. (*Placer Herald* November 26, 1887)

toll road between Iowa Hill and Illinoistown, including a bridge to replace the ferry, at a cost of $75,000. The route was later modified to be less steep, and is still in use today.

Charles and Hester had a second child, a son named Charles Hester, on November 25, 1851. Sadly, he was killed in 1872 at age 21 in an accident while driving a stagecoach on his father's road.

Charles Rice at Home on Mineral Bar

In 1880 Charles won a suit against the Orion Mine Company, which was busily hydraulicking away on both sides of the road as it entered Iowa Hill. He was barely in time. This area, known today as the "isthmus," is scarcely wider than the one-lane road passing through it.

In August 1881 Charles incorporated the Colfax and Iowa Hill Toll Road Company with himself, Jacob Neff, W. A. Himes, and William Storey as Directors. The $24,000 of capital stock was divided into 240 shares.

Charles, with William Storey, was granted patent #54507 on February 15, 1882. Consisting of 40 acres called the West Sugar Loaf Placer Mine, the property was located just west of the Isthmus.

Charles passed away in San Francisco at age 68 on July 7, 1887. He was buried in the Colfax Cemetery next to his son.

In the early 1900s Placer County purchased the Colfax-Iowa Hill Road.

Vignettes of Iowa Hill Divide Inhabitants

This chapter supplements the bios in the Founding Families and Notable Residents chapters by featuring brief bios of a variety of Iowa Hill inhabitants who have lived here over the years.

Carl W. Adamson

Carl Wendell Adamson, born on November 16, 1903 in Fayetteville, Indiana. He was the second of five children born to Walter Adamson (1876-1929) and Cora *Phillips* Adamson (1880-1960.

By 1920 the family had moved to Colorado. By 1935, Carl moved on to the town of Mountain in Siskiyou County, California where he was a miner and had married Alice (maiden name unknown) from Washington State.

For the 1940 Census, they were still living in Mountain, and Alice was a clerk at the Post Office. They had separated by the time Carl enlisted in the Army on October 12, 1942 in Sacramento.

During World War II, Carl was a Technician 5th Grade (Tec 5) in the Army. People of this rank were addressed as "Corporal" or "Tech Corporal."[87]

After the war, Carl moved to Iowa Hill, where he bought the "old" Iowa Hill Store on October 1, 1949. He also became Postmaster. On June 23, 1950 he married Evelyn M "Eva" *Rossi* (1899–1974) in Reno and together they ran the store and bar for ten years until they sold it on September 30, 1959.

---

[87] The Tec 5 insignia was two stripes with a "T" under the stripe. The "T" indicated that the soldier's promotion was based on his training and the rank did not carry any leadership responsibilities.

Carl and Eva continued to live in the Iowa Hill area until the mid-1960s, when they moved to Sonoma County, where they managed apartment buildings for Bob Yonash for several years.

Carl passed away in Santa Rosa, California on December 23, 1968 at age 65. He was buried in the Iowa Hill Cemetery next to his wife Eva.

William Harvey Booth

An Iowa Hill native, William Harvey Booth was born on March 17, 1866, the son of Garret Wood Booth (1827-1911) and Sarah E. *Haun* Booth (1837 - 1904).

William was a gold miner, a Justice of the Peace, and a member of the Native Sons of the Golden West.

In 1889, when he was 23, William married Eleanor "Ella" *Pashby* (1871-1941) and they had three daughters: Ruth, Millie, and Zylpha.

When mining output declined in Iowa Hill, he went to Siskiyou County where he was killed in a cave-in on May 26, 1903 at age 37. Friends brought his body 22 miles by mule from the mine to a wagon for a further 65-mile trip to Redding. From there, he journeyed by train to Colfax and then by another wagon to be buried in the Iowa Hill Cemetery with his parents.

Vincent J. "Johnny Pollock" Bugajczyk

Johnny Pollock was actually named Vincent J. Bugajczyk, but no one could pronounce his last name. He was from Poland, so he became Johnny Pollock to the folks in Iowa Hill. Johnny loved kids and whenever he saw one he would come over to shake hands—inevitably, he had a dime or a quarter in his palm for the child. One day someone painted "half fast" on the back of Johnny Pollock's Model T, which of course was a play on words and hilarious to everyone, including Johnny. One of his favorite sayings was "holy smoke" and this was engraved on his headstone in the Iowa Hill Cemetery when he died on November 19, 1967.

Lucius Booth "Bud" Cannon

Lucius "Bud" Cannon, an Iowa Hill native, was born on March 28, 1896. He attended school in Iowa Hill, and he served in France as a sharpshooter in the Army during World War I from 1917-1919. He later worked at a livery stable.

Bud was the grandson of Franklin "Frank" Eli Cannon, Sr. (1822-1898) and Mary *McGeachin* Cannon (1831-1899) who lived on the Divide for nearly 30 years, until the early 1890s, primarily in the Damascus area. His parents were Ransom Cannon, Sr. (1867-1945) and Lizzie Leona *Eckert*

Cannon (1866-1915).

At age 32, Bud married Dorothy *Smith* of Iowa Hill (1900-1965) and moved to San Francisco, where he was a repairman in the farm implements industry and Dorothy taught school. They had one child. However, Bud retained his ties with Iowa Hill during frequent visits, where he enjoyed hunting and fishing with his friends, including Pop Parker.

Bud Cannon on the Iowa Hill Road 1929

Bud passed away on December 1, 1980, and was buried next to his parents in the Iowa Hill Cemetery.

Joseph Colgan

Joseph Colgan was born in Baltimore ~1823 of Irish parents. After coming to California, he mined along the Middle Fork of the American River before moving to Iowa Hill and building the brick store ~1853 which survived until 1968 (see the Iowa Hill chapter for a history of the store).

He was the first postmaster in Iowa Hill (then called Iowa City), serving in that position from June 16, 1854 to March 18, 1857. In 1855, Colgan was Treasurer of the Iowa Hill Masonic Lodge. He died at age 38 on April 9, 1861 and was buried in the Catholic part of the Iowa Hill Cemetery.

Jack Dempsey

The donkey Jack Dempsey was the duly elected mayor of Iowa Hill. His platform was that he was the only elected official in the United States who would admit to being a jackass, and he won many a write-in campaign in Iowa Hill when the official candidate for election was unpopular. He is thought to have been abandoned by a miner, and then adopted by the town. Kids loved to ride him, as shown in the photo below.

Jack Dempsey and Friends 1940s
man with hat: Guy White, sitting on donkey: Patricia & Jack White, standing to right: Barbara White

One time my step-mother left the truck parked outside of the store in Iowa Hill after a shopping trip to Auburn. Her groceries were in the truck bed. When she came back out she discovered that Jack had helped himself to a loaf of bread and a bunch of bananas.

Jack took his civic duties seriously. On the opposite page he is shown participating in the 1950 unveiling of the monument commemorating the founding of Iowa Hill.

Every spring poor Jack would fall in love with my horse and she would convince him to follow her home when we returned from school. Then she would proceed to ignore him as he paced back and forth outside of her corral.

Jack Dempsey 1950
with John B. Hobson, Waldo Macy, Stanley Macy, Lawrence McCallister

On December 22, 1960 Jack Dempsey died at an estimated age of between 55 and 60. The *Colfax Record* ran his obituary on the front page.

Folly

Folly was a white dog who belonged to the teacher Zoe Belieu in the 1950s. Folly loved her beer, and she used to sit on a stool at the bar in town to imbibe it. One time she got drunk and fell off her stool. She was very embarrassed. The owner of the bar threatened to cut her off, but he later relented.

John Henry

John Henry was born on February 14, 1828 in Lorraine, France and came to the United States as a youngster. On March 15, 1847, at age 19, he enlisted in Company B of the 7th Infantry Regiment under Colonel Plympton and Lieutenant Humber. At that time, Company B was engaged in fighting the Mexican-American War. John fought in the Battle of Cerro Gordo on April 12, 1847, which was a decisive assault on the strongly fortified Telegraph Hill near Mexico City. After the war ended in the fall of 1847, he continued to serve on the frontier (Missouri, New Mexico, Kansas, and "Indian Territory" in what eventually became Oklahoma) until his discharge on March 15, 1852.

John also fought in the Civil War, serving as a Private in Company F of the 4th California Infantry. The Regiment was organized at Sacramento, Placerville and Auburn from September to October, 1861 and mustered out April 18, 1866 in Humboldt, California.

On July 11, 1874 he married Sarah *Blythe* Harlan Welch, a Cherokee from Kansas, in Monona Flat near Iowa Hill. The couple had five children: Louis, Etta, Jessie, Myrtle, and Walter. Sadly, Louis died at age 12 in a buckboard accident. They also raised Sarah's two sons by a previous marriage, John and James (the 1880 Census erroneously lists these children as being John's, but actually they were his step-children).

He was a trustee for the Iowa Hill School District in 1886.

After surviving three severe mining accidents, John died from heart disease on June 3, 1890 at age 63. He was buried in the Catholic portion of the Iowa Hill Cemetery, next to his son Louis. Their graves are still marked.

George Granville Prout

George Granville Prout was born in the District of Columbia in September 1833. He is thought to have been a runaway slave when he came to California. Some confusion exists about the source of his last name. Local lore says that he arrived in California with only a first name, and that he acquired the last name Prout by marrying a Prout woman, who was of Native-American descent.[88] However, as early as the 1860 Census, when he was living in Michigan Bluff, he was alone. The 1870 Census shows him living with Nancy Anderson, an African-American woman from Virginia. When marital status started being recorded with the 1880 Census, he said he was single rather than widowed or divorced, and he gave the same status in the 1900 Census.

George was also known by the offensive (even then) nickname "Nigger" George.[89] Nigger George Ravine, where a creek runs along Iowa Hill Road near where the road starts its drop into the east side of the American River Canyon, is named for him. The log cabin where he lived on the ravine is still there as of 2016.

A barber by trade, at one point George had a barbershop on Main Street in Iowa Hill, near the Starr Hotel. His shop was destroyed in one of the various fires that decimated the town.

George often went to the school and visited with the children as shown in the photo on the opposite page.

---

[88] Indeed, a George Prout is buried in the Colfax Indian Cemetery.

[89] The author struggled with whether or not to include this information, but to omit it would be to ignore the historical record.

George Prout (seated center left) at the Iowa Hill School ~1890

His date of death is unknown, but it was probably between 1900 and 1910 since he is not listed in the Census after 1900 when he was 66.

Ptolemy Stone

Born ~1814 in New York, Ptolemy Stone was a Notary Public and Justice Court Judge in Iowa Hill for over 15 years. He came to California in 1849 from Canton, Fulton County, Illinois, where he was a newspaper editor from 1937-1841 and also operated a job printing enterprise. He was generally recognized as a local newspaper pioneer there.

Around 1854, he and his wife Sarah settled in Iowa Hill with their adopted daughter, Mary Caroline, who was born in April 1851. They had an orchard across the street from their home, and sold apples to the local mining companies and residents.

Judge Stone served in all three of Iowa Hill's militias from 1855 until 1865. He was also a member of the I.O.O.F.

Sadly, Mary died from typhoid fever in 1862, when she was just 11 years old. Sarah passed away in 1877, leaving the Judge alone. When Ptolemy died on January 20, 1882 at age 68, his eulogy stated that "just as the sun was sinking behind the western horizon and all nature was settling down for a quiet rest, another old forty-niner passed away."

Over the years his gravestone in the Iowa Hill Cemetery disappeared, so in 2014 a new marker was added to his grave. Daughter Mary's stone was stolen in the 1970s but was subsequently found in a storage unit in Sacramento. Through some fortuitous relationship connections it was returned in September 2004 and replaced on her grave.

John Eliso Vanina

Giovanni "John" Eliso Vanina was born on June 14, 1891 in Santa Maria, Chihuahua, Mexico. His parents, Christopher Vanina (1855-?) and Guilia "Julia" *Beltramenelli* (1865-1901), were both from Switzerland and were married in Arizona on September 25, 1888. His father had previously been naturalized on August 1, 1884 in Pima County, Arizona. In addition to John, the couple had a daughter Anna Adalina "Lena," also born in Mexico.

Shortly after John's birth the family moved to California, ending up on the Iowa Hill Divide. John's father passed away (date and place unknown).

On September 23, 1895 John's mother married Henry Del Re, who was 25 years her senior. He was a miner and owned the Phillips Claim, previously known as the Roach Hill Claim and later called the Lone Oak Claim. John's mother died on February 26, 1901 in Iowa Hill when John was 9-½. He and his sister continued to live with their step-father, Henry.

At age seven, John started school in Iowa Hill and walked two miles a day each way. He attended school off and on, finally graduating in 1906 at age 16 "with the highest final examination score in the county" as he reminisced in an article in the March 8, 1979 *Colfax Record.*

Because the miners had cut down all of the trees, the walk to school could be very hot so John would walk in the Iowa Hill Ditch where it was shady and cooler. Even as a child he enjoyed hunting, and he often shot squirrels or pigeons on his way to school, hung them in a tree, and then brought them home after school. He remembered that at times it was hard to hear the teacher because of the noise from the mines.

After graduating from elementary school in 1906, John moved to Sacramento where he worked as a carpenter, and later as a foreman, for his cousin Charles Vanina. He earned $5 a week working 40 hours in construction and then taking care of the horses for the rest of the crew.

On weekends he returned to Iowa Hill, which was a challenge. Catching the 4 p.m. train from Sacramento to Colfax got him to town about 6 p.m. From there, the only affordable option was walking since the stagecoach cost $1.85 each way and didn't leave until the following morning anyway. He usually took Stevens Trail, arriving at his home in Iowa Hill in an hour and 45 minutes, only 20 minutes more than the stage would have taken.

John enlisted in the Army on June 21, 1918 and served in World War I until February 6, 1919, achieving the rank of Sergeant. He then returned to his carpentry job in Sacramento, joining the Carpenter's Union in 1927.

While constructing an apartment building, which he also owned, he met his future wife, Hazel Rose *Dutcher* (1903-1996). Rose, born in Canada, was visiting her sister, who lived in one of John's apartments. Rose and John were married in 1932. Although they had no children of their own, they raised their nephew, Allan Dutcher.

John and Rose lived and worked in Sacramento, where Rose had a business in antiques and John continued as a carpentry foreman. The couple also made frequent week-end trips to Iowa Hill where they hunted, raised animals, and had a garden.

When John retired in 1965, the couple moved permanently to Iowa Hill, where John built a house out of river rocks gathered from their property and they continued to keep numerous animals and a garden.

John passed away on October 9, 1980 at age 89 and was buried on the Catholic side of the Iowa Hill Cemetery near his mother and step-father.

Stanley "Stan the Man" Weston

Stan was born on June 13, 1915 in New York. He served in the US Army during World War II; from July 21, 1941 to September 8, 1945.

Stan was a fixture in Iowa Hill in the 1950s where he was fondly known as "Stan the Man." When asked for help on something he would say, "Let's give 'er a reading." Another favorite phrase was "goose it!" In 1951, Stan built a house for Zoe Belieu, the schoolteacher, which is still lived in today. Zoe's mother Elsie Bailey more or less adopted Stan, and he remained a part of Zoe's life until his death on June 6, 1985 just a week before his 70th birthday.

Myra Schwab with Sons Stuart & Ellard 1905

The Women

Although they were significantly outnumbered by men in the early days of the Gold Rush, women have always exerted a strong influence on the Iowa Hill Divide.

Women have operated hotels and saloons, taught school, been school principals, been postmistresses, and owned mines and ditches. They were also washerwomen, servants, and housekeepers. In addition, they performed the usual female roles of having children, keeping house, growing gardens, and raising families.

In many cases, married men traveled to the gold fields on their own, sending for their families later. This meant the women had to make the arduous journey overland or by sea on their own, often accompanied by children and even infants. The overland route required three to four months of travel in a covered wagon. Sailing around the horn took five to eight months. Sailing to Central America, crossing the Isthmus of Panama on mules, and taking another boat to San Francisco was a three to five month adventure which was eventually shortened to two months or less. Both sea routes left the women in San Francisco, and required additional overland travel to join their husbands.

Here's a sampling, in no particular order, of the contributions of women on the Iowa Hill Divide:

- In 1850 the first settlement on the Divide, Elizabethtown, was named for one of the miner's wives.
- Adelia (AKA Delia or Adelaide) *Reid* Hill, who inherited her husband's extensive ditch interests when he left her a widow in 1857 at the age of 26, went on to add several mines to her domain and fought multiple legal battles to protect her ditches. She carried one lawsuit all the way to the US Supreme Court, but the Justices

refused to hear the case. Adelia Hill Road, near the Iowa Hill cemeteries, is named for her. See her bio in the Notable Residents chapter.

- With stated losses of $10,000, Isabella Connor was one of the three property owners most affected by the fire in 1857. Mrs. Colcutt lost $3,000.
- Lucy Padman, age 35 from France, was listed as a bookkeeper in the 1860 Census.
- Anna Catherine *Murphy* Markham, an Iowa Hill native, taught school there for three terms in the 1880s, including serving as Principal during the third term. See her bio in the Notable Residents chapter.
- Leona George taught 11 terms in Iowa Hill during the 1930s, the second-longest tenure of all the Iowa Hill teachers. She commuted daily from her home near Sacramento.
- Isaline *Keysner-Develey* Power was the first white woman in Damascus and in 1857 delivered the first white child born there. She came from New York, where she was a governess for the well-off H. Crocker family, to live in a three-room miner's cabin with no indoor plumbing.
- Because medical care was either non-existent or too far to travel, women often bore their children with minimal assistance, usually from a midwife or husband. Then they bore their loss. A good 15% of the known burials on the Iowa Hill Divide were either children or infants. One story illustrates the frequent heartbreak. In 1857, Amelia, the daughter of Nancy and John Leonard of Bird's Flat died at age two. That was bad enough, but ten years later, her brother John G. was walking home from school with his mother, and dropped his lunch bucket. As he was trying to retrieve it he fell in a mine shaft and drowned while his mother stood helplessly by.
- Ida May Macy operated the Red & White Store in Iowa Hill, along with her husband Waldo, from their marriage in 1914 until the store burned in 1956.
- It was primarily the women of the town who started the Iowa Hill Community Club in 1950. Its purpose initially was to have the school reopened and to buy a new fire engine. It is still going strong today, after over 65 years, now with a focus on the fire department.
- Since 2000, the female Fire Chief and President of the Iowa Hill Fire Safe Council has acquired several significant grants to create

fuel breaks in the Iowa Hill Divide.[90] The one on King's Hill is credited with preventing a 2014 fire from reaching Iowa Hill. Creating the fuel breaks also provided several much-needed local jobs.

- Bonnie *Parker* Cantrell, who operated the new Iowa Hill store with her husband Hub for several years, was revered as the "Queen of Iowa Hill" when she passed away at age 101 in 2014.

An examination of the Census shows an unexpected trend for working women. In 1860 a major portion of the women worked at other jobs than keeping house. Occupations included ditch owner, boardinghouse keeper, seamstress, bookkeeper, servant, teacher, washerwoman, hotel/bar keeper, milliner, and house keeper. By the 1870 Census the proportion of working women had dropped significantly. The variety of jobs had also declined to servant, hotel clerk, hotel keeper, and housekeeper. This held for the 1880 Census. The 1890 Census has been lost to fire, so no details are available for that year.

In 1900 a significant portion of women were at work again, with occupations of teacher, waitress, cook, washerwoman, dressmaker, ladies nurse, dress maker, housekeeper, and servant. For 1910 and 1920, the ratio of working women had dropped once more. Occupations in 1910 were limited to teacher and waitress and in 1920 to teacher, laundress, sales lady in a millinery shop, and boarding house keeper. After 1920 the Iowa Hill Divide was merged with Colfax, Dutch Flat, Weimar, etc. so no further details are available.

As of 2016, a woman owns the Iowa Hill store and another one holds a weekly Taco Night for the community plus hosting a food bank for the residents of the Divide. The Fire Chief of the volunteer fire department is a woman, a post she has held for over a decade.

---

[90] The purpose of a fuel break is to lower the risk of the spread of wildfire by reducing the amount of vegetation on a strategic strip or block of land.

Black Banjo

African-Americans

It is beyond the scope of this book to provide a comprehensive history of African-Americans on the Iowa Hill Divide. Some anecdotal items are offered as examples of the African-American presence.

When the Gold Rush started, slavery was still in effect in the United States and many debated over whether California should be a slave state or not. It was finally admitted in 1850 as a free state, at least technically.[91,92]

Section 1669 of the California School Law enacted in 1875 stated: "The education of children of African descent and Indian children, must be provided for in separate schools; *provided*, that if the Directors or Trustees fail to provide such separate schools, then such children must be admitted into the schools for white children."

There are five known African-Americans buried on the Iowa Hill Divide:

- James Hunt was born in Virginia in 1829. He was a laborer in Iowa Hill and died in November 1869 at age 40. His burial location is unknown.
- Nelson McGee was a miner, and also praised as a good cook. He prepared food for parties, dances, and other gatherings in the community. Nelson was born in 1829 in Georgia and died at age 63

---

[91] Although California entered the Union as a free state, the framers of the state constitution wrote into law the systematic denial of suffrage and other civil rights to non-white citizens. Some authorities went so far as to attempt to deny entry of all African-Americans, free or slave, to California. Slavery persisted in California even without legal authority. Some slave owners simply refused to notify their slaves of the prohibition and continued to trade slaves within the state. Numerous state trials ruled in the favor of emancipation. (Wikipedia)

[92] In addition to Federal legislation, on April 15, 1852 California's Fugitive Slave Law went into effect, which made it illegal for slaves to run away from their owners in California. The law lapsed in 1855 and was not renewed.

on October 4, 1892 in Iowa Hill. His burial location is unknown. He was married to Susan, also African-American, who was born ~1832 in Pennsylvania. Her parents were also from Pennsylvania, so she was probably born a free woman. She died sometime after 1880, because she is listed in that Census at age 48 with Nelson, age 51.

- Mr. Power (first name unknown) was born in Baltimore County, Maryland and died in Iowa Hill on May 28, 1856 at Wisconsin Hill. His age at death and exact burial location are unknown.
- Benjamin Warren was a miner/merchant in Iowa Hill who was born in Virginia ~1804. He purchased a plot in the Iowa Hill Cemetery, so is assumed to be buried there. His death date is unknown, but it was after 1870 because he was listed in the Census that year, age 66.
- Milton Wimbish was born in Alabama ~1872 and died in a wagon accident at the Morning Star Mine on September 10, 1897 at age 25. He is buried in the IOOF section of the Iowa Hill Cemetery.

Very few African-Americans were listed in the census for the Iowa Hill Divide, almost certainly due to under-reporting. These are:

- 1860: two; a miner and a housekeeper
- 1870: six; a miner, a boardinghouse operator, a barber, and three "keeping house"
- 1880: three; a miner, a barber, and "keeping house"
- 1890: census lost to fire
- 1900: five; a barber, a cook, a laborer, and two miners
- 1910 and 1920: none listed

Two African-Americans have made their way into local legend. They are George Prout and a man nicknamed Black Banjo (actual name unknown). Banjo Hill, where the cemeteries are located east of town, is said to be named for the latter. George Prout's biography is included in the chapter Vignettes of Iowa Hill Divide Inhabitants.

Chinese Miners at the Big Dipper Mine

Chinese

This section is not a detailed history of the Chinese on the Iowa Hill Divide as that is beyond the scope of this book.[93,94] What is provided are some anecdotal items to illustrate the Chinese influence.[95]

The Census shows a major presence by the Chinese on the Iowa Hill Divide from the days of the Gold Rush to as late as 1900.

Chinese Population on the Iowa Hill Divide 1860-1920

Census	Chinese	% of Total
1860	222	14.0
1870	754	10.2
1880	70	7.4
1890 (lost to fire)		
1900	97	11.5
1910	7	3.7
1920	0	0.0

---

[93] Along with other nationalities, many Chinese immigrated to California during the Gold Rush. They also came over in the 1860s to work on the Transcontinental Railroad. In 1882 the Chinese Exclusion Act was passed by Congress, prohibiting all immigration of Chinese laborers. This law was in effect until 1943, when it was finally repealed by the Magnuson Act.

[94] In 1852, the Foreign Miners Tax, aimed at the Chinese, was passed by the California legislature. It was in effect until 1855.

[95] In Chinese the last name occurs first and a wife's and children's names are different from the man's. Many Chinese are listed in the Census with the last name "Ah," however, this is not actually a name on its own, but something more like "Mr." in English. But since that is all the records provide, it is used here as a name.

Many Chinese were employed in the mines and on the ditches, where they earned only about half of what the white miners were paid. Others were cooks. Later on, several Chinese worked as bookkeepers and servants. Almost all of them were men on their own who had come to the gold fields without their families.

The start of the major fire of March 1862 was attributed to carelessness by a Chinese man employed at the Star Bakery.

In 1882, Ah Tom & Co. owned the Vaughn Mine at Wisconsin Hill.

In the early 1890s an Ah Tom (he may or may not have been the same Ah Tom as it was a common name) owned a store in Iowa Hill. It was burned to the ground during a fight in which Ah Tom lost his life. He was 53 at the time of his death and was buried in the Iowa Hill Chinese Cemetery.

Another Ah Tom (AKA China Tom) owned Ah Tom's Store in addition to being a mine supervisor. He was a leader in the Chinese community in Iowa Hill, and very respected by the entire population of the town. After his death from rheumatism in 1901, John Papa escorted his body to San Francisco, where he was shipped to China for burial. His wife, Sub Moey, died on February 6, 1897 at age 63 in Iowa Hill and was buried in the Chinese Cemetery after a large funeral near Indian Creek.

Sub Moey
Wife of China Tom

Other Chinese known to have been buried in the Chinese Cemetery[96] are:

- Ah Chung was killed on April 17, 1895 at age 44 in a landslide at the old Blue Wing Mine, also known as the Washington Mine.
- Ah Foo was born ~1854 and died at age 45 when the Big Dipper Reservoir burst on February 8, 1899.
- Ah Sing was murdered by Boy Young, AKA Ah Young, who was subsequently convicted of manslaughter and sentenced to ten years in prison.
- Ah Yeck committed suicide due to depression over lack of work on February 12, 1900. His age is unknown.
- Lang Coak, the 3-month-old infant daughter of Ah Sing and his wife, died on April 7, 1897.

---

[96] Given the state of record-keeping prior to the early 1900s as well as the self-contained nature of the Chinese community, little information is available on Chinese deaths on the Divide. Also, most bodies were later disinterred and returned to China for final burial in accordance with Chinese custom..

- Ong Goan was a miner who died on April 17, 1895 at age 53 in a landslide at the Blue Wing Mine.
- Wing Lock (name may have been Lock Wing) died at age 45 on February 8, 1899 when the Big Dipper Reservoir burst.

A newspaper article about the 1897 fire mentions that the blaze destroyed part of Chinatown in Iowa Hill.

In the early 1900s a Chinese man named Hop Gee ran the daily pack train from Humbug Canyon to Towle on the other side of the North Fork of the American River. According to several Dorer family interviews, he wore high boots, but didn't lace them up. He could be heard coming from quite a distance.[97]

On November 11, 1927 the *Colfax Record* reported that Moy Jim Mun and four other Chinese men were starting operations in Indian Canyon near Iowa Hill. They planned to work the canyon on a big scale and would employ several local men. Mrs. Bessie Haenny, daughter of former Iowa Hill mail carrier Lawrence H. Fowler, recalled visiting the Chinese camp as a child.

---

[97] Dorer family oral histories

The Hansen Kids ~1910
Annie, John, Clayton, Henry, and Aggie

Native Americans

Little could be found specific to the Native American presence on the Iowa Hill Divide after the Gold Rush beyond the fact that the tribes who resided here prior to the invasion of the gold seekers were primarily the Maidu (including the Nisenan) and Sierra Miwok plus some Paiutes and possibly some Washoes.

Early settlers in Humbug Canyon described a Paiute tribe living there. A few years later the Federal Government moved the entire tribe to a reservation in Nevada.

Section 1669 of the California School Law enacted in 1875 stated "The education of children of African descent and Indian children, must be provided for in separate schools; *provided*, that if the Directors or Trustees fail to provide such separate schools, then such children must be admitted into the schools for white children."

The Native American population was extremely under-reported in the Census:

- 1860 and 1870: did not tabulate any Native Americans on the Divide.
- 1880: listed 23 Native Americans, all living in the Wisconsin Hill/Prospect Hill area. They were adults except for one 3-year-old and one 16-year-old. One was a servant, one a cook, one a washerwoman, six were "idle," and the occupations of the rest were not stated.
- 1890: not available (destroyed by fire)
- 1900: tabulated seven Native Americans in three households, all adults, five women and two men. Their occupations were two hop pickers, two wood choppers, two washerwomen, and one not stated. All owned their own homes.
- 1910: listed eight Native Americans, all in the Hansen family in

Humbug Canyon, two adults and five children. The adults were both mixed-race Paiutes. The man's father was American and the wife's father was Spanish.

- 1920: no Native Americans listed. (The Hansens had moved away.)

According to a Dorer family member, the Hansens lived in Humbug Canyon in a house on the Dorer property and their children attended school with the Dorer children. The five Hansen children were Henry, Aggie, Annie, John, and Clayton and the adults were Henry and Christina. The Hansens owned the first Edison phonograph in the area—the kind with the morning glory horn.

Sarah *Blythe* Harlan Welch, a Cherokee from Kansas, was the wife of John Henry. (See his bio in the Vignettes section.) After his death in 1890 she moved to Oklahoma where she joined the Cherokee Nation.

In 1993, Mescom Enterprises, Inc., a native-American-owned company in San Jose, California, purchased the Iowa Hill Telephone Company.

SUPPLEMENTARY MATERIALS

Sources

(Since so many sources are government or other publications with no author's name, sources are listed by title rather than author.)

Documents and Books

Biennial Report of the State Forester of the State of California, Volume 5, California State Board of Forestry, 1914

The Birth and Decline of Iowa Hill 1849-1899, Michael Labant Szafranski, Master's Thesis, Sacramento State College, 1962

British Columbia Mining Record, Volume X, 1903

California Blue Book, 1911

California County Boundaries, Owen C. Coy, 1923, California Historical Commission

The California Debris Commission: A History, U. S. Army Corps of Engineers, Joseph J. Hagwood, Jr., 1981

California Gold Camps, Erwin G. Gudde, University of California Press, 1975

California and Oregon Travel Diary of Artist, Illustrator And Future Yosemite National Park Advocate James Mason Hutchings, 1854-55

California's Geographic Names: A Gazetteer of Historic & Modern Names of the State, David L. Durham, 1998

Census Records, U.S. National Archives and Records Administration

The Colfax Connection, Pat Jones

Congressional Series of United States Public Documents, Volume 2031, U.S. Government Printing Office, 1882

Directory of the County of Placer for the Year 1861, C.F. Robbins, 1861

Directory of the hat, cap, and fur trades, United States and Canada, January 1880

Engineering and Mining Journal, Volume 84, No 1, 1907

Engineering and Mining Journal, Volume 93, 1912

Fifty Years of Masonry in California, Volume 2, Edwin Allen Sherman, 1898

Fire and Water Engineering, Volume VLXIII-No. 17, October 27, 1920

Gazetteer and Business Directory of St. Lawrence County, N.Y., 1873-4

Geological Map of the Iowa Hill Mining District, Placer County, J. B. Hobson, E.M., 1890

The Gospel of Beauty in the Progressive Era: Reforming American Verse and Values, Lisa Szefel, 2011

Historic Spots in California, Third Edition, Stanford University Press, 1966

Historical Context and Archaeological Research Design for Mining Properties in California, California Department of Transportation, 2008

Historical Sketch of the Mining Law in California, John F. Davis, 1902

A History of the Gold Discoveries of the Northern Mines of California's Mother Lode Gold Belt as Told by the Newspapers and Miners 1848-1875, compiled and written by Lewis J. Swindle, 2000

History of Placer and Nevada Counties, California with Biographical Sketches of the Leading Men and Women of the Counties Who Have Been Identified with Their Growth and Development from the Early Days to the Present History, W. B. Lardner and M. J. Brock, 1924

History of Placer County, California with Illustrations and Biographical Sketches of Its Prominent Men and Pioneers, Thompson & West, 1882

Hutchings' Illustrated California Magazine, Volume 4, 1860

Iowa Hill: A Demographic Analysis of a Boom and Bust Town During the California Gold Rush, Jay Shuttleworth, Dissertation, University of California at Davis, 1996

The Iowa Hill Divide Volume 1: Schools of the Iowa Hill Divide, Robin Yonash, 2015

Iowa Hill – the Town that Refused to Die, Mary Parker, 1995

List of Subscribers of the Pacific Telephone and Telegraph Co. and Sunset Telephone and Telegraph Co., March 1898

Minerals of the United States, Calendar Year 1913, Department of the Interior, United States Geological Survey

Mineral Resources of the United States, 1907--Part I--Metallic Products, United States Geological Society, 1908

Mining American, Volume 58, Mineral industries, 1908

Mining Camps of Placer County (Images of America series), Carmel Barry-Schweyer and Alycia S. Alvarez, 2004

The Northern Crown, 1904

Pacific Coast Business Directory, Langley, 1867

Pacific Coast Business Directory, Langley, 1876-8

Pacific Coast Business Directory, McKenny, 1880-1

Pacific States Watchman, 1881-1882

Proceedings of the Most Worshipful Grand Lodge of Free and Accepted Masons of the State of California, Volume 2, 1855-1856

Proceedings of the Most Worshipful Grand Lodge of Free and Accepted Masons of the State of California, Volume 70, 1919

Property Deeds, Placer County Recorder's Office

Record of Appointment of Postmasters, 1832-1971, National Archives

Report of the State Forester, California Division of Forestry, 1921

Resources of the Pacific Slope, Statistical And Descriptive Summary, 1869

The Road to Iowa Hill—Journey of Memories Road Tour, Sharon Balmain, 1999

Sacramento City & County Directory Including Counties El Dorado, Placer & Amador, McKenny, 1884-5

Seventy-Five Years of Law in California, Jeremiah F. Sullivan, 1925

Sketches of the Village of Albion ..., Albion, N.Y.: Willsea & Beach, 1853

Statistics of Mines And Mining in the States and Territories West of the Rocky Mountains, 7th Edition, Government Printing Office, 1875

Topographical Maps, U.S. National Geological Survey

The Western Shore Gazetteer and Commercial Directory for the State of California ... Yolo County: One Volume Being Devoted to Each County of the State, Giving a Brief History of Each County ... , C.P. Sprague & H.W. Atwell, 1870

USDI/NPS Registration Form, Steven's Trail, Placer County, California, National Register of Historic Places, United States Department of the Interior, National Park Service, 2002

A Volume of Memoirs and Genealogy of Representative Citizens of Northern California…, 1901

Western Express: Research Journal of Early Western Mails, Alan H. Patera, July 1987

<u>Newspapers and Magazines</u>

The Alta California, San Francisco, California

The Brooklyn Daily Eagle, Brooklyn, New York

Colfax Record, Colfax, California

Colfax Sentinel, Colfax, California

Daily Evening Star, Washington, DC

Daily Statesman, Sacramento, California
Flying Magazine
Fresno Republican, Fresno, California
Gallipolis Journal, Gallipolis, Ohio
Iowa Hill Weekly Patriot, Iowa Hill, California
Oakland Tribune, Oakland, California
Oroville Mercury Register, Oroville, California
Placer Herald, Auburn, California
Placer Republican, Auburn, California
Popular Aviation
Sacramento Daily Record-Union, Sacramento, California
San Francisco Bulletin, San Francisco, California
San Francisco Call, San Francisco, California
San Francisco Chronicle, San Francisco, California
Santa Cruz Sentinel, Santa Cruz, California
Sierra Life, Nevada City, California
Ukiah Daily Journal, Ukiah, California
The Union, Grass Valley, California
U. S. News and World Report
Woodland Daily Democrat, Woodland, California

Organizations
California Land Title Association
Colfax Area Historical Society
Placer County Historical Society
Placer County Museums
University of California at Davis, Shield Library
U.S. National Archives and Records Administration

Web Sites:
Ancestry.com
Baseball-Almanac.com
Behindthename.com
Cagenweb.com/placer
Cagenweb.com/yuba
Coinnews.net/tools/cpi-inflation-calculator
Corpun.com
Csun.edu
Davidrumsey.com
Explore.museumca.org
FindaGrave.com
Flyingmachines.org
Foresthillhistory.net

Frap.fire.ca.gov
Freepages.genealogy.rootsweb.ancestry.com
Glorecords.blm.gov
Google.com
KCET.org
Newspapers.com
NOAA.gov
Politicalgraveyard.com
Sfmuseum.org/hist3/laws.html
WesternMiningHistory.com
Wikipedia.org

Iowa Hill Community Club

The Iowa Hill Community Club was formed on May 10, 1950 for the purpose of the "welfare of the community." The primary focus was, and remains, on the school and fire protection.

The community showed strong support at this initial meeting, with attendance by ladies E. Yonash, M. McAllister, H. Wood, C. Howard, M. Watts, B. Valliere, I. M. Macy, G. Randall, and P. S. Bidstrup. The gentlemen attending were: L. F. McAllister, Andrew Anderson, Stanley Weston, Frank Yonash, Stanley Macy, G. W. Randall, E. K. Bull, Alvin Watts, Melvin Henderson, F. W. Giles, L. L. Valliere, Jud Sparhawk, O. V. Henderson, Joe Kessell, H. F. Baker, W. S. Macy, Jack Kelly, Mandus Swenson, L. F. Powell, Charles Haymes, Fred Howard, and Carl W. Adamson.

The first officers were L. F. McAllister, president; Carl W. Adamson, secretary; and Melvin Henderson, treasurer. Mrs. Esther Yonash, Mrs. Mabel McAlister, and Mrs. Mildred Watts were appointed to a proposed school board to be presented to the County Superintendent of Schools. Committees were created for finance, fire control, school, and entertainment.

On May 26, 1950 the foundation for the first fire house was laid. The women of the community served a picnic lunch and dinner. This building, while very dilapidated now, can still be seen across the street from the Iowa Hill Store. The community also purchased a fire engine.

The first of many fundraisers, a dance, was held on June 1, 1950 at the old store. Work on remodeling the schoolhouse began on July 14th, and in September the remodeled school reopened.

The following spring members of the community gathered at the cemetery to clean the grounds and dispose of the winter accumulation of leaves and brush.

As students we used to help with the cemetery cleanups and would find old bottles and arrowheads and other things from the past. It was interesting.

The Iowa Hill Community Club became a 501(c)(3) non-profit on November 5, 1959. Over the years the club has upgraded the fire engine several times, built a new fire house, trained and outfitted a formal fire department, and installed a landing pad for the CalStar air ambulance service, among other projects. The two annual fund-raisers—a chili cookoff in the spring and hillbilly games in October—are always well attended, with great fun being had by all.

Proceeds from sales of this book go to support the Iowa Hill Community Club.

Acknowledgments

Much appreciation goes to the following people for sharing their knowledge, expertise, and access to information and photos. I could not have written this book without their assistance. Thank you to Sharon and Bob Balmain, Paula Macy Bruton, Marilyn Schwab Carter, Brenda Czaya, Priscilla Daniels, Luana Dowling, Linda Love, Herbie Macy, Richard Merz, Cathy Morgan, Mary Parker, Glenda Ragan, Jay Shuttleworth, and Helen Wayland. Also, once again, to Tom McClure for all those trips up the hill.

I especially want to thank my proofreaders: Brenda Czaya, Herbie Macy, and Jay Shuttleworth for their assistance. Any remaining errors are solely my responsibility.

Jay Shuttleworth is also acknowledged for providing editorial assistance. This is a much better book because of his feedback. Thank you, Jay!

Also, ongoing appreciation to Sir Tim Berners-Lee, the inventor of the World Wide Web, which allowed me to do much of my research from the comfort of my home office.

The author, age 7, with her horse Kit

About the Author

Robin Yonash moved to Kings Hill, about 5 miles southwest of Iowa Hill, in 1949 with her grandparents, Frank and Esther Yonash. She rode a horse to attend the Iowa Hill School from September 1950 through October 1956, when she transferred to Foresthill, where she graduated as the Salutatorian in June 1957. After graduating as Valedictorian from high school at Mt. St. Mary's in Grass Valley in 1961 (a boarding school at that time), she went on to receive a B.S. in Mathematics from the University of California, Davis in 1965.

Following a successful career in the computer field, Robin retired in 1998 and moved back to her beloved Sierra Nevada foothills—but not all the way back to Iowa Hill. Having become addicted to electricity and telephones, she compromised on the Colfax area. However, she still considers Iowa Hill to be her home town and is involved with the community, serving on the Board of the Iowa Hill Community Cemetery, developing an updated transcription of the Cemetery, writing this book and the preceding one, and attending the occasional Taco Night. She is now working on Volume 3 of this series, *Gold and Fire: A History of the Iowa Hill Divide*, planned for publication in late 2016.

About the Author

Made in the USA
Monee, IL
25 November 2023